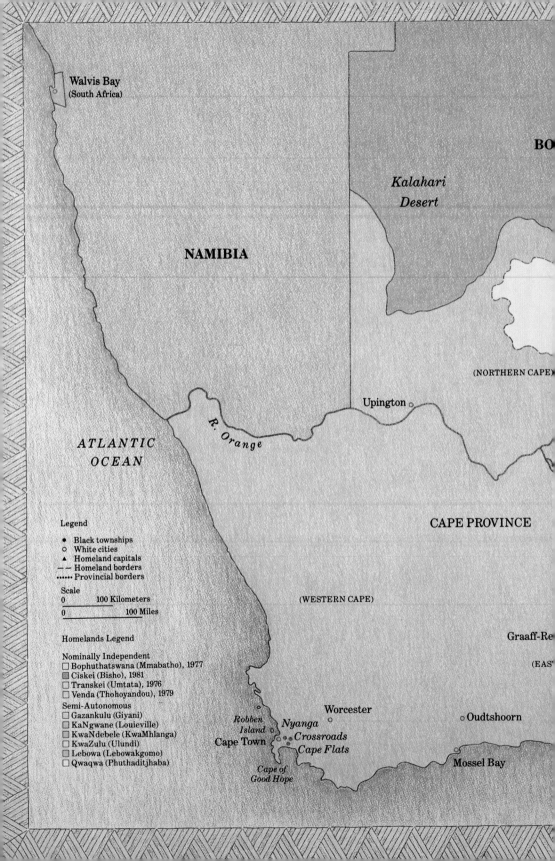

Walvis Bay
(South Africa)

BO

*Kalahari
Desert*

NAMIBIA

(NORTHERN CAPE)

Upington

R. Orange

*ATLANTIC
OCEAN*

CAPE PROVINCE

Legend
● Black townships
○ White cities
▲ Homeland capitals
— - Homeland borders
••••• Provincial borders

Scale
0   100 Kilometers
0   100 Miles

Homelands Legend

Nominally Independent
☐ Bophuthatswana (Mmabatho), 1977
☐ Ciskei (Bisho), 1981
☐ Transkei (Umtata), 1976
☐ Venda (Thohoyandou), 1979
Semi-Autonomous
☐ Gazankulu (Giyani)
☐ KaNgwane (Louieville)
☐ KwaNdebele (KwaMhlanga)
☐ KwaZulu (Ulundi)
☐ Lebowa (Lebowakgomo)
☐ Qwaqwa (Phuthaditjhaba)

(WESTERN CAPE)

Graaff-Re

(EAS'

Worcester

*Robben
Island*   *Nyanga*   ○ Oudtshoorn
Cape Town *Crossroads*
            Cape Flats

*Cape of
Good Hope*   **Mossel Bay**

CHANGING FORTUNES: WAR, DIPLOMACY, AND ECONOMICS IN SOUTHERN AFRICA

ROBERT S. JASTER
MOELETSI MBEKI
MORLEY NKOSI
MICHAEL CLOUGH

SOUTH AFRICA **UPDATE** SERIES
FORD FOUNDATION — FOREIGN POLICY ASSOCIATION

Copublished by the Ford Foundation and the Foreign Policy Association

© Copyright 1992 by the Ford Foundation

Printed in the United States of America
Library of Congress Catalogue Card Number: 92-070232
ISBN: 0-87124-144-7

Editorial assistance provided by Alicia Anthony, Sonia Kane, Margaret Nichols, and Alice Tufel

Book design by Samuel N. Antupit
Map design and illustration by Lea Cyr
Composed by The Sarabande Press
Printed on acid-free paper by Science Press

Contents

THE SUPERPOWERS IN SOUTHERN AFRICA: FROM CONFRONTATION TO COOPERATION
Michael Clough

THE FLOWERS ARE CUT DOWN: THE HUMAN COSTS OF REGIONAL CONFLICT

Appendices

Notes

PREFACE

I n 1981 the Study Commission on U.S. Policy Toward Southern Africa, funded by the Rockefeller Foundation and chaired by Franklin A. Thomas, published a report on the results of a two-year study. The report, entitled *South Africa: Time Running Out (SATRO)*, contained an extensive review of South Africa's history, people, economy, and social and political systems; a survey of South Africa's relations with its neighbors and the rest of the world; and interviews with South Africans across racial, religious, and economic lines. The book concluded with an analysis of U.S. interests in South Africa and laid out a framework for U.S. policy in southern Africa, with specific objectives and actions for U.S. public and private groups. *SATRO* has been reprinted and has become a seminal teaching and reference resource. It is probably still the most comprehensive treatment of South Africa and U.S. policy available.

Since 1981 events have moved swiftly in southern Africa. South Africa's political landscape has been transformed by a combination of internal and external pressures, the most important being a black rebellion of unprecedented scope, intensity, and duration. South Africa's neighbors in the region paid a high price in human suffering and economic dislocation as the result of Pretoria's destabilization policy and their own internal conflicts. But they also had the satisfaction of seeing both the achievement of independence by Namibia, Africa's last colony, and the initiation of a genuine dialogue between blacks and whites in South Africa itself. The international climate changed significantly, with the superpowers cooperating on regional issues, thus effectively ending the cold war in southern Africa. In the United States, southern Africa's increased importance was reflected in the controversy it aroused as a domestic issue and in its new prominence on the foreign policy agenda.

Many parts of *SATRO* have become dated, although others, particularly the policy section, remain relevant. It was therefore decided to update the work with a series of publications covering the 1980s. The intention of the series is to produce a comprehensive journal of record and an analytical resource suitable for teachers, students, and policy makers as well as for a broader audience. Each book deals with a single topic related to South Africa and is written by one or more specialists. In addition to the text, useful supplementary materials such as bibliographies and chronologies, copies of original documents, and maps are included. Together, the books provide a thorough assessment of a pivotal decade in the history of southern Africa.

The South Africa UPDATE Series is produced under the aegis of the Ford Foundation's Southern Africa Study Group and the guidance of an editorial board consisting of academics, former U.S. government and UN officials, journalists, and business, labor, and foundation executives. The opinions expressed in the books, however, are those of the authors.

John de St. Jorre
Editor
South Africa UPDATE Series

Note: This book uses the term "black" to embrace collectively Africans, people of mixed descent known as "Coloureds," and Indians. The individual terms are used when referring to each group separately. Also, money figures in the text are given in South African rand without a U.S. dollar equivalent because of the fluctuating value of the rand during the 1980s. When the decade opened, R1.00 was worth U.S. $1.25; at the decade's close, the rand's value had dropped to U.S. 40 cents.

CHANGING FORTUNES: WAR, DIPLOMACY, AND ECONOMICS IN SOUTHERN AFRICA

Introduction: Setting the Scene

During much of the 1980s, southern Africa, a region of one hundred million people and considerable strategic and economic importance, seemed locked in a grid of deepening and irreconcilable conflict. South Africa, the regional "superpower," became increasingly belligerent as internal and external pressures mounted against its white minority government. South Africa's black-governed neighbors were subjected to cross-border attacks and other destabilizing tactics that compounded their own serious political and economic problems. Rivalry between the United States and the Soviet Union exacerbated local conflicts; and attempts at international mediation, while occasionally reducing tension, failed to reconcile the opposing forces. Human suffering on a massive scale afflicted many of the countries in the region.

Yet, by the end of the decade, a remarkable transformation had occurred in southern Africa, similar in some respects to the changes in Eastern Europe. South Africa had pulled back within its borders, freeing Namibia, Africa's last colony. A large Cuban expeditionary force, which had been in Angola for more than a decade, had begun a staged withdrawal. A new leader in South Africa, committing himself to dismantling apartheid and building a genuine democracy, had initiated a dialogue with the country's long-outlawed black leaders. And the superpowers, abandoning their mutual hostility, had begun to cooperate on regional issues. These changes did not solve all of southern Africa's problems, but they removed some of the long-standing causes of instability and offered new hope for improved relations between South Africa and its neighbors.

This book examines the most important aspects of regional relationships during the 1980s, assesses their significance, and outlines trends for the decade ahead. But first it is necessary to set the scene in an area of some complexity, where history represents an indispensable backdrop to contemporary drama.

When British Prime Minister Harold Macmillan told South Africa's all-white parliament in 1960 that a wind of change was blowing through Africa, he startled his audience. South Africa and the neighboring territories in the southern cone of the continent were all under the firm control of European powers or white indigenous governments. Daily life for the white communities in places as far apart as Northern Rhodesia's prosperous Copper Belt, the bustling metropolises of Johannesburg and Cape Town in South Africa, and the scattered farms of the Portuguese settlers in Angola and Mozambique was comfortable, secure, and apparently immutable.

Challenges to the status quo by blacks, who far outnumbered whites, were ruthlessly crushed, and criticism from abroad was brushed aside. Southern Africa appeared to be immune to the effects of the momentous changes that were taking place in the rest of the continent, where imperial rule was being swept away. In its place, a new political geography was emerging in the shape of a score of independent, black-ruled states, all hostile in varying degrees to continued white domination in the south.

The erosion of white power began in the northern part of the region in the early 1960s. Events in the Belgian Congo (later Zaire), which became independent in 1960 under chaotic conditions that threatened the disintegration of the country and resulted in the dispatch of a large UN peacekeeping force, had a significant psychological effect on southern Africa. Blacks, encouraged by the rapid pace of decolonization to the north, were emboldened to make greater efforts to achieve independence. Whites, appalled at the Belgians' undignified scuttle from their hitherto wealthy model colony and at the mayhem that followed, increased their resolve to resist black pressures.

When Tanzania, in East Africa, became independent in 1961, President Julius Nyerere, a former schoolteacher, intellectual, and widely respected African leader, almost immediately began to play an important political role in the affairs of southern Africa. Also, Tanzania's port of Dar es Salaam appealed to some of its southern neighbors after they became independent, particularly landlocked Zambia and Malawi, as an alternative to the traditional trade routes that ran southward through white-controlled territory.

In 1963 the Organization of African Unity (OAU) was formed by the independent states of Africa, with its headquarters in Addis Ababa. The organization offered a forum for discussion by member states; formulated common positions on many African, Third World, and international issues; and attempted to resolve intra-African disputes. One of the OAU's principal concerns was to decolonize the parts of Africa that were still under colonial or white minority rule. It therefore put its weight behind the forces of black nationalism in those countries by granting official recognition to many liberation movements, providing them with small amounts of financial and military assistance, and giving them political and diplomatic support in international venues such as the United Nations.

Individual states added their support by allowing guerrilla forces operating against white-controlled countries to reside in or transit their territories. A few provided military training and modest supplies of weapons and channeled military aid to the nationalist movements from suppliers outside Africa. The OAU's strong commitment to finishing the task of African decolonization and achieving majority rule in South Africa also provided a unifying focus for the organization, which had great difficulty in reconciling the historical antagonisms and often conflicting interests of its member states.

Meanwhile, Africans were challenging British rule in three countries in southern Africa: Northern Rhodesia (later Zambia), Nyasaland (later Malawi), and Southern Rhodesia (later known as Rhodesia, and after independence as Zimbabwe). Britain had made the political decision to withdraw from Africa, but it found disengagement harder in these three countries than in many of its other African possessions. Both Northern and Southern Rhodesia, particularly the latter, had relatively large white settler populations, nearly all of British stock and holding British passports. Moreover, all three territories were linked by a federal structure—the Central African Federation—that Britain had put in place a decade earlier.

Most Africans in the three countries had opposed the creation of the federation. They regarded it as a device to perpetuate white rule by transferring power and responsibility from Britain to the white settler communities. (The federation's first prime minister referred to whites as the "rider" of the new state and to blacks as the "horse.") The black nationalist groups in the three countries campaigned vigorously against the federation, and in 1963 Britain agreed to dissolve it.

Later that year, the British government granted independence to Nyasaland, the smallest and poorest of the three territories, under the leadership of Hastings Banda, a doctor who had spent many years in exile in Britain. In 1964 Northern Rhodesian nationalists, led by Kenneth Kaunda, a former teacher like his friend and mentor, President Nyerere of Tanzania, successfully negotiated independence. Taking its name from the Zambezi river, which separated the two Rhodesias, Zambia joined Malawi and Tanzania as members of the OAU and began to seek ways of helping African nationalists further south pursue their independence.

The winds of African nationalism, however, faltered on the banks of the Zambezi. On the other side lay entrenched white power in Rhodesia, Mozambique, Namibia, South Africa, and to the west, Angola. Britain tried to persuade the white Rhodesians to accept independence under terms that would have led to black majority rule, but the whites rejected it. Instead, their government, led by a former Battle of Britain fighter pilot named Ian Smith, who turned out to be a tough and subtle politician, made a unilateral declaration of independence ("UDI," as it came to be known) from Britain in 1965. Smith's government suppressed the black political parties that opposed it, jailed their leaders, and sought international recognition. Britain declared the move illegal but made it clear that it would not use force to end the rebellion. It did, however, impose economic sanctions against Rhodesia and led the effort by the United Nations to make them mandatory.

Further south, Britain had an easier task with the three land-locked, undeveloped territories that it had helped to protect from South Africa's advancing settlers in the nineteenth century: Bechuanaland, Basutoland, and Swaziland. In each territory, a strong and astute traditional leader, through a mixture of military skill and diplomatic maneuvering, had resisted South Africa's attempts to incorporate it. During the 1960s the three had become self-governing territories, and when their leaders asked for independence, Britain granted it: to Lesotho (formerly Basutoland) and Botswana (formerly Bechuanaland) in 1966, and to Swaziland in 1968.

Meanwhile, Portugal, Europe's weakest but most obdurate colonial power, refused to consider the prospect of independence for its African colonies, of which the most important were Angola and Mozambique. The view from Lisbon was that all its overseas territories were part of the Portuguese state. For centuries, Portugal had managed to suppress any challenge to this concept. But by the early 1960s, a number of nationalist movements had begun to mobilize support inside and outside Portugal's African colonies. Several of them formed guerrilla armies, and a slow, spiraling pattern of insurgency and counterinsurgency warfare began.

In the southwest of the region, efforts to pry South-West Africa—or Namibia, as it was later called—from South Africa's control were equally unavailing. After driving the Germans out of the huge but sparsely populated territory during World War I, South Africa had ruled it under a mandate granted by the League of Nations. After the collapse of the League and the end of World War II, South Africa's control of Namibia became increasingly disputed, and in 1966 the United Nations formally declared Pretoria's presence illegal. The South Africans rejected the ruling and, as a result, found themselves facing a low-level insurgency launched by the South West Africa People's Organization (SWAPO), led by Sam Nujoma, a former trade union activist who had fled the country. SWAPO secured a sympathetic ally in President Kaunda of Zambia, who allowed the organization to establish its headquarters in Lusaka.

During this time, South Africa was consolidating apartheid at home as well as in Namibia. Initially, it faced considerable opposition in the form of mass protests, civil disobedience, and other political campaigns. In 1960, the year of Macmillan's "wind of change" speech, South African police shot and killed sixty-seven unarmed protesters in a black township called Sharpeville.

The international outcry and the temporary flight of capital that followed took the government by surprise. But it did not change course. Instead, it declared a state of emergency and the following year outlawed the African National Congress (ANC) and the Pan Africanist Congress (PAC), the main black political parties. These groups then turned to sabotage and other violent actions. The government jailed the organization's leaders, effectively silencing opposition for the rest of the decade. The government's ruthlessness reassured whites, who had been shaken by the political turbulence, and South Africa rode out the 1960s on an unprecedented economic boom that lifted it to new levels of prosperity, power, and confidence.

In the region, Pretoria began to focus its attention on the growth of guerrilla activity, although a buffer of white-controlled states—Angola, Rhodesia, and Mozambique—remained intact. The government was concerned about SWAPO's activities in Namibia and about the outlawed ANC and PAC, which had committed themselves to an armed struggle against the South African government and were showing signs of becoming active from bases in Zambia and Tanzania.

South Africa rejected the United Nations' call for mandatory sanctions against Rhodesia and provided that beleaguered country with a vital economic lifeline. In addition, Pretoria sent police detachments to help the Rhodesians and to intercept guerrillas moving toward South Africa itself. It also gave a limited amount of counter-insurgency assistance to the Portuguese in Angola and Mozambique and increased its spending on internal security, armaments, and military training.

In the late 1960s, Pretoria felt there should also be a diplomatic element to its regional policy to try to persuade the independent black states not to support nationalist movements hostile to South Africa. The primary objective of the "outward movement," as this strategy became known, was to reinforce the white buffer protecting South Africa with a group of neutral—or, better still, friendly—black states. But the strategy had another, broader objective. Its formulators believed that the way to South Africa's acceptance in the West lay through Africa. If South Africa could achieve a measure of respectability with the black states of Africa, its international isolation could be much reduced, if not ended altogether.

The policy was launched by Prime Minister John Vorster, the successor to Hendrik Verwoerd, the apartheid ideologue who was assassinated in 1966 in the parliamentary chamber where Macmillan had made his speech. The idea was to have good relations with as many independent African states as possible, even if those relations fell short of full public acceptance. Within the region, Vorster made some progress by meeting Chief Leabua Jonathan, the prime minister of Lesotho, and establishing diplomatic relations with Malawi—both in 1967—and building a working relationship with Botswana and Swaziland, as well as Lesotho. All three countries refused to sign nonaggression pacts or establish diplomatic relations with Pretoria, but they did join a common customs union and continued to share South Africa's currency.

The African states countered South Africa's diplomatic outreach with the Lusaka Manifesto in 1969 (see Appendix A). It was drawn up by an informal grouping of eastern and southern African countries, which included Tanzania, Zambia, Botswana, and Lesotho, under the direction of President Nyerere. The Lusaka Manifesto, which was later given the OAU's seal of approval, was a seminal document that reflected African thinking on white rule in the region, including apartheid in South Africa. The manifesto affirmed that the Africans would prefer to see majority rule come to the remaining minority-ruled countries by peaceful means, including the removal of apartheid in South Africa and the installation of a nonracial democracy there. But since the white rulers in those countries blocked peaceful transitions to majority rule, the African states had no alternative but to support armed liberation struggles.

On the broader international scene, South Africa became increasingly isolated in the 1960s. The government's racial policies, its open support for Rhodesia, and its refusal to surrender Namibia drew widespread criticism and hostility. In 1963 the United Nations voted in favor of a voluntary arms embargo against South Africa; in the latter part of the decade, there was growing talk of making the embargo mandatory, of economic sanctions, and even of the use of force if South Africa did not mend its ways.

The situation in southern Africa was deceptively calm as the 1970s opened. By then, the African drive for independence and majority rule seemed to have been decisively checked at the Zambezi. The governments of Angola, Mozambique, Rhodesia, and Namibia appeared confident that they could contain the guerrilla wars under way in their countries and maintain the status quo at relatively little cost. The lives of most whites in those countries went on much as before.

The South African government, notwithstanding the rebuff of the Lusaka Manifesto, pursued its African diplomacy in the form of trying to establish a "dialogue" with a number of states beyond the region. In the mid-1970s, Prime Minister Vorster made secret visits to President Felix Houphouet-Boigny of the Ivory Coast and President William Tolbert of Liberia. Shortly afterward, Prime Minister Vorster launched a "détente" initiative in which he met President Kaunda of Zambia in a dramatic encounter on a train over the Victoria Falls on the Rhodesian-Zambian border in an attempt to solve the Rhodesian problem. This meeting turned out to be the crowning point of the various manifestations of the outward movement. The policy collapsed when the South African–Zambian political initiative failed to produce significant results and when South Africa militarily intervened in the Angolan civil war in late 1975. For more than a decade, Pretoria's diplomatic efforts in the region and other parts of Africa would be subordinated to its military priorities.

During the late 1960s and early 1970s, several foreign powers that had had no previous involvement began to take an interest in the region. The retreat of Britain and the growing number of appeals from African nationalist movements for military and other assistance presented a unique opportunity to the Soviet Union, its Eastern European allies, Cuba, and China. Moscow, in particular, was interested in southern Africa. The Soviet Union's view of its superpower status suggested that it should be active globally and in a position to challenge and score points off its superpower adversary, the United States, wherever it chose to do so. Southern Africa had long been an exclusively Western sphere of influence, so the chance to become involved proved irresistible.

Support for the African states and the nationalist movements gave the communist countries an opportunity to put some substance behind their anticolonial and antiracialist rhetoric at the expense of the West. They also had an open door to the southern African liberation movements since no Western country was prepared to provide military training and arms to the guerrillas.

The Sino-Soviet rift, deep and apparently unbridgeable at this stage, produced a further incentive for outsiders to become involved in the region. China was determined not to be left out in this new scramble for Africa, although it was unable to match the resources of its Soviet competitor. In choosing nationalist movements to support, China usually backed rivals of movements patronized by the Soviet Union. For example, in the struggle for Rhodesia, the Soviet Union supported Joshua Nkomo's Zimbabwe African People's Union (ZAPU), the original nationalist movement, while the Chinese backed its breakaway rival, Robert Mugabe's Zimbabwe African National Union (ZANU).

The existence of three nationalist parties in Angola led to a more complicated alignment of foreign support. The Soviet Union and the Cubans decided to back the Popular Movement for the Liberation of Angola (MPLA), while the United States, South Africa, and China provided different levels of support for the other two, the National Front for the Liberation of Angola (FNLA) and the National Union for the Total Independence of Angola (UNITA). In the case of South Africa, the Soviet Union chose the ANC and China supported its rival, the PAC.

Many African states were concerned about this turn of events. One of the founding principles of the OAU had been "Africa for the Africans," meaning nonintervention by foreign powers and the resolution of African problems by the collective efforts of member states in the forum of the OAU. But the Africans' overriding goal was liberation, so no attempt was made to stop nationalist movements from soliciting help outside the continent.

Until the mid-1970s, the United States showed little interest in southern Africa, regarding the area as primarily a matter of British concern. While espousing anticolonial rhetoric, wooing the newly independent black states, and gradually distancing itself from the apartheid government in Pretoria, the United States' energies were engaged elsewhere. Even the escalating wars in Angola and Mozambique failed to produce any serious response, partly because the United States valued Portugal's membership in the North Atlantic Treaty Organization and did not want to upset the Lisbon government.

Rhodesia's break with Britain in 1965 brought about a marginally greater U.S. interest in that part of the region, and Washington supported the imposition of mandatory sanctions against the rebel colony in the United Nations. But as the 1970s opened, it was clear that many U.S. policy makers shared the perception of most of southern Africa's whites that a revolutionary transformation was not imminent and that change could come only through the initiative of the white governments.

The decade was only a little more than three years old, however, when an event occurred that radically changed the balance of power in southern Africa. In April 1974 a coalition of leftwing and centrist Portuguese army officers, radicalized by the long and apparently unwinnable wars in the African colonies, overthrew the forty-year-old dictatorship in Lisbon. Within eighteen months Mozambique and Angola were independent under revolutionary, self-styled Marxist movements that had led the struggle against the Portuguese. Rhodesia, which was beginning to feel the effects of almost a decade of sanctions and several years of escalating guerrilla warfare, suddenly found itself with a hostile neighbor—Mozambique—on its flank. The wind of change was blowing again.

Whites fled en masse from Mozambique and Angola, taking all they could with them and leaving both countries with a debilitating shortage of skilled manpower. In Mozambique, the Marxist movement, the Front for the Liberation of Mozambique (FRELIMO), assumed power without serious opposition in June 1975. In Angola, however, a bitter struggle broke out between the three nationalist parties—the MPLA, the FNLA, and UNITA—after the Portuguese left in November 1975. The fighting escalated when South Africa, supported by clandestine U.S. aid, sent in troops to support the FNLA and UNITA and the Soviet Union replied by dispatching large supplies of arms and equipment and ferrying in some twenty-five thousand Cuban combat troops. The MPLA rapidly gained the upper hand, and South Africa withdrew its forces over the Namibian border in January 1976.

In addition to ending its attempt to establish a diplomatic dialogue with black Africa, South Africa's intervention in Angola had important political repercussions. A number of African states, the most important being Nigeria, which had remained neutral on Angola up to this point, recognized the MPLA as the legitimate government of Angola. Similarly, several hesitant European countries also made up their minds and formally recognized the MPLA. In the United States, the specter of another foreign entanglement similar to the recently ended Vietnam imbroglio, and distaste at being on the same side as South Africa in an African conflict, prompted the Congress to pass the Clark Amendment. Sponsored by Senator Dick Clark, a Democrat from Iowa who chaired the Senate's subcommittee on Africa, the legislation banned U.S. assistance to any group in Angola.

In contrast to its Angolan policy, Pretoria adopted a more cautious and sophisticated approach toward Mozambique. It rejected an appeal by Portuguese and Mozambican rightwing groups to support them against the newly installed FRELIMO government and took the line that it could live in harmony with its close neighbor. South Africa had strong economic ties with Mozambique, notably the use of the railway link and the port of Maputo, which served as a trade outlet for much of the industrial Transvaal, and of hydroelectric power supplies from the giant Cahora Bassa Dam, which had just come on line when the Lisbon coup occurred. Vorster's government appeared to calculate that economic self-interest would play an important part in restraining FRELIMO from hostile actions against South Africa.

Pretoria did not, at this point, appear concerned about FRELIMO's open espousal of black nationalism in Rhodesia, a support that was soon translated into allowing Robert Mugabe's ZANU movement to establish guerrilla bases in Mozambique for training and for launching attacks across the Rhodesian border. FRELIMO also joined the international economic embargo of Rhodesia by blocking the beleaguered country's eastern road, rail, and port trade outlets. Neither of these acts, both of which proved to be extremely costly to Mozambique, seemed to rouse the ire of the South Africans, who were actively seeking ways to end the Rhodesian conflict.

Nevertheless, it was clear that the collapse of the Portuguese was a watershed in southern Africa. The formerly impervious white buffer zone around South Africa had been breached on each flank, and only an enfeebled Rhodesia remained in the center. The success of two revolutionary leftwing guerrilla movements—the MPLA in Angola and FRELIMO in Mozambique—boosted the morale of the region's other black nationalist groups and gave heart to opposition forces inside South Africa itself. The new governments of Angola and Mozambique also began to give material assistance to the ANC by permitting the organization to establish political offices and guerrilla training camps in their territories.

The United States began to show concern about developments in the region, particularly the advance of Soviet and Cuban power in Angola but also the expanding civil war in Rhodesia. In 1976 Henry Kissinger, President Ford's secretary of state, made an effort to mediate a settlement in Rhodesia with the active support of Vorster and the Frontline States, an informal grouping created in 1976 to coordinate the liberation struggle in Rhodesia and consisting of Tanzania, Zambia, Botswana, Angola, and Mozambique. Ian Smith, under pressure from Vorster and Kissinger, agreed to the principle of majority rule but refused to hand over power.

Although Kissinger was unsuccessful, he set a precedent for a more assertive U.S. diplomacy in the region designed to counter Soviet influence and stabilize the area. He also established an order of priorities that placed Rhodesia first, Namibia second, and South Africa last. By the time the Carter administration took office in 1977, it was clear that the wind of change, now fixed on its southern course, had brought with it the frigid air of superpower rivalry.

The crisis in Rhodesia deepened in the late 1970s as the Smith government became increasingly embattled. Much of the countryside was lost to guerrilla forces attacking from Zambia to the north and across the long and vulnerable Mozambique border to the east. Economic sanctions and an exodus of draft-age whites also undermined the government's resistance. In 1978 Smith made an attempt to co-opt black leaders with an "internal" settlement. This led to elections the following year and the installation of Bishop Abel Muzorewa as prime minister of "Zimbabwe-Rhodesia." A political neophyte, Muzorewa had made his name earlier by rallying opposition to Smith. ZAPU and ZANU, the two nationalist movements carrying out the guerrilla war, were excluded from both the settlement and the elections. The Muzorewa government failed to gain either international recognition or an end to sanctions, and the guerrilla war continued.

The crucial moment in the Rhodesian crisis came at a meeting of the Commonwealth countries in Lusaka in August 1979. By then, it was clear that while the guerrilla forces were not going to be beaten, their supporters in the Frontline States were not prepared to wait for a fight to the finish. Rhodesia's main ally, South Africa, under P. W. Botha, who had succeeded Vorster in 1978, also wanted a settlement to end the war. President Nyerere of Tanzania produced the formula: a round-table conference in London, chaired by Britain, to be followed by free elections leading to independence.

The result was the Lancaster House agreement of December 1979. Zimbabweans went to the polls in February 1980 and overwhelmingly elected ZANU, led by Robert Mugabe, a devout Catholic and self-proclaimed Marxist. Zimbabwe became independent in April under a government that was nationalist and strongly opposed to apartheid. The last buffer state separating South Africa from the black-ruled states to the north had fallen.

Namibia, still firmly under South African control, was the next focus of international attention in the region. Once dubbed "a dry place surrounded by a desert," Namibia, with a population of a little over a million, would seem an unlikely candidate for controversy. But Pretoria's refusal to cede to the United Nations its lapsed League of Nations mandate over Namibia ensured that South Africa's presence would be challenged.

South Africa had dropped a plan to annex Namibia but had continued to defy rulings by the United Nations and the World Court to leave the territory. In 1977, however, Pretoria agreed to take part in negotiations over Namibia's future with the Western "Contact Group" consisting of the United States, Britain, France, West Germany, and Canada. Launched by the Carter administration, this was a U.S.–led initiative to work out a formula for securing the independence of the territory through UN–supervised elections. Protracted negotiations produced a plan that was adopted by the United Nations Security Council as Resolution 435 in 1978 (see Appendix B). It called for a cease-fire between South African and SWAPO forces, the insertion of a UN peacekeeping and monitoring force, the withdrawal of South African troops, elections, and independence. South Africa agreed in principle to the plan but raised a series of objections to implementing it. The decade closed inconclusively, with the plan still on the table but with no signs of South Africa putting it into effect.

South Africa had experienced a new wave of internal political turmoil when Soweto and other black townships erupted during 1976–77. Thousands of young blacks fled the country, and many of them joined the ANC's military wing in guerrilla camps located in Angola, Zambia, and Mozambique. South Africa also had suffered further international ostracism when the United Nations made its 1963 voluntary arms embargo mandatory in late 1977. Nevertheless, Pretoria's military and economic power continued to dwarf that of its neighbors; it was an internationally recognized sovereign state;

and its white population appeared to have the will and the ability to resist outside pressures.

Yet, it was equally clear by the end of the 1970s that Pretoria had failed to translate its regional power into good relations with its neighbors. Although weak and economically dependent on South Africa, the black states remained adamantly opposed to Pretoria's control of Namibia and to apartheid. Their political hostility was expressed through continuing support for the Namibian and South African nationalist movements and by denying South Africa the acceptance it sought. The result was an uneasy standoff on the banks of the Limpopo.

The scene was thus set for the 1980s. Twenty years after Macmillan's speech, a major chapter in African history had ended. All the territories formerly ruled by European powers were independent. Zimbabwe's independence had advanced the frontiers of black Africa. Whatever the future had in store for South Africa, a sovereign nation, and its satellite, Namibia, it seemed clear that a process of dramatic change had begun.

The focus of this book is the critical decade of the 1980s, and the essays that follow concentrate on the major developments during that period and their implications for the future. The essays span the political, military, and economic dimensions of the decade; assess the actions and interests of the superpowers; and tally some of the social costs.

Robert S. Jaster, a political and military analyst, examines the rising levels of conflict that shook the region during much of the 1980s, the increasing involvement of the superpowers, and the dramatic diplomatic breakthrough that led to the independence of Namibia and the withdrawal of the Cubans from Angola. He focuses on South Africa's strategy, its military strengths and weaknesses, its quest for political acceptability in the region, and the implications of the developments during the 1980s for South Africa's relations with its neighbors in the new decade.

Turning to the economic and infrastructural links that bind South Africa to the black-ruled states of southern Africa, Moeletsi Mbeki, a journalist, and Morley Nkosi, an economist, trace the changing economic fortunes of South Africa's neighbors during this period. They analyze the rival economic strategies employed on each side of the Limpopo River as the decade opened, and profile the black states. They also examine South Africa's use of its leverage over transportation, trade and investment, and migrant labor to put pressure on its neighbors and the black states' response. They conclude with an assessment of the role of the Southern African Development Coordination Conference (SADCC) during the first decade of its existence.

Michael Clough, a political scientist, analyzes the critical role of the superpowers in the region. He traces the history of superpower rivalry in the 1970s, the escalating confrontation in the 1980s, the collapse of the United States' policy of "constructive engagement," and the underlying factors that turned superpower competition into cooperation at the end of the decade. He concludes that, with the cold war over and fundamental change under way in South Africa, the United States and the former Soviet Union have lost interest in the region and the era of superpower rivalry is not likely to be revived. The book ends with an extensive extract from the UNICEF report, *The Flowers Are Cut Down: The Human Costs of Regional Conflict*, which documents the human cost of the civil wars, South Africa's destabilization strategy, and foreign intervention in the region during this decade.

John de St. Jorre

WAR AND DIPLOMACY

Robert S. Jaster

Evolution of a Regional Conflict

After a long period of immobility, the demarcation line between black- and white-ruled states in southern Africa shifted southward in the second half of the 1970s. Portuguese rule in Angola and Mozambique collapsed in 1975, following a coup in Lisbon the previous year. A negotiated settlement ended both the guerrilla war and white minority rule in Rhodesia, transforming that country into the independent state of Zimbabwe in early 1980. The white redoubt thus was reduced to South Africa and Namibia.

Despite its fears about encroaching black nationalism, South Africa remained indisputably the military and economic giant of southern Africa, dwarfing its neighbors. Its military budget was twice the size and its economy three times as large as those of the six Frontline States combined.[1] It controlled many of its neighbors' trade outlets; supplied a considerable portion of their imports, including food and fuel; and possessed a nuclear weapons potential that they lacked.

It was not surprising, therefore, that South Africa's white leaders saw their country as the regional superpower. They believed they could best assure the survival of apartheid if they could establish a framework of close economic, diplomatic, and mutual security ties with nearby states on the basis of their country's superior military and economic strength. If necessary, South Africa's overwhelming military power could be used to keep its neighbors in line.

But South Africa—whose defense of white rule and sense of siege formed the core of its relations in the region—was unable to convert its military and economic dominance into African recognition and acceptance. The Frontline States cited South Africa's refusal to withdraw from Namibia and to share power with its black majority at home as the stumbling blocks to better relations. For those reasons, they denied South Africa the influence and legitimacy it sought and gave sanctuary to armed South African and Namibian liberation groups. That, in turn, made South Africa even more determined to defend itself by all possible means against internal and external threats and led to a more aggressive military posture against its neighbors. Thus, four factors dominated regional relations as the 1980s opened: South Africa's continuing defense of white minority rule, the black states' support for guerrillas operating against South Africa and Namibia, South Africa's superior military power, and its pariah status in the region.

During the eighties, the level of conflict in the region increased alarmingly. Low-level guerrilla campaigns against Namibia and South Africa escalated and drew increasingly punitive South African reprisals. By mid-decade, virtually every country in southern Africa was affected by the widening circle of warfare and the resulting social and economic disruption. Hostilities dislocated normal trade and transport routes through much of the region and deepened the already serious economic plight of most of the black states. Angola and Mozambique, both struggling against South African–backed guerrilla forces, were the worst affected. Angola, particularly, experienced a rapid expansion of conflict as South Africa attacked guerrilla bases, openly supported a dissident movement, and directly engaged Angolan government forces.

Outside states became increasingly involved. Cuba, which had kept troops in Angola since the mid-1970s to support the government, began raising its force level as South African military intervention intensified. The United States and the Soviet Union, competitors in southern Africa since the early 1970s, provided increasing amounts of military assistance to the opposing sides in Angola, thereby contributing to the widening war.

The result was an increasingly costly stalemate. South Africa suffered less than did its neighbors, but it, too, started to experience heavy costs. The war severely strained the South African economy, and rising battle casualties made the conflict unpopular with the country's white electorate. At the same time, South Africa was experiencing political and economic pressures due to a sustained internal black revolt and international sanctions.

The stalemate in Angola persuaded all parties to consider the idea of a negotiated settlement. The prospects for peace were enhanced by two external factors. One was a longstanding U.S.–led diplomatic initiative that had narrowed the differences between the opposing sides over the terms of a settlement in Namibia and the withdrawal of Cuban and South African troops from Angola. The other was President Mikhail Gorbachev's decision that Soviet involvement in a costly and unwinnable war in Angola had become a serious obstacle to better relations with the United States, which were necessary for the success of his domestic reforms. Although unable to dictate a settlement, the superpowers proved indispensable in brokering one, since it had become clear that none of the states in the region, either alone or in concert, could produce a solution.

The resulting Namibian-Angolan peace accords in late 1988 represented a major turning point in southern Africa, removing outside forces from Angola and bringing to a conclusion more than two decades of international conflict over Namibia, Africa's last colony. But they did not resolve the domestic conflicts in Angola and Mozambique, although they increased the diplomatic pressure on the combatants to make peace.

The decade was a remarkable one for southern Africa. It witnessed the final act of African decolonization, the end of serious superpower rivalry, and the beginning of political change in South Africa itself. As the 1990s opened, South Africa was finding that its withdrawal from Namibia and its moves toward genuine reform at home were bringing it a degree of acceptance by its neighbors that armed might and economic strength had failed to achieve.

This essay analyzes the conflicts of the 1980s in southern Africa: how they came about, how they developed, and why, after a decade of failed diplomacy and expanding violence, a Namibian settlement was reached. The roles of the major actors are traced, with the focus on South Africa, the mover-and-shaker in southern Africa.

The first section provides a brief explanation of the conflicts in the region, their origins, and their relation to each other, particularly from the standpoint of South Africa's strategic and domestic political interests. The second part examines the characteristics of South Africa's war machine that enabled it to conduct military operations against its neighbors with virtual impunity for much of the

1980s. The constraints on the South African military, notably those revealed by the war in Angola in the late 1980s, are also analyzed. The third section explains the developments leading to the Namibian-Angolan peace accords of 1988, analyzes their significance, and discusses the ensuing shifts in South African relations with other regional states. The essay concludes with an analysis of the changes in the relationship between South Africa and its neighbors in the new era of a free Namibia, an Angola without Cuban forces, and superpower détente.

Escalating Warfare: 1978–88

At the opening of the 1980s, the stage was set for a rapid expansion of conflict in southern Africa. The black-governed states, bolstered by an independent Zimbabwe under a militantly anti-apartheid leadership, had rejected Pretoria's appeal for formal economic and security ties and were forming an economic grouping that pointedly excluded South Africa. Namibian and South African black nationalist movements were stepping up their guerrilla operations. South Africa, under an aggressive new leader and driven by the notion of a Soviet-orchestrated "total onslaught" against it, had already begun to strike at guerrilla sanctuaries across its borders. The superpowers remained locked in a cold war that was reflected in their support for opposing sides in the region and their refusal to cooperate on seeking peaceful solutions there.

Prelude to Conflict

When Pieter W. Botha became prime minister in September 1978, South Africa had already embarked on a policy of destabilization against its neighbors that Botha himself had devised. Botha had been defense minister for twelve years before becoming prime minister and was known for his hawkish views on foreign policy and for his impulsiveness. (His nicknames were "Piet Wapen"—Afrikaans for "Pete the Gun"—among his colleagues and "Bomber Botha" with the press.)

In 1975 Botha and the generals had prevailed on B. J. Vorster, then prime minister, to invade Angola—an ill-conceived and ill-fated attempt to prevent the Soviet- and Cuban-backed Popular Movement for the Liberation of Angola (MPLA) party from coming to power. In May 1978 Botha won the physically ailing Vorster's approval to launch South Africa's first deep penetration raid against a South West Africa People's Organization (SWAPO) guerrilla camp inside Angola. South Africa was also providing vital supplies of weapons, fuel, and small military units to protect transport routes to Ian Smith's embattled white minority government in Rhodesia. In defending the incursion into Angola, Botha reiterated a major precept in South African military strategy: "The Government's view is that we do not want war on our own soil, and we therefore want to stop the enemy before he comes over our borders."[2]

During the late 1970s, Botha and his generals formulated the twin concept of a total onslaught against South Africa and the need for "a total national strategy" mobilizing all the country's resources to meet it. Botha asserted that South Africa was the target of a Communist-orchestrated "total onslaught under the guidance of the planners in the Kremlin" whose objective was "to overthrow this State and create chaos in its stead, so that the Kremlin can establish its hegemony here."[3] SWAPO and African National Congress (ANC) operatives based in neighboring countries were seen as the military spearhead of the alleged onslaught.

The threat was perceived to be wide-ranging and to include such diverse activities as anti-apartheid demonstrations abroad, black protests and boycotts at home, and even Western pressure on South Africa for domestic reform and Namibia's independence. Botha blamed the United Nations and the Organization of African Unity (OAU) for joining in the onslaught, and he was particularly bitter over the lack of Western sympathy. "We can do nothing," he said, "to turn the hungry beast of Marxism to peaceful intentions regarding us. We can do nothing about the demands made on us by the weak, concessions-politics of Washington."[4]

Based on the writings of the French military strategist General André Beaufre, the total strategy notion had been harnessed by Botha to win support for larger defense budgets and a more aggressive posture in the region. In government circles, the perceived need for such a strategy was given added urgency by the uprising in the black townships in 1976–77 and growing external pressures, notably the imposition of the UN mandatory arms embargo in 1977.

During 1978–79 President Botha took a number of steps to put the total national strategy into practice. A national security management system was established and senior military personnel were brought into prominent positions in the policy process. The State Security Council (SSC), a cabinet committee chaired by the prime minister (later state president), was reinforced with a large secretariat headed by military staff members. Under President Botha, the SSC became a sort of inner cabinet that sometimes made decisions on issues of national strategy and security without the participation of the full cabinet.[5] As a result, the military's influence on regional policy became decisive during the Botha years. The length of military service was doubled, an emergency radio network was established along the border to link commando (local defense) units to nearby military bases, and construction was begun on new army and air bases near the Mozambican border. Faced with a limited reservoir of white conscripts, President Botha sought to attract more black volunteers into the armed forces. South Africa also began to support and train Angolan, Mozambican, and Zimbabwean dissidents to carry out sabotage and military operations against their governments.

But President Botha also offered an olive branch to his neighbors in the form of economic cooperation and mutual security pacts. The object was to woo them away from Soviet and Western influence and, in particular, to induce them to stop giving support and sanctuary to the ANC and SWAPO. The most ambitious of these initiatives was launched early in 1979, when President Botha and his foreign minister suggested a grand scheme of regional cooperation under which South Africa and the other states in the area would resolve their problems without outside interference. The proposal envisaged a "constellation" consisting of seven to ten southern African states, totaling up to forty million people, with South Africa at its center. It would involve close collaboration in "all important spheres," including mutual security arrangements. Eventually "international secretariats" might be formed to regulate the affairs of member states.[6]

The first setback to the constellation idea was its outright rejection by the leaders of the Frontline States, who responded with their own plan, the Southern African Development Coordination Conference (SADCC). SADCC's twin goals—to strengthen economic cooperation and development among the black states and to reduce their dependence on South Africa—flew in the face of Botha's scheme. Botswana, Lesotho, Malawi, and Swaziland, four of the states South Africa had hoped to include in a regional organization, promptly joined SADCC. The five other SADCC member-states are Angola, Mozambique, Tanzania, Zambia, and Zimbabwe.

In early 1980 the constellation proposal was dealt a mortal blow by the election of Robert Mugabe as the first prime minister of an independent Zimbabwe. Mugabe was an outspoken critic of apartheid and declared that Zimbabwe would join SADCC. South African officials had been pinning their hopes on the election of the conservative Bishop Abel Muzorewa, who, they felt, would seek close economic and security links to Pretoria.

The victory of black nationalism in Zimbabwe was a watershed event in the region. Its effects were multilayered and complex. While it ended a bloody bush war and thus removed a source of growing regional conflict and instability, it also raised fears among South African whites that Namibia and then South Africa would be the next "dominoes" to fall. The defeat of Muzorewa led South African officials to express concern that what they termed the "Muzorewa syndrome"—that is, the defeat of a South African–supported candidate—would occur if free elections were to be held in Namibia, where Pretoria was backing a loose coalition against SWAPO. The Botha government's resolve to resist holding free elections in Namibia was thus stiffened.

Mugabe's victory also raised expectations among black South Africans. Coming only five years after the takeover of Angola and Mozambique by groups that had fought long bush wars, Mugabe's triumph encouraged the belief among South African blacks that armed insurgency could topple the South African white regime. Events in Zimbabwe also had an effect on Pretoria's regional strategy. Although taken by surprise, the government had no illusions that Zimbabwe would adopt a friendly stance toward Pretoria. The new nation, Botha predicted, would "probably be pressurized to play an active role in the onslaught" against South Africa.[7]

South Africa, the African National Congress, and the Sanctuary States

By the early 1980s, the governments of Angola, Botswana, Lesotho, Mozambique, Swaziland, Zambia, and Zimbabwe had allowed the ANC to establish offices and maintain sizable numbers of personnel in their countries. Angola and Mozambique offered virtually full sanctuary to the ANC, including military bases and training camps. The other states were more cautious; they restricted the ANC presence to nonmilitary personnel and prohibited cross-border attacks against South Africa. With the exception of Zimbabwe, however, these sanctuary states lacked the capability, and in some cases the will, to monitor ANC activities.

The ANC consequently was able to plan and execute a series of sophisticated attacks against South African targets from relatively close range. Among the more spectacular was a night attack in June 1980 on the prestigious Sasol oil-from-coal complex, which destroyed fuel storage facilities and sent flames high into the night sky. The ANC mounted nineteen separate actions in 1980 and fifty-five in 1981, including a rocket attack on South Africa's main army base near Pretoria and the blacking out of several towns through sabotage of power stations. In December 1982 carefully placed limpet mines caused extensive damage to South Africa's only nuclear power complex at Koeberg. Six months later a car bomb attack on the air force headquarters in Pretoria killed sixteen people and wounded two hundred.[8]

Although often daring and headline-catching, the ANC's guerrilla activities did not threaten the government's ability to maintain control. Yet President Botha could not afford to be seen as "soft" in the face of this growing challenge. This was particularly important since his program for domestic race reform was already under attack by the rightwing of South Africa's ruling National Party.

To win broad support for his reforms, President Botha had to demonstrate that his government was in control of events, that it was implacable in the face of outside provocation, and that armed insurgency would not be allowed to succeed. Botha, who had a reputation for toughness, decided that the sanctuary states should be made to pay a price, in a highly visible way, for sheltering the ANC. Thus, the destabilization policy was spurred by a vital link between South African domestic politics and the ANC offensive.

South Africa responded to the upsurge in ANC actions with *blitzkrieg* raids against suspected ANC targets in neighboring capitals. A South African attack on ANC headquarters in Maputo in January 1981, carried out by a unit of the South African Defense Force (SADF), disguised as Mozambican troops, killed a dozen ANC members. The timing of that raid—two days before Botha announced a general election for whites—indicated its domestic political importance for him. The 1981 attack was followed by others: an airborne commando raid on suspected ANC personnel in Maseru (Lesotho's capital) in December 1982 and a second attack on Maputo in October 1983 against an alleged ANC planning office that turned out to be a local jam factory.

Mozambique was a major target of South African attacks because it was perceived to be the principal staging area for ANC cross-border operations. In addition to enduring the two SADF raids on its capital, Mozambique was reeling under the impact of sabotage and disruption caused by the Mozambique National Resistance (RENAMO). This was a force of mercenaries and Mozambican dissidents originally organized by Smith's government in Rhodesia to fight the Marxist Front for the Liberation of Mozambique (FRELIMO) guerrillas who were challenging Portuguese colonial rule in Mozambique. After the collapse of white minority rule in Rhodesia, RENAMO was trained, armed, financed, and directed by South Africa to destabilize the victorious FRELIMO government in Maputo headed by ex-guerrilla Samora Machel.

In late 1983 the Mozambican government decided that it must come to terms with South Africa and sought U.S. intervention to arrange a rapprochement. The result was the Nkomati Accord, "a nonaggression and good neighborliness" pact, signed by Botha and Machel at a flag-decked ceremony in the small South African border town of Nkomati on March 16, 1984 (see Appendix C). The treaty obliged both sides to stop aiding each other's enemies and to set up a joint security commission to monitor the agreement. In practice, this meant that Mozambique would expel ANC operatives from the country and curb the organization's political activities there, while South Africa would end its support for RENAMO.

Machel's government kept its side of the bargain. Some eight hundred ANC operatives were expelled, and ANC attacks on South Africa from Mozambique ceased.[9] Although South Africa claimed to have ended its support for RENAMO, the movement expanded its operations. In late 1984 South Africa's foreign minister, Roelof F. ("Pik") Botha, tried unsuccessfully to mediate the dispute. Then, in August 1985, Mozambican troops overran Gorongosa, one of RENAMO's provincial headquarters, and documents captured there revealed that the South African military had violated the Nkomati Accord by continuing to provide aid to the dissident group.[10]

South African officials admitted the charges. They explained that they had maintained links with RENAMO to facilitate negotiations between the movement and the Mozambique government, and that since September 1985 all aid had been ended. Evidence showed, however, that South African military intelligence officials, with or without the knowledge and approval of higher authority, continued to provide clandestine assistance to RENAMO.[11] As late as April 1986, U.S. Secretary of State George Shultz stated that the South Africans "were not keeping their side of the bargain."[12] The breaches in the Nkomati Accord revealed serious divisions within the South African bureaucracy over the policy toward Mozambique. The Department of Foreign Affairs favored strict adherence to the pact, while elements in the military were reluctant to withdraw support for RENAMO.

In September 1986 the fighting in Mozambique took on a regional dimension as Zimbabwe and Tanzania intervened militarily on a substantial scale to help the hard-pressed government's counterinsurgency against RENAMO. By 1987 Zimbabwe had deployed about twelve thousand troops in Mozambique, mainly to protect the Beira corridor containing the vital road, rail, and oil lines from Zimbabwe to Mozambique's Indian Ocean port of Beira. Tanzania sent in about one thousand troops, who held various towns after Mozambican and Zimbabwean forces had cleared them of RENAMO elements. Malawi, another neighbor but not a member of the Frontline States, provided a contingent of two hundred soldiers to guard its rail link with the Mozambican port of Nacala. This joint military cooperation put considerable pressure on RENAMO, which suffered serious reverses in 1987.

By then the Botha government appeared to have curbed the South African military's clandestine aid to RENAMO and to be seriously pursuing a rapprochement and closer economic ties with Maputo. In August 1987 the two governments revived the Nkomati Accord and began negotiating technical and economic cooperation. RENAMO suffered another setback at that time, when the Reagan administration resisted rightwing pressure to assist RENAMO, and instead reiterated its support for the government. The publication in April 1988 of a U.S. State Department–commissioned report on Mozambican refugees further damaged RENAMO's public image. Prepared by Robert Gersony, an independent expert on refugees, the report charged RENAMO with systematically carrying out the murder of an estimated one hundred thousand civilians and causing well over two hundred thousand to become refugees.[13]

RENAMO lacked credentials as a legitimate nationalist movement, a clearly defined leadership, or a coherent political program. Yet, neither international ostracism nor the cutoff of South African aid seemed to reduce its capacity to survive and wreak havoc inside Mozambique. It continued to terrorize the population, disrupt the economy, and threaten the survival of the Mozambican government. In the latter part of the decade, RENAMO's depredations finally became a source of embarrassment to the Botha government. Pretoria discovered that it was far easier to organize a proxy force than to curtail its activities when it was no longer useful.

* * *

At the time of the 1984 Nkomati Accord, it was revealed that Swaziland had signed a similar security pact with South Africa in 1982 and had expelled ANC personnel. In 1985, after South African raids on the capitals of Lesotho and Botswana, these states began to monitor the ANC more closely and arrest or expel members suspected of being guerrillas. But both countries refused to sign nonaggression treaties with Pretoria despite considerable pressure from South Africa to do so.

RENAMO was not the only dissident movement that South Africa assisted. Pretoria also helped organize and support armed groups fighting the governments of Lesotho, Zimbabwe, and according to some reports, Zambia. Dissident groups were provided with weapons, training, communications, and money. These three countries were targeted because they were thought to be allowing ANC guerrillas to launch attacks against South Africa or to be turning a blind eye to such activities.

Zimbabwe was particularly vulnerable because a sizable group of disaffected nationalist guerrillas, who had fought against Smith's government in the 1970s, fomented a rebellion in the southwest of the country during the mid-1980s. South Africa provided assistance to the rebels, who carried out a series of attacks on isolated farms and other civilian targets. Mugabe's government crushed the uprising with considerable brutality but made an effort to negotiate a political accommodation with the dissidents' leaders.

In addition to military force, South Africa employed an array of economic measures in its destabilization strategy. The black states' economic dependence on South Africa, inherited from the colonial era, played into Pretoria's hands. (See the essay by Moeletsi Mbeki and Morley Nkosi in this book.) The rail network was the trade lifeline for many of South Africa's landlocked neighbors. It gave Pretoria an important lever to use in what became known as "railway diplomacy." By manipulating the flow of traffic, South Africa sought to deter hostile actions and encourage good behavior among its neighbors.

Zimbabwe was again a principal target. Mugabe's South African policy had been clear and consistent throughout a decade of uneasy relations. While he denied bases and transit rights to ANC guerrillas and maintained extensive trade and transport links with South Africa, he refused to deal with Pretoria at the ministerial level and maintained a steady flow of anti-apartheid rhetoric.

On several occasions, Pretoria applied pressure to landlocked Zimbabwe's trade and transportation lifeline in retaliation for Mugabe's hostility. In 1982 supplies of fuel were cut off, causing the Zimbabwean government to ration gasoline and diesel fuel. In August 1986, after the Commonwealth states adopted a package of sanctions against South Africa, Foreign Minister R. F. Botha announced the imposition of "strict border controls," namely, a slowing of rail traffic, on goods transiting South Africa en route to Zimbabwe and Zambia. This action, he said, would force them "to put their money where their mouth is."[14] Zambia and Zimbabwe had agreed to end all air links with South Africa as part of the Commonwealth sanctions package. But after South Africa's threats, neither country followed through.

Lesotho, a small, impoverished state surrounded by South Africa, was also subjected to economic pressures. Chief Leabua Jonathan, the autocratic leader who had ruled Lesotho since its independence in 1966, had incurred Pretoria's ire by protecting ANC activists and refugees and establishing ties with Communist countries. In the mid-1980s, South Africa tried but failed to persuade Chief Jonathan to hand over suspected ANC personnel living in Lesotho. At that time, Chief Jonathan was having serious difficulties with his opposition. At the height of the crisis, in January 1986, Pretoria imposed a blockade cutting off all supplies of food, fuel, and other goods. A military coup, encouraged by South Africa, quickly followed, and Chief Jonathan was overthrown. The new government agreed to expel ANC personnel but refused Pretoria's demands that they be turned over to South African authorities. The blockade was then lifted.

By 1984–85 the exiled ANC leadership, recognizing that South Africa's military power and the loss of sanctuaries close to South Africa ruled out a traditional insurgency, changed its strategy. Since ANC military planners were forced to move to Zambia, which was too distant from South Africa to plan and oversee complex operations, attacks were limited to simple sabotage operations that could be carried out by one or two people with little training or preparation.

The ANC was also preoccupied with the mass protests and turbulence that were spreading through South Africa's black townships at this time. The United Democratic Front (UDF) emerged as the organizational leader of the revolt. A coalition of anti-apartheid organizations formed to organize opposition to the proposed constitution (which gave a measure of power to Coloureds and Indians but excluded Africans), the UDF identified with the ANC's political philosophy but remained formally independent of it. The ANC, which had not anticipated the uprising, began to look for a role to play. At a major conference held in Zambia in June 1985, the ANC leadership decided on a new strategy: the "people's war." It would use armed actions by ANC recruits inside South Africa to supplement the nonviolent protest movement led by the UDF. Operationally, this meant recruiting and giving basic training in explosives and hand weapons to "part-time guerrillas." Their targets would be apartheid institutions, particularly the police, in their home communities.[15]

This shift resulted in less centralized control over ANC operatives and an increased prospect of attacks against civilian targets, something the ANC had generally, but not always, been able to avoid. ANC operations became less sophisticated and more indiscriminate, and the number of incidents increased. In 1985, for example, they exceeded 100, more than twice the 1984 total. Of the 245 attacks that occurred in 1988, 73 were directed at civilian targets.[16] Although the ANC was not responsible for all these incidents, its leadership publicly acknowledged responsibility for attacks on civilian targets and announced that it had taken steps to prevent them in the future.[17]

As ANC attacks continued, South Africa retaliated with new raids across its borders. In May 1986 simultaneous attacks were made on alleged ANC targets in three neighboring Commonwealth states: Botswana, Zambia, and Zimbabwe. They were launched during the week that the Eminent Persons Group—a mediating delegation of Commonwealth notables—had come to South Africa to discuss the prospect of exploratory talks between the Botha government and the ANC and other opposition groups. The motive for the raids clearly was political rather than military—a gesture of defiance and a rejection of the Commonwealth mission. The raids led to strong condemnation by virtually all Commonwealth, African, and Western states: Canada recalled its ambassador, Argentina severed diplomatic relations, and a bipartisan group of U.S. senators and representatives called for tougher sanctions against South Africa.

The Botha government, surprised by the diplomatic repercussions and concerned that the costs might outweigh the benefits, reduced its cross-border activities in frequency and scale, but did not immediately end them. It also shifted the focus of its campaign against the ANC to individual clandestine actions: kidnappings and assassinations of ANC personnel in Europe and nearby African countries by anonymous hit squads. South Africa is widely believed to be responsible for the assassinations of thirteen ANC members in foreign countries in 1987 alone, including Dulcie September, a longtime ANC representative in Paris.

The ANC did manage, however, to continue to operate at a low level inside South Africa. The Pan Africanist Congress (PAC), a rival nationalist movement, after a long period of inaction, also was able to penetrate South Africa's security and conduct a few isolated acts of sabotage and other attacks. But as the struggle between Pretoria and the ANC showed signs of retreating into the shadows, South Africa's focus shifted to its de facto colony, Namibia, and to the escalating conflict in the vast savannahs of southern Angola.

The Struggle Over Namibia

South Africa's refusal to relinquish control over Namibia was driven by the twin imperatives of territorial security and domestic politics. Although Namibia's minerals are of considerable importance, economic factors had little impact on the policy. The South African military, in particular, viewed Namibia as a buffer against guerrilla incursion or a conventional attack on South Africa itself. Defense Minister Magnus Malan and Foreign Minister R. F. Botha outlined these interests in a joint interview given in an Afrikaans newspaper, *Die Transvaaler*, in March 1981. "The security interests of South Africa and South-West Africa are irrevocably and inseparably tied to each other," they said. A South African withdrawal, they noted, would place "the enemy closer to the heartland of the Republic," make a conventional attack on South Africa more imminent, and reduce its ability to withstand such an attack.[18]

The military establishment was also concerned over its base in Walvis Bay, Namibia's only major deep-water port, which South Africa claimed as an integral part of its territory. Defense Minister Malan voiced the military's concern in a confidential discussion with U.S. officials in 1981, asserting:

> . . . the [South African government] can't accept prospects of a SWAPO victory which brings Soviet/Cuban forces to Walvis

Bay. . . . *This would result from any election which left SWAPO in a dominant position*[19] [emphasis added].

The government also feared the possible political costs of the loss of Namibia to SWAPO—an event that would be widely perceived as the fall of the penultimate domino, with South Africa the next in line. Black South Africans would see it as another example of how armed insurgency eventually pays off. It was thought that the morale of white South Africans, as well as that of co-opted blacks (such as the leaders of the nominally independent tribal "homelands"), would be seriously affected. Moreover, Namibia's seventy thousand whites—5 percent of the total population—were politically active and for the most part extremely conservative. The territory's white politicians maintained close links with their South African counterparts and were able to exert pressure on the government in Pretoria. South Africa's foreign minister complained that even his government's cautious moves to negotiate a Namibian settlement had led to "frequent allegations that it has sold South West Africa's whites down the river."[20] Thus, the stakes for the Botha government were high, and it mounted a broad and determined campaign to prevent a settlement that might lead to a SWAPO government in Namibia.

Botha's Namibian strategy had three objectives. The first was to destroy SWAPO as a credible military force. Second, Botha sought to build a strong, multiethnic coalition inside Namibia that could offer a viable alternative to SWAPO in the event of free elections. Third, while engaging in various diplomatic initiatives on the Namibian issue, South African diplomats studiously avoided committing their government to the implementation of the UN plan for free elections in Namibia and the country's independence (see Appendix B).

The South African military was only partially successful in its efforts to crush SWAPO. By 1983 it had prevented SWAPO from establishing permanent guerrilla bases in southern Angola and had forced the guerrillas to operate from staging areas far north of the Namibian border. This complicated SWAPO's logistical planning and limited its ability to recruit among the Ovambo people, who straddle the border and provide the bulk of SWAPO's membership. SWAPO's credibility as a military threat was thereby undermined. Yet, despite South Africa's claims that it had reduced SWAPO's troop strength from sixteen thousand in 1978 to nine thousand in 1985, the SADF failed to destroy SWAPO as a guerrilla force or prevent its annual rainy season infiltration of twelve hundred to fifteen hundred guerrillas into northern Namibia as late as 1987.[21]

Most seriously, what had originally been a classic counterinsurgency war against SWAPO turned into a conventional conflict between South African and Angolan government forces. After 1981, the SADF intensified its ground-and-air assaults on SWAPO bases in Angola. The Angolan government steadily strengthened its defenses in southern Angola with Soviet-supplied armor, artillery, and advanced radar and ground-to-air missiles. In August 1981 the SADF launched a major offensive against Angolan forces. In the eight-day campaign, the South Africans captured thirty Angolan soldiers and thirty tons of equipment, including tanks, missile launchers, and anti-aircraft weapons.

A brief respite occurred in 1984, however, when the United States helped to bring the South Africans and the Angolans to the negotiating table in Lusaka, the Zambian capital. The Lusaka Agreement, signed in February 1984, called for a cease-fire, to be followed by a withdrawal of the South African forces. In return, Angola would prevent SWAPO infiltration into Namibia. The pact led to an easing of tensions, even though South Africa's doubts about SWAPO's intentions slowed the SADF withdrawal, which dragged on for more than a year. The truce soon broke down. In May 1985 a South African commando unit was ambushed by Angolan forces as it attempted to blow up a U.S.–owned oil installation at Cabinda, the Angolan coastal exclave between Zaire and the Congo. The next month South African troops recrossed the Angolan border in force to attack SWAPO units twenty-five miles inside the country. But by then, SWAPO was of less concern to South Africa than was the growing conventional war against the Angolans.

Meanwhile, in pursuit of its attempt to build a viable electoral alternative to SWAPO, the Botha government was trying to strengthen the Multi-Party Conference (MPC), an anti-SWAPO coalition of ethnic—including white—parties that South Africa had put together in 1983. In 1985 South Africa installed a "government of national unity," drawn from the MPC, to serve as "an interim mechanism" to administer Namibia "pending internationally accepted independence."[22] If an internationally acceptable solution did not materialize, Pretoria would then have the option of handing power over to this body and declaring Namibia independent. Meanwhile, real power in the territory remained in the hands of an administrator-general appointed by Botha.

The MPC's credibility was weakened by divisions within the coalition and between the MPC and Pretoria. An MPC committee appointed to draft a constitution took eighteen months, only to have the proposal rejected by the Botha government in 1987. The proposed constitution, which called for a dismantling of the territory's apartheid structures, was too liberal for the majority of Namibia's whites and for the South African government.

South Africa's diplomats played an astute game of calculated ambiguity on the third track of President Botha's Namibia policy—stalling the UN plan for a settlement in Namibia. They would agree "in principle with" or "to cooperate with" various elements in the negotiations, yet avoid making binding commitments. On several occasions, after winning a major concession, they raised a new objection. In 1980, for example, after gaining important concessions on the size and composition of the UN monitoring force, South Africa announced that it was still not willing to implement the plan and demanded that the United Nations must first demonstrate its "impartiality" on the Namibian issue. South Africa, it was implied, would be the judge.[23]

At a January 1981 conference in Geneva, attended by the major parties to the dispute, South Africa flatly refused to implement the UN plan, saying that it would be "premature" to do so. But negotiations, led by the United States, were soon renewed and produced some progress. By 1982 the election formula, the location and monitoring of SWAPO forces, and the composition of the international peacekeeping presence had been agreed upon. Agreement on South African implementation, however, remained elusive.

South Africa's success in stretching out the talks and in winning substantially more advantageous terms for a settlement reflected primarily its strong bargaining position vis-à-vis its adversaries. The combined military strength in Angola of the South African military and the National Union for the Total Independence of Angola (UNITA) reduced the pressures on South Africa to seek a settlement and intensified those on Angola and SWAPO. The Reagan administration's concern with overcoming Pretoria's objections to the UN plan also strengthened South Africa's position. A critical point was the U.S. proposal in 1981 that South Africa's withdrawal from Namibia be formally linked to the removal of Cuban forces from Angola.

This "linkage," as it came to be known, was opposed by the Frontline States, SWAPO, and the United States' negotiating partners in the Contact Group (Britain, France, West Germany, and

Canada) because they felt it introduced another complication into an already extraordinarily complicated affair. They were also opposed because it put the onus on the Angolans to send the Cubans home, rather than on South Africa to leave Namibia. It also gave the South Africans a further pretext to stall on the Namibian issue. Dissension over "linkage," which dominated the Namibian negotiations for several years, brought about the de facto collapse of the Contact Group. After 1982 the United States assumed a virtual solo role in orchestrating diplomatic efforts to end the conflict.

By 1984 South Africa, apparently convinced that it could not secure a settlement through the United Nations on its own terms, decided to exclude the United Nations, bypass the U.S. initiative, and devise an "African solution." In March of that year, Pretoria proposed a regional peace conference in Africa in which South Africa, Angola, SWAPO, UNITA, and Namibia's MPC would participate. The initiative failed when Angola and SWAPO rejected the proposal. In May Zambia's president, Kenneth Kaunda, hosted talks between SWAPO and the MPC. This mediation attempt collapsed when the MPC's white parties refused to endorse the UN peace plan. In yet another independent initiative in 1984, President Botha offered SWAPO a secret deal. If SWAPO agreed to give up the armed struggle and join the MPC parties in a coalition, it would be given nominal leadership of the government. But such key government portfolios as security, finance, and foreign affairs would be reserved for non-SWAPO parties.[24] SWAPO rejected the offer. By the end of 1985, it was clear that South African attempts to negotiate a settlement outside the UN framework had failed.

During the next three years, the Botha government directed its Namibia policy toward shoring up the moderate anti-SWAPO political parties inside Namibia in preparation for a possible internal settlement. Meanwhile, the Angolan government concentrated its attention on launching major military campaigns against UNITA. Thus, the diplomatic impasse remained, despite continuing low-key U.S. efforts to move the opposing parties toward serious negotiations.

The War in Angola

Angola, a potentially rich but tragically devastated and divided country, became the center of the regional conflict in the 1980s. Unlike Mozambique, where a single party assumed uncontested power after the departure of the Portuguese in 1975, Angola entered into a three-sided civil war when it became independent later that year. By the beginning of the eighties, the Angolan combatants were down to two: the MPLA government in Luanda and UNITA, whose strength lies in southern Angola, where it has widespread support from the country's largest ethnic group, the Ovimbundu.

Foreign powers became involved early in the struggle, with the Soviet Union and Cuba supporting the MPLA and South Africa and the United States siding with UNITA. U.S. aid to UNITA was cut off by Congress in early 1976 by the Clark Amendment, which prohibited assistance to all the factions in Angola. But when the Reagan administration took office, a groundswell of support for UNITA occurred inside the administration, in Congress, and among right-wing public interest groups.

UNITA served South Africa's strategy of destabilizing the Angolan government. It had strong nationalist credentials and received support from other countries, including some African states. Its leader, Jonas Savimbi, demonstrated considerable military skills, political deftness, and personal charisma. His headquarters were located at Jamba, close to the Namibian border and SADF bases, which greatly facilitated military cooperation. With extensive South African logistical and financial help, and some direct involvement of South African forces, UNITA conducted a punishing campaign of sabotage and hit-and-run attacks against the Angolan government for over a decade. From Jamba, UNITA's forces carried their guerrilla campaign throughout most of Angola, isolating agricultural areas from the urban centers and causing severe economic dislocation and a flood of refugees into the cities. By the late 1980s, the war had brought the Angolan economy to the brink of collapse.

In return for Pretoria's support, UNITA assisted South African counterinsurgency operations against SWAPO and the ANC in Angola by providing intelligence on the guerrillas' bases and movements. After the closing of ANC bases in Mozambique and the expulsion of ANC personnel from other countries in the region during the 1980s, the ANC's half dozen or more camps in Angola were its nearest bases to South Africa. UNITA forces also provided a buffer against SWAPO infiltration into Namibia from Angola.

The Botha government made its commitment to UNITA clear on several occasions.[25] Its good faith was tested when Angolan forces, equipped with newly supplied Soviet helicopters and armored vehicles, launched a major ground-and-air assault on UNITA's stronghold at Jamba in September 1985. The Angolans were turned back, with heavy casualties on both sides, after South

Africa sent a mechanized battalion to UNITA's rescue and its jets attacked the advancing Angolan columns.[26]

During 1986–87 outside states increased their support to the belligerents and the conflict took a more serious turn. Following the failure of the Angolans' 1985 offensive against Jamba, the USSR resupplied Luanda with large numbers of late-model tanks, fighter aircraft, helicopter gunships, missiles, and other weapons in preparation for another major assault against UNITA. The chief of Angola's air force said the goal was to "go over to the offensive and liberate the territory occupied by UNITA and cut off its supply lines from South Africa."[27]

In 1986 the United States responded to the Angolans' growing weapons buildup by supplying UNITA with Stinger anti-aircraft missiles and TOW antitank weapons. U.S. aid was resumed following the repeal of the Clark Amendment in 1985. Strong conservative pressure, inside and outside the Reagan administration, led to the decision to become militarily involved in Angola again. Arming UNITA also meshed with the "Reagan doctrine"— the administration's view that by supplying weapons and other aid to "freedom fighters" opposing Soviet-supported regimes it could check and possibly roll back what was perceived to be Soviet expansionism.

Cuban combat forces, deployed since 1975 to defend major installations and population centers against UNITA and the South Africans, had played a predominantly defensive role until 1986–87, consciously neither provoking nor engaging the South Africans. At the conference of nonaligned nations in July 1986, however, Castro took a hard line on the Angola-Namibia issue, declaring that Cuba was prepared to keep its troops in Angola "as long as apartheid exists in South Africa" if the Angolans wanted them to stay.[28]

Meanwhile, by 1986 Angola had acquired close to one hundred Soviet fighter aircraft, including six advanced Mig 23 fighter-interceptors, and its southern bases were ringed by surface-to-air missile sites, as well as advanced radar capable of monitoring South African flights inside Namibia and South Africa.[29] South Africa's air force chief described the war in Angola as "a very high intensity, sophisticated, high-technology conflict in which air power is paramount":

> . . . as the air umbrella [over Angola] has become more effective, it is . . . becoming increasingly difficult to neutralize it. And unless it is neutralized, *no long-range operations in the host country [Angola] are possible without heavy casualties*[30] [emphasis added].

This advantage showed up in late summer 1987, when Angola launched a major new offensive against Jamba. The campaign, planned and directed by Soviet Major-General Konstantine Shaganovitch, employed some ten thousand regular Angolan troops and hundreds of tanks. Although UNITA's forces were at least as numerous as their opponents', they were not trained or equipped for conventional warfare. To prevent UNITA's defeat, South Africa intervened with a mechanized force of around five thousand soldiers backed up by heavy artillery. In the ensuing battles—the heaviest fought on African soil since World War II—the combined South African–UNITA forces routed the Angolans, who retreated to their base at Cuito Cuanavale after sustaining an estimated thousand or more killed and the loss of several hundred armored vehicles. The South African force suffered several hundred casualties, mostly among the black Namibian troops who had fought alongside UNITA. White units sustained an estimated one hundred fifty or more dead and wounded, the highest number for any similar period in the ten years of conflict.

South Africa followed up its victory by besieging Cuito Cuanavale in the fall of 1987. At this critical point, the Angolan president, José Eduardo dos Santos, flew to Havana for urgent talks with Cuba's president, Fidel Castro. The outcome was a new strategy that led to a dramatic escalation of the war. The Cubans agreed to dispatch fifteen thousand to seventeen thousand seasoned troops immediately to Angola. The troops began arriving in Angolan ports in December, and a detachment was sent to help defend Cuito Cuanavale.

In the spring of 1988, as the United States stepped up its efforts to mediate a negotiated settlement, a heavily mechanized Cuban force of fifteen thousand moved directly south. For the first time in the conflict, the Cubans took up positions within a few miles of the Angolan-Namibian border. They deployed along a two hundred–mile front and built forward bomber and fighter bases to support their ground forces. Castro later explained these moves as "necessary to change the correlation of forces."[31] It was a bold move calculated to deter further South African incursions and to put pressure on Pretoria in the peace talks, which were still at an indecisive stage.

The Cuban deployment to the south also increased the likelihood of serious armed clashes between the Cubans and South Africans for the first time since 1975. South Africa charged that the move was a "provocative action" and ordered a partial mobilization of its reserves. More troops were sent to bases in northern Namibia. On June 27, 1988, a South African mechanized unit on reconnaissance in Angola opened fire on a Cuban tank force near Calueque, twenty miles north of the border, killing some Cuban soldiers and destroying two tanks.

That apparently unplanned attack led to a retaliatory Cuban air strike the same day that killed a dozen white South African soldiers. By then the Cuban combat force in Angola had risen to fifty thousand.

The two clashes reminded both sides of the risks of a sudden and unwanted escalation in warfare between two well-trained forces equipped with advanced weapons. In South Africa, the clashes led to growing misgivings in the white community about the Angolan war. An antidraft campaign was gaining strength, with many young men either leaving the country or refusing to serve, an act that could lead to a six-year jail term. *Die Kerkbode*, an influential journal of the Dutch Reformed church, caused a stir in Afrikaner circles by questioning the morality of the South African presence in Angola. The war also divided South Africa's leaders. In an interview given a fortnight after the Calueque clash, Foreign Minister R. F. Botha gave his "personal opinion":

> If the enemy is dug in over a broad front and is equipped with a deadly arsenal, you must think twice before you simply allow hundreds of your sons to be killed. You are surely in a more favorable position . . . if you can wait for the enemy to cross the border from your own established positions.[32]

The South African leadership was also concerned about the growing financial burden of the war. The economy, which had been stagnant for several years, was further hobbled by some $20 billion of foreign debt and by a drying up of foreign capital. By 1988 the bite of Western economic sanctions was also beginning to be felt.

During 1987–88 the Angolans, too, came under heavy pressure to end the war that had devastated the country for more than a decade. The disastrous failure of the government's offensive against UNITA in 1987 had convinced the USSR that the war was unwinnable. The Gorbachev leadership, recognizing that continued Soviet involvement in the war was incompatible with the diplomatic and economic imperatives of *perestroika,* was pressing Angola to seek a political settlement of the conflict.

During the summer of 1988, as the peace talks gained momentum, the buildup of Cuban forces in southern Angola and of South

African troops in northern Namibia continued, although no more clashes occurred. The Calueque engagements proved to be an important catalyst, since both South Africa and Cuba realized that they faced a steep rise in casualties if the fighting continued. This shared perception encouraged them to intensify their efforts to achieve a negotiated settlement.

South Africa's Military Strengths and Weaknesses

W hile South Africa's military fortunes fluctuated on Angola's battlefields, its underlying military strength and dominance of the region remained unimpaired. South Africa has a large defense force and an impressive inventory of air, ground, and naval weaponry compared to the military resources of its neighbors (see Table 1). Moreover, its armed forces are well educated, well trained, and well led. Although subject to a mandatory UN arms embargo since 1977, South Africa has been able to field a highly mechanized and mobile force equipped with a range of late-model artillery, aircraft, missiles, tanks, and naval craft.

South Africa's military strength was built up by a sustained and costly program of arms purchases and production and through modernization and expansion. Most of this growth took place from 1966 to 1978 under the personal direction of P. W. Botha, who was then defense minister and the government's leading advocate of a hard-line foreign policy and a military response to perceived security threats from within the region. The programs were technically and economically possible because of South Africa's developed economy, notably its modern industrial sector, its pool of skilled laborers, and its world trade. The economy was strong enough to sustain a growing defense budget that was roughly twice that of the six Frontline States combined.

By the late 1980s, South Africa was among the world's ten leading arms producers. With some critical exceptions, it was able to supply nearly all its own requirements, and its weapons exports were

TABLE 1: South Africa and the Frontline States, the Military Balance—1989–90

	South Africa	Angola	Botswana	Mozambique	Tanzania	Zambia	Zimbabwe
Armed Forces	103,000	50,000	4,500	71,000	46,700	16,200	49,500
Army	77,500	91,500	N/A	60,000	45,000	15,000	47,000
Air Force	11,000	7,000	N/A	4,250	1,000	1,200	2,500
Navy	6,500	1,500	—	750	700	—	—
Medical Service	8,000						
Combat Aircraft	338	179	14	66	24	68	81
Helicopters	136	84	5	20	4	37	26
Surface-to-Air Missiles	74+	172	10	10+	21	N/A	N/A
Tanks	250	550	—	150	126	60	43
Other Armored Vehicles	4,600	455+	52	264+	75	101	218
Naval Combat Ships	24	40	—	31	18	—	—
Defense Budget* (mill. U.S. dollars)	3,910	819	46	116	223	127	397

*Budget data are not strictly comparable across the board: the latest Tanzanian figure is for 1985, for Zambia, 1987, and for Angola and Zimbabwe, 1988. The rest are 1989–90 data.

Source: Adapted from *The Military Balance 1989–1990* (London: IISS, Autumn 1989). The above data are only gross indicators of relative military capabilities, since they do not take into account differences in age or quality of weapons (e.g., heavy vs. light tanks), nor do they reflect such critical measures of performance as operator training, maintenance and repair capabilities, availability of replacements.

a major source of foreign exchange. Its arms technology was sufficiently advanced to warrant widespread belief among the nuclear states that South Africa either has produced and tested a nuclear device or is on the threshold of having such a capability.

Yet South Africa's military power and competitiveness in the region were adversely affected by a number of factors. One was the rapid development of global weapons technology that made it difficult for a relatively small country to keep its armed forces equipped with the latest weapons. And while the global arms embargo forced South Africa to seek clandestine sources of arms, its neighbors were free to acquire advanced weapons openly on the world market.

The lack of potential recruits was another problem. Since the South African Defense Force recruited mainly from the small pool of skilled and educated whites who also were needed to keep the civilian economy growing, the annual military service requirement cut into the available white work force. This led to a broader recruitment of black volunteers.

These two vulnerabilities—the growing costs of acquiring advanced weapons and the shortage of skilled soldiers—became critical when the conventional warfare in Angola escalated. While South Africa's technological base and number of troops could have sustained a low-level bush war indefinitely, it was a different matter in the late 1980s, when South African forces were confronted with sophisticated air defenses and heavy concentrations of Angolan and Cuban armor. The South African military performed well. But unlike in earlier years, when operations in Angola involved negligible losses, South Africa suffered substantial human casualties and significant losses of hard-to-replace aircraft and tanks.

With the signing of the 1988 peace accords and the end of South African intervention in Angola, the military faced a new problem. For the first time in almost three decades, the government signaled its intentions to reduce defense expenditures. Although South Africa continued to seek and acquire ballistic missiles and other sophisticated conventional weapons, sharp cutbacks were planned in most major weapons programs by the end of 1989.

The Arms Industry

In the 1960s the South African government gradually came to realize that its racial policies and its refusal to surrender Namibia precluded the possibility of a military alliance with the West, although South African leaders continued to nurture hopes of such an alliance for another decade. In the words of former prime minister H. F. Verwoerd, "South Africa must have her own striking power and must be able to stand on her own feet."[33] In 1963, when the United Nations imposed a voluntary UN arms embargo on South Africa, the government had already established a fledgling armaments industry.

South Africa was in a far better position to develop an indigenous arms industry than any other African state. It is a leading producer of ferrous and nonferrous metals, and has a well-developed modern industrial sector. Large seaports at Cape Town and Durban are connected to the interior by a first-class transport and communications network. South Africa has a sizable number of scientists who have continued to maintain close professional relations with the West. A complex web of financial, trade, and corporate connections binds South African industry to the global economy. As a result, by the early 1970s South Africa was producing a variety of small arms, ammunition, explosives, and armored cars— almost all the weapons needed to conduct a low-level war against guerrillas.[34]

After Angola and Mozambique became independent in 1975, however, South Africa's military planners saw the need to prepare for a different type of warfare. They were concerned that the introduction of sophisticated weapons in those countries and the presence of Cuban troops in Angola might undermine their ability "to counterattack *or to take preventive action against bases supporting aggression against us*"[35] [emphasis added]. In short, South African attacks on the South West Africa People's Organization and African National Congress sanctuaries might invite retaliation by the host countries' armed forces.

Defense spending rose steeply in the 1970s as South Africa strove to expand and modernize its conventional capabilities. But the 1977 UN mandatory arms embargo made the acquisition of advanced weapons from abroad both costly and difficult because South Africa was forced to pay premium prices under the table for clandestine deliveries. The embargo, together with the military's rapidly growing demand for more sophisticated weapons, also spurred the development of indigenous arms production.

By the early 1980s, the arms industry was employing ninety thousand people, including more than twenty thousand who worked for Armscor, a parastatal corporation established to manage the development, production, and acquisition of weapons.[36] During the 1980s South Africa was the world's tenth largest arms producer, and was officially said to supply as much as 85 percent of its own weapons requirements.[37] According to South African press reports, the country's arms exports totaled roughly $200 million in 1987.[38] Virtual self-sufficiency had been established in the manufacture of explosives, ammunition, and small arms, including a multipurpose machine gun and a new semiautomatic rifle. South Africa's industry also met almost all the military's needs in artillery, light attack helicopters, and armored vehicles except heavy tanks. Other weapons, including missile patrol craft, Puma helicopters, and the Cheetah jet fighter, were assembled in South Africa but were dependent on imports for key components.[39]

Dependence on foreign technology constituted a serious vulnerability. This was particularly true of subassemblies and component parts, including aircraft engines and advanced avionics. Even South Africa's much publicized G-5 155mm howitzer, although assembled locally, used a motor made in West Germany and a targeting system that had a computer imported from Canada.[40] Its assembly was made possible in the first place by the clandestine purchase of blueprints and projectiles from a U.S. firm whose executives were subsequently prosecuted and jailed for violating the U.S. arms embargo. The Cheetah supersonic jet fighter, unveiled in 1986, was an upgraded version of the Mirage III, incorporating advanced navigational and electronic equipment acquired from Israel, which also helped South Africa develop a surveillance aircraft and an aerial refueling capability.[41] In 1986 it was reported but never verified that a German shipyard had provided South Africa with blueprints for the U209 submarine, and that an engineer from that shipyard was supervising the submarine's construction in Durban.[42]

South Africa's success in keeping pace with developments in military technology also depended on its ability to evade the UN arms embargo. A 1984 report by the American Friends Service Committee described numerous violations of the embargo by the United States and other Western countries that allowed "a brisk flow" of weapons technology to South Africa.[43] That flow seems likely to have been diminished somewhat by the imposition of Western sanctions against South Africa in 1985–86. U.S. sanctions, for example, banned the sale of computer equipment to South African government agencies concerned with security matters.

More important, the Comprehensive Anti-Apartheid Act, passed by the U.S. Congress over President Ronald Reagan's veto in October 1986, required the State Department to report by April 1987 on other countries' arms sales to South Africa "with a view toward ending U.S. assistance to countries engaged in that trade."

Israel, fearful of jeopardizing its relationship with the United States—which was already strained from recent spy revelations—announced on March 18 (two weeks before publication of the critical State Department report) that it would sign no new military contracts with South Africa.[44] That still left open the question of Israel's existing contracts, whose content and duration were not made public, and whether these contracts would be modified or extended.

The issue resurfaced in late 1989, when U.S. officials confirmed press reports that in July South Africa had tested a medium-range ballistic missile built with Israeli help.[45] U.S. officials also delayed approving the sale of a supercomputer to Israel because of suspicions that the Israelis had transferred sensitive U.S. nuclear technology to South Africa in violation of U.S.–Israeli agreements.[46]

Given the wide availability of modern weapons through public and private agencies, the network of international arms dealers, and South Africa's past success in evading the arms embargo, it was unlikely that extensive U.S. and European sanctions could effectively block South African access to new military technologies. But sanctions undoubtedly made Pretoria's purchase of advanced weapons more difficult, costly, and subject to delays. Obtaining the more sophisticated weapons systems that used proprietary U.S. or Western European technology was particularly difficult because their illegal sale to South Africa risked the termination of technology transfers to the exporting state and its manufacturers.

Military Personnel

South Africa's other major military vulnerability was the size of its army. At the end of the 1980s, the standing army was a force of approximately twenty thousand career professionals, large numbers of whom were training and support staff. This Permanent (i.e., full-time) Force was augmented by an annual intake of some thirty thousand white inductees. Until 1990 conscripts served an initial two years, plus up to four months' additional service every two years if needed, for a total service liability period of twelve years. Since they served with regular units and often went directly into combat, the conscripts were an essential component of the army's active force. The defense forces were backed by commando (local militia) units and one hundred fifty thousand active reservists, enabling the government to muster over two hundred thousand trained troops on relatively short notice.[47]

Since only white males have been subject to the draft in South

Africa, the annual call-up seriously strained labor resources in South Africa's skills-short economy. The labor force was also affected negatively by increases in white emigration and decreases in immigration. Moreover, many young whites were reluctant to serve in the military, particularly after 1984, when the army was called upon to patrol the troubled black townships following the beginning of the mass protests.

Some draft-age youths simply left the country. Although the penalty for avoiding military service could be six years' imprisonment, 143 young whites publicly declared their refusal to serve in 1988. The End Conscription Campaign (ECC), a nationwide organization formed to mobilize and assist people opposed to the draft, was banned in August 1988, reflecting the seriousness the government attached to this issue.[48] These developments came at a particularly bad time for the military, when it needed more men to guard the country's borders against ANC infiltration, to patrol the townships, and to fight in Angola as the war intensified.

These problems were not so serious as to weaken South Africa's defense capabilities. But they added to the chronic tension between the demands of the economy and the army's need for skilled workers to keep its highly mechanized forces in a state of combat readiness.

The military sought to alleviate the manpower crunch by expanding the recruitment of black volunteers. Unlike the police force, roughly half of which is black, the army had moved slowly in this area. Coloureds had a long association with the military, going back to before World War II; yet by the mid-1980s, only an estimated five thousand were serving.[49] Recruitment of Africans went even more slowly. Beginning with a training company recruited in 1977, eight African ethnic battalions had been trained for defense duty in the homelands by the end of the 1980s.

Initially, concern over the political reliability of black troops was a factor in their slow recruitment, but military officials denied that this was a concern. They said the major constraint was the shortage of qualified personnel to train the African recruits, most of whom were from rural areas.[50] Nor was there a shortage of volunteers. The defense force accepted about half of the seven thousand blacks who volunteered for service in 1988. By that time, blacks comprised around a quarter of the Permanent Force.

In Namibia, the military went further, training six ethnic Namibian battalions during the 1970s and incorporating them into a separate combat command, the South-West Africa Territorial Force (SWATF), under regular South African officers. By the mid-1980s, these ethnic units accounted for two-thirds of South Africa's fighting strength in Namibia. Together with a battalion of Angolan dissidents, these troops bore the brunt of fighting along the border and inside Angola.

In October 1987, however, the Namibian press reported that hundreds of Namibian troops in the 101 (Ovambo) and 202 (Kavango) battalions had mutinied over their deployment to fight in Angola alongside UNITA. The military denied that a mutiny had occurred, but acknowledged that forty-seven soldiers of the 101 Battalion had been discharged and that members of 202 Battalion had protested about "the way they were being utilized."[51] Whatever the scale of the protest, it was the first such incident reported among South Africa's black troops. It was clearly a source of concern to South Africa, which had become heavily dependent on these local troops for its Angola operations.

The Namibian-Angolan peace accords had a significant impact on the manpower issue. In April 1989 the South African defense minister announced that the annual "camps" (i.e., service stints for men who had earlier completed their initial two-year full-time duty) would be no longer than thirty days. In December 1989 President F. W. de Klerk announced that the draft would be reduced from two years to one.[52] Thus, a major consequence of the end of South African involvement in Angola in 1988 and the gradual withdrawal of South African forces from Namibia during 1989 was to reduce military personnel requirements and to free skilled workers for the civilian sector.

The sudden change in South Africa's security outlook caused a lag in its strategic planning. Although the SADF quickly recognized the need to reduce requirements for military service, the peace accords and the closing of ANC camps in Angola left South Africa without an identifiable external threat. It was thus clear that plans to acquire sophisticated conventional weapons could be sharply cut back, as could the military budget for the first time in more than two decades. In April 1989 Defense Minister Malan spoke to Parliament of the prospect of "an entirely new order . . . with far-reaching implications for South Africa." The shifting relationship between East and West, he said, meant that South Africa would have to revise its strategy and engage in "new thinking, preparation, and a new attitude to the problems, opportunities, and challenges" it faces.[53]

The Nuclear Option

Senior South African officials over the years denied that South Africa was developing nuclear weapons. Yet on numerous occasions they referred to South Africa's capability to do so. They even sometimes issued thinly veiled threats that they might find it necessary to develop such weapons.[54]

The question of South Africa's nuclear weapons capability first drew global attention in 1977, after Soviet and U.S. reconnaissance satellites detected what appeared to be a nuclear test complex under construction in South Africa's remote Kalahari Desert. Confronted by U.S. and West European officials, South African leaders issued ambiguous assurances that they had no plans to develop or test nuclear weapons, but their explanations about the purpose of the Kalahari site were unconvincing. U.S. technical intelligence assessments concluded that its configurations resembled those of a nuclear test site and nothing else. Toward the end of 1977, South Africa dismantled the Kalahari site. The government, however, would not allow international inspection of its nuclear facilities and would not sign the Nuclear Non-Proliferation Treaty.

Concern was rekindled in the autumn of 1979 when a U.S. Vela satellite recorded a double pulse of light—the telltale signature of a nuclear explosion—somewhere in the south Atlantic near the tip of Africa. Several independent pieces of technical evidence supported the Vela indicator, leading the Carter administration to appoint a special scientific panel to investigate. Although the intelligence community was sharply divided as to whether or not South Africa had detonated a nuclear device, the panel found "no smoking gun" and decided that the evidence was inconclusive.[55] By 1981, when South African officials announced that their uranium enrichment plant at Valindaba was producing 45 percent enriched uranium for their nuclear research reactor, it was clear that South Africa had the capability to produce enough weapons-grade uranium for several nuclear weapons each year.[56]

How would a nuclear weapon fit in with South Africa's security strategy? While the prestige of being a nuclear power might have appealed to South Africa's isolated and embattled government, the military utility of a nuclear weapon was unclear. Given the primary threats to the regime—guerrilla attacks and internal unrest—South Africa's conventional weapons capability offered a more appropriate response than could a nuclear weapon. Nuclear weapons would be unlikely to deter clandestine infiltration by small guerrilla groups. Nor was there any real prospect that the ANC would be able to mount large-scale guerrilla offensives, like those launched against Rhodesia in the late 1970s. Conventional counterinsurgency tactics were enough to force South Africa's neighbors to deny sanctuary to ANC guerrillas.

The use of nuclear weapons against South Africa's black townships is simply inconceivable, given the proximity of such communities to major cities and the high risk of radioactive fallout. Furthermore, township residents are an essential component of South Africa's integrated economy, which depends on them to work the mines, run the railroads, and staff the factories. A major concern of the government during the state of emergency was to prevent black rebellion from totally disrupting the flow of black workers to and from their jobs. The spreading chaos and collapse that would follow a nuclear attack on Soweto, for example, are beyond description.

Another contingency, defense against a conventional attack from across the borders, possibly with the active participation of Cuban or Soviet troops, was seen by most outside observers as an extremely remote possibility.[57] The economic and military weakness of the nearby states, the defensive nature of Soviet and Cuban strategy in Angola, and the absence of aggressive military moves toward South Africa by either Communist or African states suggested that the threat of a conventional assault on South Africa was negligible. Although Cuban troops moved to within a few miles of the Namibian border in 1988, that was a preemptive—though purposely provocative—move taken to deter South African incursions and to put pressure on Pretoria at the conference table. It did not appear to be a prelude to an invasion of Namibia. The withdrawal of Cuban forces in Angola during 1989, following the timetable laid down in the 1988 peace accords, made the threat of conventional attack even more remote.

During the 1980s, however, South Africa's military leaders repeatedly cited conventional attack as a worst-case scenario for which they had to be prepared, and emphasized the importance of planning military exercises and defense budgets responsive to it. A 1984 White Paper on Defense, warning of a conventional attack, noted that the USSR's "sustained supply of advanced weapons and personnel to these [black-ruled] states is disturbing the military balance" in the region. This was depicted as a situation that the USSR could exploit "should it decide on direct action" against South Africa.[58] A 1986 White Paper noted that the buildup continued, compelling the defense force "not only to maintain its conventional strike capability, but also to introduce more sophistication."[59]

Heavy armaments, advanced jet fighters, ballistic missiles, and submarines—hardly the weapons for a low-level bush war—continued to dominate defense procurement activities through the end of the decade.

Although South Africa's severe security laws discouraged serious public discussion of its nuclear intentions, numerous statements by senior military officials over the years suggested that, far from dismissing the need for such weapons, the military favored a nuclear weapons program.[60] To the extent that Pretoria's military leaders anticipated that shifts in the regional military balance might eventually reduce South Africa's margin of superiority in conventional weapons, tactical nuclear weapons remained attractive. Such weapons might have been viewed, for example, as a deterrent against attack or as a means for breaking up formations of conventional forces before they crossed the border. As with most other nuclear threshold states, however, the appeal has rested less on specific contingencies than on the new options such a weapon might offer.

Regional Peacemaking: 1988–90

$\mathbf{B}$y 1988 the conflict between South Africa and its neighbors was imposing serious and growing political and economic costs on all the participants. Moreover, the military stalemate in Angola, the increasing international isolation of South Africa, and the Soviet Union's reassessment of the Angolan situation had created a more favorable climate for negotiations. Yet neither South Africa, despite its regional superpower status, nor any combination of regional states could bring about a resolution of the conflict on its own. No mechanism for consultation between South Africa and the Frontline States existed, nor was there any basis for mutual trust. As in the earlier major peace talks in the region, outside mediation and pressure were indispensable for the negotiating process that began in early 1988.

Diplomatic Breakthrough in Southern Africa

In January 1988, as the first Cuban reinforcements were arriving at Cuito Cuanavale, the Angolan government informed Washington that it was ready to resume negotiations. Chester Crocker, U.S. assistant secretary of state for Africa, who had been working for a settlement since 1981, flew to Luanda for talks with the Angolans and Cubans. The meeting was particularly significant. For the first time, the Angolan delegation included Cuban representatives, thereby signaling Cuba's willingness to accept the United States' role as mediator. Moreover, the talks also produced important results: Angola and Cuba agreed in principle for the first time to a total withdrawal of Cuban forces from Angola as part of an overall settlement.

In February 1988 Manuel Pacavira, Angola's ambassador to the United Nations, set forth initial hard-line conditions for the proposed four-year withdrawal. "Angola's security is the fundamental question," he said, and it "can only be assured with the independence of Namibia, the withdrawal of South African troops from our territory, stopping aggression against our country, and stopping U.S. and South African aid to UNITA."[61] The South Africans, fresh from their success in blunting the Angolan army's assault against UNITA, were not yet prepared to make concessions. The Cuban troop withdrawal plan was rejected in scathing terms, and in March President Botha defiantly declared, "We are staying in Angola until the Cubans leave."[62]

In May, as large numbers of Cuban mechanized troops were moving into southern Angola, senior diplomatic and military officials from Angola, Cuba, South Africa, and the United States met for the first time in London. With Assistant Secretary Crocker chairing the meeting, the South Africans pledged to implement the UN plan once the issue of Cuban troop withdrawal was settled but rejected the Angolan proposal of a four-year withdrawal period. South Africa also sought but failed to win Cuba's assurances that its troops would not cross into Namibia. The talks made little progress; but the participants agreed that Crocker should continue to mediate.

South Africa then took the diplomatic initiative by convening a meeting with the Angolans in Brazzaville; Cuba and the United States were not present. The South Africans maintained a hard line, demanding an end to the Cuban troop buildup and a reconciliation between the Angolan government and UNITA as prerequisites for a settlement.

During the U.S.–Soviet summit meeting in Moscow at the end of May, the United States encouraged Soviet officials to take an active interest in the peace initiative. Although the Soviets did not participate in the actual meetings, they were always on hand for consultation. Assistant Secretary Crocker and his colleagues had a number of informal bilateral discussions with the Soviets and found them particularly helpful in explaining to the Angolans and Cubans possible trade-offs and nuances that could not be voiced in plenary sessions. For example, at a critical point Crocker persuaded the Soviets to suggest to the Angolan and Cuban negotiators that South Africa might agree to an extended Cuban troop withdrawal if Angola and

Cuba would propose a "heavy front-end loading"—that is, for large numbers of Cubans to withdraw in the early stages.[63]

At the next meeting of the negotiating parties, held in Cairo in late June, South Africa reiterated its demands and proposed that Cuba remove all its troops from Angola over a seven-month period. Meanwhile Castro had responded publicly to South Africa's intransigence, asserting that South Africa "was in no position to demand anything" and refusing to give assurances against Cuban attacks on Namibia.[64]

The Calueque clash in southern Angola, in which Cuba and South Africa suffered significant casualties, occurred the day after the Cairo meeting ended. It had a sobering impact on all the combatants and contributed to the first real breakthrough in the negotiations. This took place in New York in July when the delegates agreed to a set of "Fourteen Principles for a Peaceful Settlement in Southwestern Africa."

The two key principles committed Angola and South Africa to name a date for implementing the UN plan for Namibia's independence and provided for the redeployment of Cuban forces to the north and for their "total and staged withdrawal." The three governments agreed to a number of nonbinding rules of behavior, such as respect for territorial integrity and noninterference in the internal affairs of states. Implicit in these rules was the understanding that South Africa would stop aiding UNITA while Angola would close the African National Congress's military bases. Angola dropped its demand for an end to U.S. aid to UNITA, and Pretoria no longer insisted on reconciliation between the Angolan government and UNITA.

Recognizing that the military leaders on each side were uneasy with the broad agreements reached in New York, Assistant Secretary Crocker set up a secret meeting between them at Cape Verde in late July. It turned out to be a crucial two-day discussion. The South African, Cuban, and Angolan generals gradually moved from open suspicion and hostility to mutual respect and eventual agreement on a step-by-step process for the withdrawal of South African and Cuban forces from Angola. The key concession was the acknowledgment by General Jannie Geldenhuys, chief of the South African Defense Force, that South Africa's withdrawal could be accelerated, provided the Cubans "stay off our backs."[65] The South African defense minister, Magnus Malan, initially opposed the idea but was eventually persuaded by General Geldenhuys. In sum, the Cape Verde talks laid the groundwork for disengagement and withdrawal.

Formal negotiations resumed in early August and led to the Geneva Protocol, which endorsed the Fourteen Principles and confirmed the rules of mutual force disengagement. Angola, Cuba, and South Africa announced an immediate cease-fire in Angola and Namibia, to be followed by the meeting of a joint military monitoring committee appointed to oversee its implementation. It was also agreed that guerrillas from the South West Africa People's Organization would be kept north of the 16th parallel, approximately a hundred miles north of the Namibian border. The South African withdrawal from Angola began and the last soldier crossed the border into Namibia ahead of the August 31 deadline.

Hard bargaining over a precise schedule for Cuban troop withdrawal continued during a series of meetings that took place between August and November. Final agreement came in Geneva in early November and was formalized in Brazzaville the following month. The Protocol of Brazzaville committed the parties to sign two interlocking peace accords and set up a joint Angolan–Cuban–South African commission to monitor implementation. The United States and the Soviet Union, continuing their collaborative roles, were given observer status in the commission. The first accord, between Angola, Cuba, and South Africa, provided for the implementation of the UN plan for Namibia, beginning on April 1, 1989. The second, between Angola and Cuba, laid out a twenty-seven-month phased withdrawal schedule for the removal of the Cuban forces from Angola that would be complete by mid-1991. The accords were signed at the United Nations on December 22, 1988, at a ceremony attended by the U.S. secretary of state and the Soviet foreign minister. This formality marked the end of a diplomatic quest that had begun in the same place eleven years before (see Appendix D).

Assistant Secretary Crocker's astute diplomacy and President Gorbachev's decision that Soviet involvement in remote regional conflicts posed a threat to *perestroika* at home were critical to the success of the negotiations. With an acute sense of the strengths and weaknesses of the opposing sides, Crocker negotiated a succession of changes in the proposed settlement terms that eventually brought the war-weary combatants to see that the costs and risks of a deal were preferable to continuing conflict. The key to Crocker's strategy was an accord that would enable each of the parties to declare itself a winner. His efforts were enhanced by a cool detachment. When, for instance, Castro's troops advanced to the Namibian border, Crocker quietly warned the Cubans that they were playing with fire. But he refused to join in South Africa's shrill denunciation of the Cuban move, which he saw as a risky but effective means of putting pressure on Pretoria to make vital concessions in the negotiations.

The Soviet Union, for its part, sent a clear signal to Angola in 1988 that it considered the Angolan conflict unwinnable and that a political settlement should be reached. Soviet diplomats also helped the negotiating process by lending quiet offstage support to Crocker's efforts.

The 1988 accords introduced dramatic shifts in the regional security balance between South Africa and the black states. The settlement had important implications for all the countries in the region, but its greatest impact was on Angola, Namibia, and South Africa.

For South Africa, the accords restored its military superiority in the region and left it more secure. The end of SWAPO's insurgency and the closure of the ANC bases in Angola removed one guerrilla threat and seriously weakened another. The immediate expulsion of several thousand ANC operatives from Angola in late 1988 and their relocation in countries far from South Africa's borders further reduced the ANC's capability to mount an effective guerrilla war against South Africa. The departure of SWAPO and the ANC from Angola also ended a major source of conflict between that country and South Africa. The withdrawal of the Cubans removed what South Africa's military leaders had long considered the nearest physical threat of a conventional attack.

South Africa's military strategists were reluctant to give up the eight hundred–mile deep Namibian buffer zone that separated South Africa from Angola. They favored the principle of keeping real and potential enemies as far as possible from South Africa's borders. But an independent Namibia, under a SWAPO government, did not have the negative political impact on white South African politics that had been widely predicted. Most whites seemed to accept it as a fair price to pay for ending a war that they felt was not critical to South Africa's security interests.

For the ANC, the removal of its camps in Angola was a military setback. The Soviet Union, the ANC's principal supplier of arms and military training, had already indicated that it preferred a negotiated solution in South Africa's internal conflict. Accordingly, the ANC began to revise its strategy. While not repudiating the armed struggle at that stage, the movement directed its energies toward developing closer links with the opposition forces within South Africa and establishing a set of constitutional and negotiating guidelines.

For Angola, the accords brought an end to South African intervention and support for UNITA. But the withdrawal of the Cuban forces, with the last units due to leave in July 1991, meant that Angola would lose the defensive shield around its cities that the Cubans had provided. The country would be free of foreign troops for the first time since independence in 1975, leaving the MPLA and UNITA facing each other without their powerful foreign allies.

The withdrawal of the South Africans and Cubans, and the end of South African support for UNITA, did not immediately lead to a resolution of Angola's internal conflict. But each side found that it could no longer count on its superpower patron for arms because both the United States and the Soviet Union made it clear that they wanted a political settlement in Angola. These new circumstances and the continuing efforts by African states, Portugal, and others to broker a settlement substantially increased the pressure on the MPLA government and UNITA to seek a political solution to the fifteen-year-old conflict.

For Namibia, the accords cleared the way for the implementation of the UN plan and independence. Although bloody fighting broke out between SWAPO guerrillas and South African security forces along the border on the eve of the transition period, the territory soon settled into an uneasy peace as some forty thousand refugees returned and campaigning began for the elections. UN–supervised elections for a constituent assembly were held in November 1989, and SWAPO, led by Sam Nujoma, won 57 percent of the votes. The ensuing negotiations between SWAPO and other political parties produced one of the world's most democratic constitutions, and the country became independent under a SWAPO government on March 21, 1990.

Elsewhere in the region, Mozambique's problems continued into the new decade, apparently resistant to the changes that were taking place. RENAMO managed to sustain its destructive activities although deprived of official South African aid and thoroughly discredited internationally. A low-key African peace initiative was launched to seek an end to the conflict, but no resolution was in sight by the end of the decade. Meanwhile, a number of Western states, including the United States, sent substantial amounts of food and economic aid to Mozambique, and Britain also supplied some military training.

Pretoria's New African Dialogue

Throughout most of the 1980s, South Africa's relations with its neighbors were characterized by the paradox of cross-border violence and business-as-usual contacts. With the exception of Malawi, South Africa had no diplomatic ties with the countries of the region. But it had trade missions in several of them, including rhetorically hostile Zimbabwe. Road, rail, and air links between South Africa and its neighbors functioned with only occasional interruptions. Joint ventures were undertaken with Botswana, Mozambique, and Lesotho.

Pretoria encouraged the private sector to invest in and trade with its neighboring states. Its motives were mixed. The expansion of trade demonstrated goodwill and brought economic advantages, but it also tied the black states more closely to South Africa and provided Pretoria with a way of evading sanctions. Swaziland and Mozambique, in particular, were used as conduits for exporting South African goods bearing non–South African labels of origin. Trade with the whole of sub-Saharan Africa expanded sharply, from an estimated $650 million in 1984 to more than $1.5 billion in 1988, and increased from 6.5 percent to 10 percent of South Africa's total trade.[66]

During 1988 Pretoria took advantage of the easing of hostility toward South Africa that resulted from progress in the Namibian-Angolan negotiations. Pretoria's diplomats had long acknowledged that the most effective way of improving relations with the West, and of reducing or ending sanctions, was to be accepted in Africa. The diplomats were also eager to take the initiative for bureaucratic reasons. They calculated that successful diplomatic outreach to Africa would enhance their role in foreign policy and would diminish the influence of the military, which had prevailed during the years of destabilization.[67]

South Africa's new diplomatic overtures to its neighbors began in May 1988, when Foreign Minister R. F. Botha traveled to Brazzaville, capital of the Congo, for direct peace talks with Angolan officials. No progress was made, despite his plea that "African problems should be solved by Africans."[68] Six months later, as Crocker's diplomatic initiative advanced, South African diplomats arranged meetings between President Botha and a number of African leaders. In September President Botha visited President Joaquim Chissano, who had succeeded Samora Machel after his death in a plane crash in 1986. This was the South African leader's first state visit to an African country. Reactivation of the Cahora Bassa hydroelectric complex was discussed, and Botha promised substantial economic aid for Mozambique. He also reiterated his support for the government's struggle against RENAMO, Pretoria's former client. Visiting Malawi the following day, President Botha announced a financial and food aid package.

Botha met with President Mobutu Sese Seko on October 1, 1988, in Zaire, where the two leaders discussed the Namibian-Angolan peace talks and South Africa's race policies. The real significance of the meetings, however, lay in the symbolism of Botha's welcome by the leader of a major African state. Botha made sure this was not lost on his constituents back home. A large group of South African reporters was invited to fly with him on his own plane, and he responded to Mobutu's welcoming address with a speech in Afrikaans. Upon his return home, Botha announced that "Africa is talking to South Africa," and called for a summit meeting of all southern African heads of government.[69] The last stop in P. W. Botha's summitry took place in late October, when he visited President Felix Houphouet-Boigny, the Ivory Coast's leader since its independence. The talks apparently were less than cordial, however, and no communiqué was issued.

The prolonged leadership crisis in South Africa following President Botha's stroke in January 1989 led to a break in the dialogue initiative. Talks were resumed in July 1989, when F. W. de Klerk, the new National Party leader, visited Mozambican President Chissano to seek his support for a regional summit. Chissano was noncommittal, and the summit did not materialize. But South Africa was consulted by its neighbors when an African-mediated cease-fire in Angola's internal conflict collapsed. In early August Zairian and South African officials met secretly in Pretoria with Jonas Savimbi, UNITA's leader, and De Klerk discussed the problems of reconciling the MPLA and UNITA with Mobutu in Zaire and Kaunda in Zambia.[70]

By the end of 1989, however, South Africa's dialogue initiative seemed to be running out of steam. The call for a regional summit conference had made no progress, and South Africa's effort to play a mediating role in the Angolan civil war did not produce any identifiable results. While individual countries opened their doors to South Africa's leaders, the collective leadership of the African states remained wary. As early as October 1988, African representatives at the United Nations had expressed a growing unease about the new dialogue, declaring that only the "total abolition of apartheid" would make South Africa acceptable to the rest of Africa.[71]

In August 1989 the Ad Hoc Committee on Southern Africa of

the Organization of African Unity, meeting in Harare, endorsed the ANC's guidelines for a new constitution in South Africa and its conditions for entering into negotiations with Pretoria. The Harare Declaration, as it came to be known, called for the release of political prisoners, the unbanning of political parties, the removal of troops from the townships, the end of the state of emergency, and the cessation of political trials and executions. Meanwhile, economic sanctions and other measures designed to isolate South Africa were to be maintained. The declaration was adopted, with some modifications, by the United Nations in December 1989 (see Appendix E).

Nevertheless, the ice was broken. South Africa had been included in the Africans' efforts to reconcile the opposing sides in Angola. A new dialogue, which held out greater promise than previous attempts, had begun. With De Klerk in power and Botha's securocrats reined in, South Africa seemed serious about establishing a new relationship with its neighbors. They, in turn, proved to be receptive to the De Klerk initiative. Their reluctance to deal with Pretoria had been eroded by the Namibian settlement, the improved political climate inside South Africa, the need to address their own pressing economic and social difficulties, and the fading prospects of large-scale aid from the outside world.

The prospects for regional détente improved considerably in early 1990 when President De Klerk launched a full-fledged internal dialogue with credible black leaders by unbanning the ANC and other groups and releasing Nelson Mandela. Talks between Pretoria and the ANC in the first half of the year led to the ANC's official renunciation of violence and the promise of further discussions about a democratic constitution for South Africa. The ultimate success of the regional dialogue, however, will depend on the success of those negotiations.

Conclusion

A decade of war and diplomacy brought profound changes to the political and military landscape of southern Africa. As the 1990s began, the major causes of conflict between South Africa and its neighbors had either been eliminated or were being dealt with by peaceful means. What are the implications of these changes for the region? How will relations between South Africa and the black-governed states be affected?

Of the four major factors that shaped South Africa's relations with its neighbors, one had disappeared by the beginning of the 1990s while the other three will have less relevance in the decade ahead. First, the defense of white minority rule that drove South Africa's regional policy under President Botha underwent a major transformation in the hands of his successor, Frederik W. de Klerk. The new South African leader committed his government to dismantling apartheid and negotiating a new constitution with the leaders of the country's black majority. President De Klerk's stated goal was to find a formula for sharing power with blacks while assuring the protection of the white minority.

Second, the commitment of the Frontline States to support guerrillas operating against Namibia and South Africa lost its rationale. The Namibian-Angolan peace settlement permitted the South West Africa People's Organization guerrillas to return home. In South Africa the release of black political prisoners, the return of exiles from abroad, the beginning of negotiations between the South African government and the African National Congress, and the suspension of the armed struggle by the ANC meant that the need for armed support and sanctuary for South African guerrilla movements by the Frontline States fell away. These developments also removed the major external security threat perceived by South African military and political leaders.

The third factor, South Africa's clear military superiority, remains largely the same. But military power is likely to prove far less relevant to the country's regional relations in the 1990s, largely because of the government's changed relationship with Namibian and South African black nationalist movements. Moreover, the end of the 1980s saw a decline in the military's role in shaping South African foreign policy, sharp cuts in military spending, and a significant reduction in the length of service for white conscripts. All these developments point to a diminished importance for the South African military in the decade ahead.

Overarching these developments was the unexpected end of the cold war in southern Africa. The Soviet Union's decision to pursue political rather than military solutions in the region led it to exert pressure on its African clients to seek political settlements. It also produced a close collaboration with the United States that resulted in the Namibian-Angolan peace accords. The end of the cold war further meant that regional states could no longer obtain military and economic support by playing one superpower against the other.

The convergence of Soviet and U.S. interests in southern Africa sharply reduced the threat that the region might become a flash point for armed confrontation between the superpowers. As the 1990s opened, neither was willing or politically able to abandon its clients in the region. But each was sending clear signals that it wanted a quick end to armed conflict and that a political solution was the only available option.

The cumulative effect of these developments was a change in the fourth influence on South Africa's relations with its regional neighbors: its pariah status. South Africa's isolation began to erode when it signed the Namibian-Angolan peace accords and fulfilled them conscientiously. A sign of growing trust by the black states came when South Africa was invited to help in negotiations between UNITA and the Angolan government. President De Klerk's more conciliatory policies, both in the region and at home, sent favorable signals to South Africa's nervous neighbors. One of his most important early moves was to reduce the policy-making functions of the military that had played a leading part in promoting Botha's destabilization strategy. De Klerk's moves toward reconciliation with black political groups in South Africa greatly strengthened the country's bona fides.

The war and diplomacy of the 1980s opened the way for a more benign and cooperative regional environment in the 1990s. Although South Africa retains a decisive, long-term military edge over the rest of the region, economic and political factors will probably have greater impact on its regional relations in the decade ahead. Several neighboring states have already shed some of their reluctance to engage in joint economic ventures with South Africa. The continuing economic malaise in most southern African countries, together with fading prospects for large-scale development aid from the outside world, are likely to weaken further their resistance to South Africa's economic and technical overtures, particularly if the dismantling of apartheid is seen to progress. South Africa, for its part, appears eager to expand such links in order to encourage closer relations and to bypass or weaken international sanctions.

Some regional conflicts, however, remained unresolved as the 1990s opened. In Angola and Mozambique, armed dissident movements, which had thrived due largely to South African support during the 1980s, continued to cause massive social and economic upheaval. By 1990 the United States and the Soviet Union recognized that their intervention might be required to bring about a settlement in the stalled Angolan peace talks. Their joint efforts succeeded in 1991: A cease-fire took effect and a formal peace accord was signed at the end of May. Angola's first free, multiparty elections were scheduled for 1992.

The likely long-term scenario, however, is a reduction of superpower engagement in southern Africa's affairs. The end of the cold war, the collapse of Soviet power in Eastern Europe, and the Soviet Union's own internal problems have all diverted superpower attention from southern Africa. Moreover, Western economic aid to southern Africa, as well as to the rest of the continent, seems likely to diminish during the coming decade given the donors' priority of helping Eastern Europe and their continuing budgetary constraints. This trend should enhance the prospects for closer technical and economic ties between South Africa and its poorer neighbors and should further lower the political barriers between South Africa and the rest of Africa. These changes may propel South Africa toward becoming the acknowledged regional superpower, a status that its vaunted military power failed to achieve.

ECONOMIC RIVALRY AND INTERDEPENDENCE IN SOUTHERN AFRICA

Moeletsi Mbeki
Morley Nkosi

Introduction

The military struggle that flickered and flared between South Africa and the black states through the 1980s lit up the international headlines and preoccupied the diplomats who sought to defuse it. But this struggle was only one aspect of a broader confrontation in the region. Another trial of strength was taking place in the less spectacular but equally important realm of economics. As Pretoria strove to buttress white power against external and internal challenges by using an array of economic pressures against its neighbors, so those countries tried to reduce South Africa's economic hegemony by increasing cooperative efforts among themselves and expanding their options. This struggle, like its military counterpart, proceeded unevenly and was punctuated by lulls, changes of direction, palliative diplomacy, and rapprochements.

Colonial whim, combined with geography and the historical pattern of development, gave Pretoria powerful economic levers for influencing the destinies of its neighbors (see Figures 1 and 2). In the nineteenth and early twentieth centuries, Britain created six landlocked southern African colonies, which later became Botswana, Lesotho, Malawi, Swaziland, Zambia, and Zimbabwe; meanwhile Portugal controlled Angola and Mozambique, which had access to the Atlantic and Indian Oceans.

The dramatic events of the 1970s, which culminated in Zimbabwe's independence in April 1980, brought the dividing line between black- and white-ruled states in the region down to the Limpopo River, which flows along Zimbabwe's and Botswana's bor-

FIGURE 1
Southern Africa Population—1984

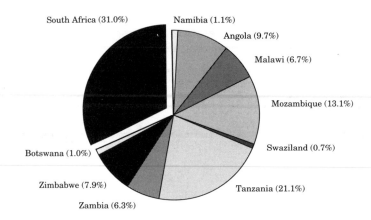

South Africa (31.0%) Namibia (1.1%)

Angola (9.7%)

Malawi (6.7%)

Mozambique (13.1%)

Swaziland (0.7%)

Botswana (1.0%)

Zimbabwe (7.9%)

Tanzania (21.1%)

Zambia (6.3%)

FIGURE 2
Southern Africa GDP—1984

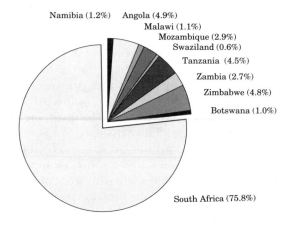

Namibia (1.2%) Angola (4.9%)
Malawi (1.1%)
Mozambique (2.9%)
Swaziland (0.6%)
Tanzania (4.5%)
Zambia (2.7%)
Zimbabwe (4.8%)
Botswana (1.0%)

South Africa (75.8%)

Source: Francis Wilson, "Economic Interdependence and Rivalry in Southern Africa" in report of The Southern Policy Forum Second Conference, August 14–17, 1989 (Queenstown, Maryland: The Aspen Institute, 1989), 10.

ders with South Africa and reaches the sea through Mozambique. The political shape of the region had been changed, but the historical pattern of economic and infrastructural links between the countries of southern Africa was virtually undisturbed. The balance of power and control was still weighted heavily, although not exclusively, in South Africa's favor.

As the countries of the region digested the new geopolitical realities, rival economic strategies emerged. South Africa was the first in the field with its blueprint for a "constellation of southern African states," which was an attempt to draw its closest neighbors into a loose but formal economic grouping under its control. The black states, however, had been devising their own economic strategy with the aim of reducing their inherited dependency on South Africa and coordinating development of their own economies. While South Africa's constellation never went much further than the drawing board, the black states' Southern African Development Coordination Conference (SADCC), launched in 1980 and significantly strengthened by newly independent Zimbabwe's membership, established firm roots and became a relatively successful model for modest but pragmatic regional planning.

The SADCC states, however, were not a homogenous group. They varied widely in virtually every respect, including the character of their dependence on South Africa. While they all subscribed to the Organization of African Unity's (OAU) political goal of working for the independence of Namibia and the end of apartheid in South Africa, and shared SADCC's economic and developmental aims, their diversity led them down different paths during the volatile 1980s.

Each country was preoccupied with its own economic problems, which in most cases grew steadily more severe during the decade. Periodic drought, unstable commodity prices, a heavy debt burden, political instability, economic mismanagement, corruption, and lack of foreign investment contributed to their plight and helped maintain their dependence on South Africa. On top of all this was Pretoria's strategy of destabilization. A few countries managed to cope, even prosper in a modest way; others succumbed to the debilitating combination of these forces.

The economic struggle between South Africa and its neighbors centered on the elements that bound them most firmly together: transportation routes, trade and investment, and migrant labor (see Table 1). It was in these sectors that the principal drama between South Africa and the black states was played out.

The balance sheet at the end of the 1980s showed reduction by a few countries in transport and trade dependency and increased ties in other cases. Overall, the black states were not successful in achieving SADCC's goal of reducing their historical economic dependence

TABLE 1: Economic Linkages in Southern Africa—1984

	Botswana	Lesotho	Swaziland	Malawi	Mozambique	Zimbabwe	Zambia
Trade							
Main partner	SA	SA	SA	SA	SA	SA	UK
Exports to SA (%)	17	—	20	6	5	17	1
Imports from SA (%)	88	95	90	36	14	22	16
Migrant Workers							
Number (000s)	29	150	13	31	59	17	—
Wage earners (% of)	23	86	15	8	20	2	—
Remittances (£ m.)	21	99	9	11	43	20	—
Tourists							
Number from SA (000s)	150	50	50	25	—	63	ban
Total (% of)	67	70	60	39	—	24	—
South Africa Supplies							
Electricity (%)	19	100	50	—	33	1	—
Oil (%)	100	100	100	70	some	some	—
Food	most	most	some	some	some	some	some
Overseas Trade via SA (%)	100	100	33	some	—	66	33

Source: Africa Research Bulletin 22, no. 8, September 30, 1985, 7873.

on South Africa. But the political changes that took place as the new decade opened, notably the independence of Namibia and the beginning of a genuine political dialogue within South Africa itself, raised questions about the relevance of this facet of the SADCC vision and the future role of the organization.

Rival Strategies: The Constellation vs. SADCC

Most of the black states in 1980, whatever their internal differences and problems, could not ignore the influence of their powerful southern neighbor. This was particularly true when South Africa undertook a panregional economic initiative that challenged the political cohesion of the black group.

The concept of a loose confederation of southern African states had first been canvassed in South Africa by Prime Minister John Vorster in the early 1970s. In 1979 his successor, Pieter W. Botha, formally launched the "constellation of Southern African States." The initial membership, in addition to South Africa, was to include Botswana, Lesotho, and Swaziland; the four "independent" homelands (Transkei, Venda, Bophuthatswana, and Ciskei) in addition to any others that might emerge; and Namibia, which was still under South African control. A place was reserved for Zimbabwe, whose location and relatively sophisticated economy made it a key component of the scheme.

The acceptance of the constellation by any of the region's independent black states would have been a valuable prize in the eyes of Pretoria's planners. It would have placed the homelands on the same footing as several genuinely independent states, granting them a degree of international legitimacy that had eluded them. Since the independent homelands were an essential part of the apartheid strategy, any formal recognition of them would have been a major breakthrough. Moreover, if countries such as Zimbabwe or Botswana could be persuaded to acknowledge that their economic future lay permanently within the South African orbit, they would be tacitly accepting a role as buffer states between the white south and the black north. Mutual security arrangements were part of Pretoria's plan.

Then, as the constellation gathered momentum, other hostile states like Zambia and Mozambique might soften their antagonism and conceivably be drawn in. In effect, Botha was offering his black neighbors a deal: We will cut you in on our prosperity, and give you access to our aid, investment, and markets, but you will have to accept that we are in the driver's seat—which means giving up the idea that our political arrangements are any of your business.

Viewed in purely economic terms, the constellation had clear attractions for many of the black states, but none of them showed the slightest interest in it. Pretoria's gambit turned out to rest on a number of misconceptions. One was simply a wrong guess about the sort of government that would emerge from Zimbabwe's elections. South Africa believed that Bishop Abel Muzorewa, viewed as moderate and malleable, would prevail; instead, Robert Mugabe, Pretoria's "worst-case scenario," won decisively. Another miscalculation was the belief that however critical African leaders might be of South Africa in public, they would, when it came to hard policy decisions, put economics before politics. Perhaps South Africa's leaders were so used to controlling the region and getting their way that they could not conceive of a rejection. Or perhaps it was psychologically impossible for those in authority in Pretoria to grasp that apartheid was highly offensive to all Africans and that blacks would make significant economic sacrifices in defense of their principles.

The dilemma posed by the black states' political hostility to South Africa on the one hand and their economic dependence on it on the other had already alerted them to the need for defining a collective relationship. This need was heightened by the prospect of Zimbabwe's independence—only Namibia and South Africa itself then remained under white rule—and Pretoria's new economic strategy. Thus, while the finishing touches were being put on the constellation in South Africa, the black states were laying the foundations for their own regional economic grouping. Formally established on April 1, 1980, it was called the Southern African Development Coordination Conference, sometimes dubbed the "counter-constellation." The nine founding member states were Angola, Botswana, Lesotho, Malawi, Mozambique, Swaziland, Tanzania, Zambia, and Zimbabwe. Their primary goals were to reduce their economic dependence on South Africa and to foster and coordinate regional development. South Africa's constellation project effectively collapsed when the newly elected government of Zimbabwe, led by Robert Mugabe, decided to join SADCC.

South Africa found that instead of creating and controlling a mutual prosperity sphere, whose members would be in no position to cause it any trouble, it faced a united front of countries pledged to do as little business with it as possible. Even the states that had been relatively docile (Swaziland), economically captive (Lesotho), or even friendly (Malawi) chose to cast their lot with SADCC.

In symbolic terms, the birth of SADCC was an event of prime importance. The member states committed themselves to a clear statement of where they wanted to go, which meant at a minimum that they would be under an obligation to justify their economic relations with South Africa and to reduce them where possible. The SADCC secretariat also provided a mechanism for developing strategic goals, designing specific programs, and raising funds (see Table 2).

TABLE 2: SADCC's Sectoral Programs

Sector	Coordinating Country
Energy	Angola
Food, Agriculture, and Natural Resources:	
• Overall Coordination	Zimbabwe
• Agricultural Research and Training	Botswana
• Fisheries, Forestry and Wildlife	Malawi
• Food Security	Zimbabwe
• Livestock Production and Animal Disease Control	Botswana
• Soil and Water Conservation and Land Utilization	Lesotho
Industry and Trade	Tanzania
Manpower Development	Swaziland
Mining	Zambia
Tourism	Lesotho
Transport and Communications	Mozambique

Source: Unpublished SADCC report, 1989.

SADCC's founding members were well aware that previous attempts to create regional economic groupings in Africa had not been successful. Arrangements that had appeared to transfer power from national governments to international bureaucracies had run into severe difficulties. SADCC's creators decided that decisions would be made only by consensus—all members were given a veto—and that national sovereignties and sensitivities would not be infringed. These concerns were reflected in SADCC's structure: a small central secretariat together with a much larger apparatus of meetings for national delegations at all levels—from technical experts in the various program sectors through senior civil servants to ministers and from there to the annual summit for heads of state.

SOUTHERN AFRICAN DEVELOPMENT COORDINATION CONFERENCE (SADCC)

Formed: *1 April 1980*
Membership: *Angola, Botswana, Lesotho, Malawi, Mozambique, Swaziland, Tanzania, Zambia, Zimbabwe. Namibia joined 1 April 1990*
Overall Coordination: *SADCC meets annually, usually in June or July, at heads of government level, with an additional two Council of Ministers meetings. The latter is the effective programme decision-making body, while the annual Consultative Conference with donors, usually held in January/February, has become very important for funding the projects that form the traditional core of SADCC's activities.*
Project Status: *Over 600 projects have been identified and are in various stages of funding, implementation or completion. Total project cost (as of January 1990) was $6.3 bn, of which transport and communications accounts for $5.1 bn, agriculture, fisheries, forestry, etc., $670 mn and energy $427 mn.[1]*

The SADCC States

A more ambitious or tightly structured organization would have been undermined by the reluctance of the Southern African Development Coordination Conference's member governments to surrender any of their prerogatives. It was not just a question of nationalism. The reality was that SADCC's nine members, apart from sharing a common history of colonialism and a rejection of apartheid, were a group of extremely diverse countries. Their differences ranged over size, population, political system, history, official ideology, economic performance, geography, and natural resource endowment.

The BLS States—Botswana, Lesotho, and Swaziland

In the most general sense, the SADCC countries shared an experience of geographical closeness to South Africa as the dominant power in the region. But even here there were fundamental differences. Three countries, Botswana, Lesotho, and Swaziland (the BLS countries), had always been firmly tied to the South African economy. It was through quirks of history and the shrewdness of their nineteenth-century leaders that these small nations emerged in the 1960s as independent states rather than as components of South Africa.

In most economic respects, however, they have always been satellites of South Africa. They belong to the Southern African

Customs Union (SACU), which allows the free movement of goods throughout the four member states. South Africa collects customs duties for SACU's members and distributes the money under a revenue-sharing formula. The BLS states obtain a large proportion of their government revenues from this arrangement, but are bound closely to the South African economy by it, since Pretoria determines the customs rates and operates the system to protect its own economic interests.[2] Lesotho, Swaziland, and South Africa signed the Rand Monetary Agreement (RMA) in 1974, which tied them to South Africa's monetary policies. Botswana, larger and more distant from South Africa than Lesotho and Swaziland, later achieved a greater degree of autonomy through the development of its mineral wealth, notably diamond production. Botswana established its own currency in 1976 and took control of its own monetary policy. South African companies, however, own the bulk of Botswana's productive enterprises. South Africa supplies most of Botswana's goods and services and provides a market for most of its products. Lesotho, completely surrounded by South Africa, and Swaziland, sandwiched between South Africa and Mozambique, are even more closely tied to their large neighbor.

Angola and Tanzania

At the other end of SADCC's geographical range are distant Angola and Tanzania. Neither of these large countries—Angola in land area, Tanzania in population—has ever had much to do with South Africa. Under colonialism, Tanzania was part of East Africa, not southern Africa, whereas Angola, under Portuguese rule, had little to do with any other state. In economic terms, their access to the sea was their principal value to the other SADCC states. The Benguela railroad, which links Zambia and Zaire to the Atlantic Ocean at Lobito, Angola, was the cheapest way of moving those two countries' vital copper exports to their overseas markets. But during Angola's civil war, the railroad was constantly sabotaged and was inoperative for most of the 1980s.

In Tanzania, the Tanzania-Zambia Railway Authority (Tazara) railroad, linking the Zambian copperbelt with Dar es Salaam on the Indian Ocean, was built by the Chinese and opened in 1975. The express purpose of the railroad was to reduce Zambia's trading dependency on white-ruled Rhodesia and South Africa. But due to poor management and congestion in the port of Dar es Salaam, the railroad was not an operational success. It did, however, help to strengthen political ties between Tanzania and countries closer to South Africa, which suited Tanzania's president at the time, Julius Nyerere, who was a driving force in Africa's efforts to bring about political change in Rhodesia and South Africa.

Zambia, Zimbabwe, Mozambique, and Malawi

Between these two extremes—three countries umbilically attached to South Africa and two on the periphery of the region—are SADCC's four other members. They have certain characteristics in common. They all are closely linked to South Africa in economic terms, without being satellites like the BLS countries, but none has any formal economic ties to South Africa. Each of their economies is profoundly affected by its South African connections, although the nature of these connections differs greatly from one to another.

Yet classifying the four as a group is misleading. A brief look at some of the more striking economic features of these countries helps to illustrate the varied and complex background against which the struggle to reduce dependence on South Africa was waged during SADCC's first decade.

Zambia. At its independence in 1964, Zambia wanted to exert greater control over its copper industry, its principal export and source of foreign exchange. Much of the copper revenues during colonialism had gone to Southern Rhodesia, and the mines were owned by foreigners, mainly South Africans. Zambia also aimed to diversify its economy, particularly by directing national resources toward agriculture.

The country started life with high hopes and much international goodwill. But it spent its copper revenues freely during the early years of independence, when the price of copper was high, leaving itself in a weak position to withstand the collapse of the market from the mid-1970s onward. The government borrowed heavily to maintain living standards, plunging the country into a prolonged and acute shortage of foreign exchange. The situation was aggravated by a determination to maintain a high exchange rate for the currency, thereby discouraging exports and stimulating demand for imports.

In addition to earning less for each ton of copper, the mines also produced less, partly due to the inefficient management that followed their nationalization. The economy was further damaged by too much state intervention, including the establishment of a large number of state-owned companies that operated at a loss. Policies to invigorate the farm sector proved unsuccessful. They were undermined by the low prices paid to farmers for their produce in order to keep down the cost of living in the towns and by the inefficiency of the supply and marketing systems operated by the government.

By the mid-1980s, Zambia was in a state of severe economic distress, with a crippling debt burden, a heavy deficit on the government budget, rampant inflation, and growing unemployment. Having run out of international credit, the country turned for help to the International Monetary Fund (IMF), which prescribed a painful restructuring of the economy featuring reduced government spending, even higher prices, less state intervention, and a massive devaluation of the currency.

When these measures led to food riots in 1987, President Kenneth Kaunda decided that the political costs of the austerity program were too high. He broke off relations with the IMF, curtailed the country's debt service payments, and reverted to earlier policies of rigid state controls, including the managed allocation of foreign exchange at a fixed rate. But after two years of this strategy, billed as "growth through own resources," and despite an improvement in the copper price, the economy was still limping badly. By the end of the decade, Zambia was again working with the IMF and its other creditors and was once again committed to structural reform along market-oriented lines.

Zambia is a landlocked country whose foreign trade traditionally went either south, via Southern Rhodesia to the ports of South Africa and Mozambique, or north and west, through Zaire and Angola. After Zambia's independence, the Rhodesian, Angolan, and later the Mozambican civil wars made many of these routes either politically undesirable or physically impassable. In the late 1960s, Zambia began to move some of its exports and imports via the long and slow route to the distant port of Dar es Salaam, at first along the hazardous Great North Road and subsequently along the newly constructed Tazara railroad. While self-sufficient in hydroelectric power and coal, it obtained all of its oil through a pipeline running from Dar es Salaam in Tanzania to the Zambian copperbelt. Road connections to Botswana and Malawi, linking up with rail systems to South Africa and Mozambique, respectively, were also developed.

But all of these new routes had problems. The road and rail links through Tanzania suffered from delays at Dar es Salaam port, and the Tazara railroad was affected by shortages of rolling stock and operational difficulties. The Mozambican corridors, through Malawi to Nacala and via Zimbabwe to Beira and Maputo, were severely disrupted by the Mozambique National Resistance (RENAMO) insurgents during much of the 1980s.

Zambia has no common frontier with South Africa, but throughout the 1980s it was reminded of Pretoria's presence by the Caprivi Strip, a long tongue of Namibia that separates southwestern Zambia from northern Botswana. Its main economic linkages with South Africa were in trade and transport. The country had long been dependent on South African manufactured goods, especially equipment for the crucial mining industry. This dependence tended to be accentuated by its foreign exchange shortage and the difficulty in obtaining credit. For example, when Zambian importers had to pay cash in advance, South Africa's shorter delivery time gave it an edge over more distant suppliers.

Zambia's contribution to SADCC's policy of reducing economic ties with South Africa was thus adversely affected by its own pressing economic difficulties and its failure to develop efficient and dependable alternative trade routes.

Zimbabwe. When Zimbabwe became independent in 1980, plausible reasons existed for optimism about the new state's economic prospects. Zimbabwe had the most developed and vigorous economy in the region, second only to that of South Africa. Its export base was well diversified by African standards, consisting of a relatively wide range of mineral and agricultural commodities as well as some manufactured items. It thus enjoyed a degree of protection against the vagaries of world markets that had proved so destructive for a country like Zambia, which relied on a single product.

The economic challenge facing Prime Minister Robert Mugabe and his team was how to utilize the country's strengths while moving away from the closed economy that had been forced on Rhodesia under Ian Smith's white minority government. One factor in their favor was that except for getting modest loans from South Africa, Rhodesia had not been able to borrow abroad during its fifteen years of isolation. The country's foreign debt burden consequently was extremely low in the African context, which meant that there was room to raise money for the necessary capital investment.

But it was clearly not going to be easy to ensure economic stability and at the same time satisfy the pent-up political demands unleashed by majority rule. The voters who had given Mugabe his electoral triumph thought that the war had been fought to bring in a government that would redress past injustices. They expected rapid and radical land redistribution, considerably higher wages, and many more schools, hospitals, and business opportunities. An economy that had supported the minority white population in comfort would now have to be squeezed to provide services previously denied to blacks, thereby putting severe pressure on the national budget.

The most productive sectors, including mining, manufacturing, and commercial farming, were owned and managed almost entirely by whites. In theory, the presence of an efficient managerial and technical class gave the country a big advantage, since it would not have to rely on expensive outside experts with little local knowledge. But it was difficult to reconcile the continued economic predominance of whites with the new political realities.

It was also difficult to reconcile the capitalist nature of the nation's economy with the official Marxist-Leninist label that the ruling Zimbabwe African National Union (ZANU) party had attached to itself. While Smith's government had found it necessary to administer a strong dose of state intervention, this had been done from a position of sympathy with businesspeople and a knowledge of how business worked. Few in the Mugabe government had any such knowledge or sympathy; the new rulers represented interests that to a large extent saw themselves as being in conflict with business.

The South African connection was another important factor in the development of Zimbabwe's economy. South Africa was Zimbabwe's largest trading partner, and the relationship was formalized in a preferential trade agreement. There was also substantial South African investment, notably in the mining and larger manufacturing industries. Zimbabwe's transport and trade links with South Africa, which had grown stronger under Smith, made it highly dependent on that country. The road and rail links were particularly critical, at least until the shorter outlets through Mozambique could be made safe and rehabilitated to function at full capacity. The air link, operated by both Air Zimbabwe and South African Airways, was also important.

Other links between the two countries were weaker. Unlike Mozambique and Lesotho, Zimbabwe sent relatively few migrant workers to South Africa. It was also more independent in energy than the other border states, since it had its own coal, produced its hydroelectric power from the Kariba Dam, and obtained its oil through the Beira pipeline in Mozambique. A major problem, however, which also applied to rail transportation, was the vulnerability of the Beira corridor to sabotage by RENAMO.

Robert Mugabe was the man the South Africans least wanted to win the elections in 1980, and relations between the two countries throughout the 1980s were frigid at best and hostile at worst. Relations were limited to maintaining trade missions in each other's capital and discussing security matters at an official but not ministerial level. The Zimbabwean government, like Botswana's but unlike Mozambique's, resisted any suggestion of a nonaggression pact with South Africa. Mugabe consistently criticized both apartheid and the destabilizing tactics pursued by Pretoria against its neighbors.

In response, South African forces attacked African National Congress (ANC) offices and personnel in Zimbabwe. South Africa also gave a measure of support to the armed dissidents in Matabeleland province who, until their surrender at the end of 1988, posed the sharpest political threat to the Mugabe government after independence. Furthermore, Pretoria put intermittent pressure on Zimbabwe's economic arteries by cutting off supplies of fuel and imposing border controls in order to slow the flow of goods from South Africa to Zimbabwe, thereby reminding Zimbabwe of its vulnerability.

The combination of political hostility and economic interdependence posed awkward problems for Zimbabwe's policy makers. The country's voice was among the loudest of those calling for comprehensive and mandatory sanctions against South Africa at the United Nations or at summit meetings of the Commonwealth and nonaligned movement. Yet it was not prepared to accept the heavy economic damage that it could suffer if it adhered to that policy itself. In 1987, for example, the Zimbabwean government ruled that all future import licenses would exclude South Africa as a source of procurement other than in exceptional circumstances. But the proposed restriction was quietly shelved after an alarmed business community warned the government of the severe disruption it would cause. Similarly, Mugabe and Zambia's President Kaunda had to abandon a public pledge that they would end all airline flights between their countries and South Africa. In practice, Zimbabwe's attempts to reduce its dependence on its large and powerful neighbor were mainly concentrated in efforts to protect and upgrade the Mozambican corridors.

The unpalatable necessity of continuing to do business with South Africa was a distracting background element in economic policy making and could be seen in areas such as foreign investment policy. The Zimbabwean government's attitude toward foreign investment was ambiguous. It said it would like to attract such investment in carefully selected fields, but equally, it wanted to reduce the proportion of the economy owned by foreigners. The government showed itself ready to buy out existing investors wishing to leave, especially when the sellers were South African. The predictable result of this ambiguity, reflected in the heavily bureaucratic way in which the government handled foreign investment proposals, was that little new investment came in. By the end of the 1980s, concerned at the economy's patchy growth record and rising unemployment, the government decided it had to do more to attract investors. But it continued to move slowly and cautiously, and did nothing to promote Zimbabwe to South African investors who—politics apart—would have been among those most likely to respond. It is plausible to conclude that behind these uncertainties was the government's uneasiness at its dependence on South Africa, combined with its inability to do much to reduce it.

The main point is that Zimbabwe's aspiration to reduce its South African ties had to take its place among the many objectives and complications that preoccupied the framers of economic policy through the 1980s. While the country started with some advantages, it soon encountered difficulties. The first year saw economic growth of more than 10 percent, reflecting the end of international sanctions and an inflow of aid, but thereafter the picture was a mixed one.

The economy's performance was strongly affected by factors outside Zimbabwe's control, notably the annual rainfall and the trend of world commodity markets. A severe drought for three consecutive years in mid-decade caused the growth rate to turn negative. When it picked up again after good rains, it was not enough to make a significant impact on the rising unemployment, as more and more school-leavers poured out of the country's rapidly expanding educational system. Meanwhile, the political need to show positive benefits arising from independence meant a large budget deficit, which in turn led to inflation and placed a heavy tax burden on the population.

Although the government borrowed substantially from abroad, Zimbabwe's external debt never became unmanageable. But the repayment obligations placed an additional strain on the public purse, particularly the availability of foreign exchange. The government maintained the battery of tight controls it had inherited from the days of Ian Smith and added a few of its own. Virtually everything any business might want to do required government permission, from raising product prices to firing employees to importing the smallest item. The overall effect was to place the economy in a bind that made it barely possible to maintain existing operations and stifled new initiatives.

The picture was not one of unrelieved gloom, however. Agriculture, for instance, saw major success. Mugabe, who had learned from the experiences of other African countries that had ceased to be agriculturally self-sufficient, was careful not to do anything that would drive away the experienced white commercial farmers. At the same time, encouragement for peasant farming paid off handsomely in rising production.

The country's economy avoided the disasters that had taken place in much of Africa, but its performance fell far short of the upsurge expected by many at the time of independence. It proved unable to generate new jobs and thereby keep pace with the rise both in the total population and in the number of educated job-seekers, many of whom could no longer hope to make a living on the land as their parents had. That was the background against which any economic struggle against South Africa had to be waged. It was not a situation that allowed much scope for experimentation or maneuver.

Mozambique. If Zimbabwe started life with special advantages, Mozambique's birth in 1975 was attended by equally special difficulties. The country has a potentially viable economy, with good agricultural land, abundant hydroelectric power, some minerals, including coal and possibly many more (little exploration had taken place under Portuguese rule), and adequate ports. But following independence, Mozambique was afflicted by a series of disasters, both natural and man-made.

The country had always been a backwater under Portugal, but the general underdevelopment was made far worse by the mass exodus of Portuguese capital and skilled labor at the time of independence. Military confrontation and closed borders with Rhodesia from 1975 until 1980 imposed additional burdens. Many of the economic policies adopted at independence were inappropriate. They were drawn largely from Soviet models and had little relevance for an African economy based mainly on peasant farming. A succession of devastating droughts and floods took place. Most damaging of all was the protracted and draining RENAMO insurgency, fueled by South Africa, that began as soon as the struggle with Rhodesia was over.

From the mid-1980s onward, Mozambique began modifying its socialist policies and turning to the West for assistance, a process that accelerated after Samora Machel, the country's first president, died in a plane crash in October 1986 and was succeeded by Joaquim Chissano. In an even greater shift of policy, in the mid-1980s the government clearly began to move toward dismantling the one-party state. Mozambique became a member of the IMF and the World Bank and, in 1987, with the two organizations' support and encouragement, it instituted an economic recovery program that featured devaluation and a more market-oriented economic approach. Throughout the 1980s, however, the economy continued to be ravaged by the civil war with RENAMO. Few areas outside Maputo, the capital, were immune from violence and sabotage. The effects of the insurgency made it virtually impossible to assess the success or failure of the country's new economic policies.

The economic links between Mozambique and South Africa historically have been close. They are important in three different areas. First, the large port of Maputo is the most natural trade outlet for South Africa's Transvaal province and before the Portuguese withdrawal handled one-fifth of South Africa's total trade. During the 1980s this traffic dropped by over 80 percent. Second, a large number of migrant workers, mostly miners, continued to work in South Africa, although their numbers dropped by more than half after Mozambique's independence. Their remittances remain important, however, in Mozambique's slender foreign exchange earnings.

Finally, at Cahora Bassa, Mozambique has Africa's largest hydroelectric dam, built at the end of the colonial era. In theory, it can supply all of Mozambique's electric power needs and 10 percent of South Africa's. In reality, sabotage of the transmission lines by RENAMO, with the help of its South African friends, shut the dam down, leaving Mozambique dependent on South Africa for almost half its electricity. A series of meetings in the late 1980s between South Africa, Mozambique, and Portugal, which still owns the dam, resulted in an agreement that revived hopes of restoring the transmission lines and resuming power supplies.

Mozambique, accused by Pretoria of permitting itself to be a conduit for ANC guerrillas, found itself a major target of the South African strategy of destabilizing its neighbors. In March 1984 Machel's government in effect sued for peace by signing the Nkomati Accord with South Africa, a nonaggression and good neighborly pact that required it to expel almost all the ANC personnel in the country in exchange for South Africa's ending its support for RENAMO (see Appendix C). The pact broke down within a year, when it became obvious that South Africa was still helping the RENAMO dissidents. A second rapprochement took place in September 1988, when South Africa's President P. W. Botha paid a state visit to Mozambique and the two countries reaffirmed their adherence to the accord. Political and security issues continued to dominate the relationship, but both sides promised to cooperate more closely on economic issues.

Mozambique offers the clearest example of the clash between political aspirations and economic realities in southern Africa. At the time of its independence, no country could have been more determined in its opposition to apartheid and its refusal to do South Africa's bidding. That determination was symbolized by Mozambique's strong support for the black nationalist forces fighting against Smith's government in Rhodesia, its backing of the ANC in the struggle against South Africa, and its close relations with the Soviet Union, Pretoria's most feared opponent.

Yet during the 1980s, Mozambique was obliged to change course in a most drastic fashion. Such a complete economic and political reversal can be explained partly by South Africa's policy of destabilization, including its support for RENAMO. But that is not the whole story. The country's economic weakness, the product of colonial neglect compounded by inappropriate postindependence policies and natural disasters, ensured fertile ground for insurgency. Its close economic links with South Africa reduced its scope for independent action. Throughout the 1980s Mozambique remained the prisoner of its history.

Malawi. It came as a surprise to some observers that Malawi decided to join SADCC when it was formed in 1980. It alone among the member states had full diplomatic relations with Pretoria and had received substantial South African aid. The country had been ruled since independence in 1963 by the autocratic Dr. Hastings Kamuzu Banda, whose idiosyncratic personality and great age—he is believed to be at least ninety-one years old, although nobody knows for sure—made him a unique figure in the region.

Banda took over a landlocked country that was extremely poor, with no mineral resources and little manufacturing industry. The economy relied on agriculture, with tobacco, tea, and sugar as the main export crops. Malawi traditionally had sent a large contingent of migrant workers to South Africa's mines and farms. Banda believed in capitalism, under his own firm guidance. His top priority was to strengthen the farming sector, and he was prepared to do business with any country he thought could help Malawi's development, including South Africa. Establishing formal diplomatic relations with South Africa ran counter to all conventional African thinking and breached the rules laid down by the Organization of African Unity for isolating South Africa. But none of that seemed to worry Malawi's president, and he was rewarded for his approach by considerable amounts of South African aid, including the construction of a new capital at Lilongwe.

Banda's pragmatic if unorthodox program resulted in considerable economic success until the early 1980s. The emphasis on agriculture enabled production to grow, particularly on the larger farms. Raising the yields of peasant farmers proved harder because of the shortage of land and the rapidly increasing population. But even there, progress was made. The country prided itself on producing all the food it needed, plus a surplus for export in most years.

In the early 1980s, Malawi fell on harder times. This was due partly to a relaxation of previously strict government spending policies. The foreign debt rose to an unsustainable level, the balance of payments ran out of control, and Malawi was forced to ask its creditors for relief. Financial disciplines were reimposed, and the country embarked on a restructuring program with help from the IMF and, particularly, the World Bank.

Malawi also suffered badly from the effects of regional instability, despite all of Banda's efforts to steer clear of it. In the past, it had relied for most of its trade on the rail links through Mozambique to the ports of Nacala and Beira. When these were disrupted by RENAMO's activities, Malawi had to turn to far longer and more expensive outlets through Zambia, Zimbabwe, Botswana, and South Africa, using road transport to reach the railheads in those countries. Official estimates suggest that this added no less than 40 percent to the cost of Malawi's imports, a crippling burden and one that the economy was ill equipped to bear.

As a further consequence of the Mozambican civil war, more than half a million refugees crossed the border by the end of the 1980s. The Malawi government showed itself admirably ready to receive them and did its best to assimilate them into village life. But the influx threw a heavy additional strain on the land and the fragile environment, as well as on government services that were already fully stretched.

The experience of Malawi during this decade showed that no country in the region was immune to the effects of its neighbors' instability, no matter how great its determination to insulate itself and prevent regional politics from interfering with its economic development. In many respects, Malawi had started from a position diametrically opposite that of a country like Mozambique, by shunning ideology, by disassociating itself from the sanctions campaigns against Rhodesia and South Africa, and by uncompromisingly putting its own national self-interest first.

Yet when South Africa decided to support the RENAMO rebellion, Malawi's diplomatic friendship with Pretoria failed to shield it from the devastating effects of the conflict. The relationship with South Africa cooled, and Malawi came under pressure from its SADCC neighbors to play a part in defending the vital transport routes through Mozambique. In 1987 Banda, while maintaining diplomatic relations with Pretoria, sent a battalion of troops to help protect the railroad connecting Malawi to the port of Nacala.

Pressure on the
Economic Arteries

South Africa's regional strategy during the 1980s was shaped by its determination to prevent its neighbors from posing any threat to its own security. This meant deterring the black states from providing sanctuary and conduits for African National Congress and South West Africa People's Organization (SWAPO) guerrillas. It was also in South Africa's interest to keep its neighbors economically weak and to remind them of their vulnerability. To do so, South Africa used direct military action, indirect support for dissident movements within those countries, and economic pressures. While military action played a major role, Pretoria often resorted to the use of pressure on the black states' economic lifelines, notably the transportation routes, the flow of trade and investment, and the migrant labor system.

Transportation

> The single-track railway bridge drenched in the spray of Victoria Falls on the Zimbabwe-Zambia border is a lifeline for black Africa. Every thirty minutes or so a Zimbabwe steam train carrying coal and food arrives to be met by a Zambian engine which will take over. From the opposite direction a Zambian train carrying copper heads south for Bulawayo and for a port in South Africa's long coastline. Victoria Falls is a key rail link between Africa and racist Pretoria despite political differences.[3]

Transportation, especially the regional network of railroads, was pivotal in the economic relationship between South Africa and the black states in the 1980s. Yet South African dominance of the regional railroads was relatively recent. Most of the countries in the region have rail connections to the ports of friendly neighbors that do not pass through South African territory. There are five such rail-port systems that could more than cope with all the black states' trade if they were functioning at full capacity and were properly protected. The theoretical capacity of these routes is twenty-five million tons a year. The Southern African Development Coordination Conference's figure for the total overseas trade of its nine founding members amounted to between eight and nine million tons a year.

It was clear, therefore, that if during the 1980s the rehabilitation and security problems of the black states' transport routes had been resolved and the routes had operated at peak efficiency, they could have served all the black states' transport needs with capacity to spare.[4] This would have reduced South Africa's transport leverage to zero. But Pretoria was careful to ensure that this did not happen.

Southern Africa's Rail-Port Systems. The five rail-port systems controlled by the black states include three in Mozambique, one in Tanzania, and one in Angola. A sixth is controlled by South Africa.

Mozambique. Mozambique's three rail-port systems are located in Beira, Maputo, and Nacala. Beira is particularly important because it is the terminal point for a short and theoretically cheap system of parallel rail, road, and oil pipeline links known as the Beira corridor, which connects Zimbabwe to the sea. As well as serving Mozambique and Zimbabwe, the corridor is used by Malawi and Zambia and could also serve Botswana if necessary.

Before Zimbabwe's independence, Rhodesia was denied access to the corridor when the Mozambican government closed the border between 1976 and 1980 in compliance with international sanctions. The pipeline had been inactive since 1965 when the refinery at the Rhodesian end was mothballed by Lonrho, its British owners. The corridor was reopened in 1980 after Zimbabwe's independence but it soon became unreliable because of maintenance problems and sabotage by RENAMO. Beira is particularly critical to Zimbabwe since it is a quarter of the distance to South Africa's ports and the pipeline provides Zimbabwe with nearly all its petroleum needs.

Maputo, the black states' largest port, is another vital outlet for the landlocked countries, notably Zimbabwe and Swaziland, but also

Zambia and Botswana. The port, connected to Zimbabwe by the Limpopo Railroad, had traditionally been Rhodesia's main external trade outlet. Reopened after Zimbabwe's independence, disrepair and RENAMO attacks closed the line again in the early 1980s.

Maputo is linked by road and rail to South Africa in a connection that, when functioning, is of mutual benefit to the two countries. When Mozambique was under Portuguese control, the port was the most economical trade outlet for South Africa's heavily industrialized Transvaal province. But following Mozambique's independence, South African traffic through Maputo declined due to a combination of factors: deterioration of the port's facilities, sabotage by RENAMO, and a deliberate policy by Pretoria to divert business away from Maputo to South African ports. Ironically, the South African government provided technical assistance for the port, and the country's private sector played a role in its rehabilitation in the late 1980s.

Nacala is the smallest of Mozambique's three main ports, but it is of great importance to landlocked Malawi and, to a lesser extent, to Zambia. Nacala is a natural deep-water port that, unlike Maputo and more particularly Beira, does not require dredging and is in good working order. But the connecting railroad to Malawi was another victim of Mozambique's civil war. Malawi was forced, at enormous financial cost, to reroute its trade through much more distant ports in Tanzania and South Africa, utilizing a combination of road and rail transportation.

Tanzania. Tanzania's port of Dar es Salaam is linked to Zambia by the Chinese-built Tazara railroad and the Tazara oil pipeline. It also serves Malawi and Zaire. Malawi's link consists of the "northern corridor," a road from Blantyre to the railhead at Mbeya in Tanzania. The Tazara line, which opened in 1975, was plagued by managerial and technical problems. While its total capacity is two and a half million tons a year, by mid-1986 it was carrying less than one million tons.[5] Two years later, however, that figure had risen to over one and a half million tons.[6]

The railroad and port were upgraded to increase their capacity, and through most of the 1980s they handled Zambia's copper exports as well as its crude oil imports. The Dar es Salaam route was the only one controlled by the black states that was not under a security threat.

Angola. Lobito is the only major west coast port in the region and offers the closest access to European and American markets. Linked to Zaire by the Benguela Railway, Lobito serves Zaire and Zambia, as well as the interior of Angola. The Benguela line was once the main artery for Zaire's and Zambia's mineral exports. But it was effectively closed from the time of Angola's independence in 1975, when civil war broke out and continued through the 1980s. While a small amount of local traffic continued to be handled, the line ceased to serve central and eastern Angola.

South Africa. Durban, Richards Bay, East London, Port Elizabeth, and Cape Town are all under South African control and constitute what is sometimes called the "southern route." The major rail network that feeds these ports runs south from Zaire, through Zambia, and then forks in Zimbabwe. One branch goes directly into South Africa; the other runs south through Botswana and then into South Africa. Once inside the country, they link up with other regional rail and road routes that carry freight to and from Zaire, Zambia, Malawi, Zimbabwe, Botswana, Swaziland, and Lesotho. Although distant and costly for many of the black states, the southern route was often their only option.

South Africa's Transport Strategy. In the early 1980s, it became apparent that South Africa, through a combination of economic and military measures, was forcing the black states to use its transport infrastructure. Government officials in South Africa called the phenomenon "transport diplomacy," while opponents referred to it as Pretoria's "transport weapon." While South Africa cooperated with many of its neighbors on a technical level, it used tactics varying from light pressure to a virtual siege when it wanted to make a specific political point or to remind its neighbors of their vulnerability.

South Africa's transportation system is owned and operated by South African Transport Services (SATS), a huge parastatal organization that is formally independent of the government but intimately connected with it. SATS, which runs the country's railroads, its ports, its national airline, and some of its road haulage, maintains a close working relationship with many of the border states.

The invention of transport diplomacy is commonly credited to—or blamed on—J. G. H. Loubser, general manager of SATS from 1970 until 1983. Loubser denied using South Africa's transport leverage as a "weapon," but acknowledged that it was "a highly strategic deterrent to political isolation and a key to relations with Africa in transport as well as other fields." He added: "I cannot but use these opportunities to the full to the benefit of South Africa in various areas and particularly in the political field."[7]

Loubser, who regularly attended meetings of the State Security Council (SSC), South Africa's top decision-making body for defense, security, and foreign affairs, saw transport as helping South Africa's "outward movement," a policy designed by Prime Minister Vorster in the 1970s to establish more friendly relations with South Africa's neighbors and with other African states. Transporting its neighbors' goods was also a useful source of income, providing South Africa with $240 million in foreign exchange in 1980–81.[8]

Loubser and his successor, E. L. Grove, regarded themselves as "diplomats"—or even "doves"—in the way they handled South Africa's transport leverage. But that was not how most of the black states viewed SATS and its policies. Actions such as refusing to renew leases on vitally needed locomotives, holding up critical petroleum supplies, and arbitrarily manipulating tariffs to deter exporters and importers from using non–South African routes were seen by the black states as hostile at best and punitive at worst.

By a curious irony, the first time the South African government used its transport leverage was against a white ally, when it put pressure on Ian Smith's Rhodesian government to reach a political settlement in the mid-1970s. The target soon shifted to the black border states, and pressure was increased steadily in the early to mid-1980s. Pretoria's techniques ranged from relatively minor administrative and technical pressures to all-out military destabilization that closed down major railroads for periods of years.

Rental of locomotives and freight cars to neighbors gave Pretoria a powerful lever. At any given time during the 1980s, around five thousand South African freight cars and fifty locomotives were on lease to neighboring states.[9] When South Africa was annoyed by statements made by Zimbabwe's leader, Robert Mugabe, in late 1980 and early 1981, it delayed Zimbabwe-bound freight carried by South African rolling stock. Zimbabwe then voted in favor of sanctions against South Africa in the United Nations. A month later, South Africa demanded the return of twenty-four diesel locomotives leased to the National Railways of Zimbabwe. Fuel imports from South Africa were increasingly subject to delay, and Zimbabwe was forced for a time to introduce fuel rationing.

South Africa's transport minister, Hendrick Schoeman, said that the delays and the issue of locomotives could be solved if two conditions were met. First, the Zimbabwe government would have to deal with Pretoria at the ministerial level, as opposed to the customary lower-ranking official contact. Second, Harare would have to guarantee that the ANC would not be allowed to operate within Zimbabwean territory.

Zimbabwe refused the first condition and pointed out that while the ANC—as well as its rival, the Pan Africanist Congress (PAC)—had diplomatic representation in Zimbabwe and the Zimbabwean government supported their goals, they were not allowed to launch military operations against South Africa from Zimbabwean territory. South Africa accepted this explanation, ended the delays of Zimbabwe-bound goods, and agreed to lease the locomotives.[10] The outcome of this confrontation could be seen as a draw, but Pretoria had unmistakably demonstrated its economic muscle.

South Africa took similar action against Mozambique for two weeks in mid-March 1981 by imposing a rail embargo on goods destined for Maputo. This move was apparently triggered by both Mozambique's growing role as the coordinator of SADCC's transport program and Pretoria's belief that Mozambique was permitting the ANC to launch operations from its territory. The same technique was later used against Botswana. In 1986 South Africa withheld refrigerated trucks for beef exports from that country in what was seen as a response to the strong anti-apartheid language in a speech delivered by Botswana's vice president, Peter Mmusi, who was also chairman of SADCC's Council of Ministers.

A second South African technique for punishing "uncooperative" governments was the imposition of special bond requirements on freight destined for its neighbors. In August 1986 President Mugabe and Zambia's President Kaunda argued vigorously at a Commonwealth meeting for mandatory international sanctions against South Africa. Soon afterward they announced they would consider imposing their own sanctions on South Africa by the end of the year.

South Africa promptly imposed a 25 percent bond requirement, payable in foreign exchange, on goods entering South African ports in transit for Zambia. It also introduced lengthy customs searches for the purpose of "gathering statistics" on all Zimbabwe- and Zambia-bound goods crossing the South African–Zimbabwean border.

The move seemed clearly intended to focus the two countries' attention on their transport dependence prior to the summit meeting of the nonaligned countries that Zimbabwe was due to host in September 1986. The summit was expected to explore the possibility of the nonaligned nations imposing sanctions against South Africa on their own or in coordination with other parties. Zimbabwe and Zambia duly muted their rhetoric—and South Africa eased its restrictions.[11]

Luring freight away from non–South African routes by offering concessional rates was a third South African technique. This earned South Africa additional revenue in hard currency, deprived the alternative routes of funds for development, and by entrenching dependence on South African routes, gave increased credibility to the threat of cutting off the black states' lifelines. For example, it became cheaper to send a container of coffee from Mutare, in eastern Zimbabwe, to the South African port of Durban, a distance of 1,250 miles, than to the Mozambican port of Beira, only 190 miles away.[12] A variant of this strategy was Pretoria's policy of manipulating its own shipments so that only low-tariff goods went to foreign ports, keeping the high tariff freight for South African routes.

South Africa imposed undeclared but effective trade sanctions on Mozambique. In 1980 SATS provided Transvaal shippers with freight cars that were allowed to go to the port of Durban only. Ferrochrome exports were shifted from Maputo to the South African port of Richards Bay. In 1983 South Africa ended fuel shipments through Maputo. Trade statistics tell the story best. In 1979 four million tons of South African goods passed through Maputo; by 1983 that figure had fallen to one and a half million tons.[13]

A fourth element of Pretoria's strategy involved its air services. South Africa often granted subsidized freight rates on its airlines, both to protect its market share and to further its political ends. For example, it reportedly offered heavy subsidies on air freight rates from Malawi, with which it had diplomatic relations, in order to ease the impact on Malawi of RENAMO's disruption of the country's rail routes through Mozambique.

The fifth and by far the most powerful element in the transport strategy was the military component of South Africa's destabilization strategy. Above all, the civil wars in Mozambique and Angola, directly fueled by South Africa, proved disastrous. Four of the black states' five major transport routes were shut down or severely crippled by the activities of RENAMO in Mozambique and the Union for the Total Independence of Angola (UNITA). Direct South African military action, particularly in Angola, also took an economic toll.

RENAMO, whose origins lay in the irregular forces organized in Mozambique by Rhodesia in the 1970s and which was later backed by Pretoria to keep Mozambique weak and divided, severely curtailed the operation of virtually all the Mozambican routes. According to documents discovered by the Mozambican authorities in 1985, the South African military specifically instructed RENAMO to target transportation facilities. RENAMO's transport sabotage often occurred at times and places that served South Africa's interests. For instance, in January 1985, a week before an important SADCC meeting in Swaziland, RENAMO damaged a key rail facility linking Swaziland and Mozambique.[14]

In Angola, South Africa's ally, UNITA, kept the Benguela route closed from 1975 on by sporadic attacks and acts of sabotage. After 1984 UNITA guerrillas increasingly targeted the Benguela Railway, and from late 1987 they began capturing towns along the line rather than simply cutting the track.

South Africa also intermittently launched its own military raids against ports in Mozambique and Angola. In Angola, South African forces, attacking by sea, sabotaged Lobito's oil terminal in 1980 and Luanda's oil refinery in 1981.[15] And in the weeks leading up to the second SADCC annual conference in 1981, South Africa attacked the Zimbabwe-Beira corridor as well as the port of Beira itself.[16] In December 1982 South African forces blew up a Beira depot containing supplies bound for Zimbabwe and Malawi.[17]

The outcome of South Africa's tactics was a massive growth in regional dependence on its transport system. In the colonial period, relatively little of the region's trade traversed South Africa because the alternative ports were able to handle most of the traffic. However, by 1981, 50 percent of the extraregional trade of the landlocked black states passed through South Africa, and by 1985 that figure had risen to 85 percent.[18] "By 1987 the vast majority of trade of the landlocked SADCC states was being carried through the ports of South Africa, not through the SADCC ports in Angola, Mozambique, and Tanzania," wrote Stephen R. Lewis, an economist who studied the region in the 1980s.[19] The sight of giant trailer trucks with Johannesburg license plates hauling mining gear through Lusaka, Zambia's capital, on their way to the nation's copper mines no longer provoked comment. South Africa's presence on the region's roads and railroads and in its air space had become a fact of life.

The Black States' Transport Strategy. The growing transport dominance of South Africa ensured that transport became SADCC's top priority and the cornerstone of its regional strategy. SADCC's primary objective was to restore the natural routes to the sea for the six landlocked member countries. It quickly set up the Southern African Transport and Communication Commission (SATCC), based in Maputo, Mozambique, to deal with transport and communications.

As SADCC got into its stride, two features stood out in its strategy to free itself from Pretoria's dominance of the trade routes: rehabilitation and protection. The rehabilitation program aimed at mobilizing international aid and technical expertise. This was needed not only to rebuild the damaged networks but to increase their capacity so that they could handle all the black states' trade should South Africa restrict or totally deny access to its ports. The governments of the member states tacitly acknowledged that their own deficiencies, in management, technical know-how, and cross-border coordination contributed to their plight and that they would need outside help to correct the situation.

During the 1980s SATCC developed 182 projects in ports and water transport, railroads, roads and road transport, civil aviation, telecommunications, meteorology, and postal services. The program called for an investment of $4.6 billion for these projects and represented more than two-thirds of the total costs of all of SADCC's programs.

The Beira corridor was the natural choice for SADCC's highest priority transportation project. By 1987 the corridor was sufficiently rehabilitated to handle two million tons of freight.[20] In that year it was estimated to have accounted for 30 percent of Zimbabwe's foreign trade and 20 percent of the black states' total trade.[21] The Maputo port system, particularly the Limpopo Railroad, which links the port with Zimbabwe, became another top SADCC project, and improvement of the port facilities in Dar es Salaam in Tanzania was also undertaken. Rehabilitation of Angola's Benguela line was placed on the agenda, but it was realized that little could be done until UNITA's guerrilla activities were ended.

Rehabilitation made little sense without protection, and once again SADCC's members focused their efforts on Mozambique. In 1986 Zimbabwe and Tanzania sent military units to help the Mozambique government protect the key routes. Zimbabwe provided the largest contingent and concentrated on the Beira corridor. A year later Malawi sent a battalion to safeguard repair operations and prevent further sabotage along the Nacala route. Without these forces, the Beira and Nacala railroads would have been much more vulnerable to guerrilla attack, and work to restore the Limpopo line would have been seriously hampered. Britain also helped the SADCC security effort by training officers of the Mozambican and Zimbabwean armies.

Trade and Investment

Pretoria's grip on the black states' transport system was relatively new and could be loosened by specific actions to revive the alternative routes. But the more general power of the South African economy in the region was another matter, since it was both deeply rooted and pervasive.

The great advantage that South Africa possessed was its industrial strength. The far smaller economies of its neighbors were confined mainly to agriculture, minerals, and energy, with the partial exception of Zimbabwe. South Africa, with slightly less than a third of the region's total population, produces three-quarters of its gross national product and two-thirds of its exports. It predominates even in sectors where the SADCC countries could be expected to be strong, producing 98 percent of the region's electricity, 87 percent of its wheat, 70 percent of its corn (maize), and 67 percent of its sugar.

South African companies are heavily invested in mining and manufacturing in the black states, apart from Angola and Tanzania, and are also active in agriculture and services. A few examples illustrate the degree of this penetration. In Botswana, just under two-thirds of the mining sector is controlled by South African interests, while the wholesale and retail trades are 90 percent South African–controlled. In the late 1980s, the Botswana government went into partnership with a South African company to set up a major soda ash project, with the South Africans providing the management.

In Swaziland, approximately one-third of all foreign investment is South African. The Zambian copper mining industry was developed largely by South Africans, and although the government acquired majority control in 1969, it continues to depend on South Africa and South African–controlled firms for many essential services and supplies. Zimbabwe's mining industry is 90 percent South African and an estimated 60 percent of its manufacturing sector is controlled by South African companies. A study prepared for the Canadian government in the mid-1980s on the possible impact of anti-South African sanctions on the SADCC states concluded: "South African entrepreneurs predominate in the production and distribution of goods in the modern sector of most SADCC countries."[22]

South African manufacturers sought to expand their markets in the region, but they faced two handicaps. First, they had to contend with the political stigma that South Africa and its products carried. Many African states did not observe the Organization of African Unity's trade embargo against South Africa, but its existence, as well as SADCC's emphasis on reducing its members' dependence on South Africa, had some effect in inhibiting the growth of South African trade.

The second handicap was the quality of South African goods, which were often inferior to the products of overseas competitors. On the other hand, they were usually cheaper, especially since the value of the South African rand declined considerably during the 1980s. And South African suppliers, because of their proximity, could offer shorter delivery dates and better after-sales service, particularly for capital equipment. For instance, it was much quicker and cheaper to fly an engineer in from Johannesburg than from London, New York, or Tokyo.

Given the huge disparity between South Africa's industrial base and that of its neighbors, it was hardly surprising that South Africa recorded consistently high trade surpluses on a bilateral basis in the 1980s, or that its trade with its neighbors far outstripped trade among the black countries themselves. Only Angola and Tanzania, on the outer periphery, did more business with other states in the region than they conducted with South Africa.

Nor did the black states have much to sell to South Africa, which has its own abundant supplies of the minerals and agricultural products that are the mainstay of the black states' economies. Oil is South Africa's single major deficiency. Angola, the only major oil producer in the region, observed the Organization of Petroleum Exporting Countries' (OPEC) boycott of South Africa. Zimbabwe was the exception among the black states in that it exported some manufactured goods to its southern neighbor. It also sold maize to South Africa when that country's usually large crops were afflicted by drought.

In the latter part of the 1980s, some of the black states' trade with South Africa was artificially inflated by South African firms that used these states as a means of evading international economic sanctions. Swaziland, in particular, became an important conduit for such "sanctions-busting" operations. This small, landlocked country had good access to foreign markets through its preferential trade status with the European Economic Community (EEC), the Commonwealth, and the Preferential Trade Area for Eastern and Southern Africa (PTA). Under local laws, only approximately a third of the value of a manufactured product had to be generated in Swaziland to qualify for a "made in Swaziland" label. A number of South African companies arranged to have their goods finished in Swaziland so that their products could be exported to the outside world with a Swaziland label of origin.[23]

As with transportation, South Africa used its trading relationships for political as well as economic ends. For instance, when Zimbabwe became independent in April 1980, it became apparent that Pretoria was uncomfortable with the new nation's rhetoric, its apparent success in reconciling blacks and whites, and its pivotal role in SADCC as the transport hub of the black states. The South African government-run Credit Guarantee Insurance Corporation cut its coverage on new exports to Zimbabwe by 75 percent, threatening to deprive the country of many vital basic commodities. Pretoria's price for a change of mind was a ministerial meeting to resolve the issue.[24]

Zimbabwe, whose position was that it would only deal with South Africa on a technical or official rather than a political level, refused. In March 1981 the South African government announced that it intended to cancel its preferential trade agreement with Zimbabwe at the end of a twelve-month period. It was only after the United States brought strong diplomatic pressure to bear that Pretoria reversed its decision and the agreement was allowed to continue.

While South African goods, services, and investments are of great importance to many of the black states, it is equally true that these markets make a significant contribution to the South African economy. Precise figures are hard to ascertain, but it was reliably estimated that South Africa's surplus with its neighbors in the mid-1980s was running between $1.25 billion and $1.6 billion a year.[25]

Given the deterioration of the South African economy in the latter part of the 1980s, and the fact that most of the trade was done on a cash basis, this surplus assumed even greater significance. Any action by South Africa to reduce or cut off trade with its neighbors, or to damage their economies, inevitably entailed economic costs for South Africa itself.

Thus, it was clear that, despite the trade imbalance, a significant degree of economic interdependence existed between South Africa and its neighbors. Just as the black states had to go on trading with South Africa while they argued for and supported international sanctions, a similar pragmatism encouraged Pretoria to limit the use of its power to reduce or cut off trade with its hostile neighbors.

Migrant Labor

Although South Africa imported few goods from its neighbors, it relied on them for large numbers of migrant laborers, most in the mines. Originally, South Africa had found it hard to persuade its own black population to go into the mines and had turned to the surrounding countries for an alternative source of labor. Coordinated recruitment in neighboring countries by South African mining companies helped them to keep the price of black labor down even as the demand in South Africa grew. Migrant laborers also had a reputation for being more docile than the indigenous work force.

For their part, foreign laborers and their families became heavily dependent on the wages they earned in South Africa. Those wages were, and still are, an important source of foreign exchange for some of the black states, particularly Lesotho and Mozambique and to a lesser extent Malawi, Botswana, and Swaziland. In the mid-1980s, the value of these remittances was estimated at between $200 million and $350 million annually. The flow, however, was not only one way. Foreign exchange received by South Africa from its nationals working in the black states, small in number but highly paid, amounted to between $50 million and $100 million a year.

During the first half of the 1980s, about 350,000 workers from the black states were officially employed in South Africa. Of that total, 300,000 worked in the mines, making up almost half the South African mining industry's total labor force. The countries involved were Lesotho (130,000–140,000 workers), Mozambique (60,000), Malawi (30,000), Botswana (25,000–30,000), Swaziland (15,000–20,000), and Zimbabwe (5,000–10,000).[26] During the latter part of the decade, some changes took place. Mozambique's contingent, for example, dropped to 40,000, and the overall figure for foreign migrant workers probably dropped to around 300,000. But since a large number of nationals from the black states were working illegally, the overall picture may not have changed significantly.

As with its transport and trade leverage, Pretoria used its control of the migrant labor system for political purposes. When the South African government became dissatisfied with Chief Leabua Jonathan, the leader of Lesotho, for being too sympathetic toward the ANC and for refusing to sign a nonaggression pact in 1984, it threatened to repatriate migrant workers to Lesotho.[27] Since their remittances constituted a remarkable 50 percent of Lesotho's gross national product and paid for 79 percent of the country's imports, repatriation would have been a crippling economic blow. In the end, Pretoria chose an even blunter weapon. By closing its borders with Lesotho, it helped engineer a military coup that overthrew Jonathan's government in January 1986.

South Africa used a similar tactic against Mozambique later that year. Shortly after six South African soldiers were injured by a land mine that Pretoria alleged had been planted by ANC operatives based in Mozambique, the government banned further recruitment of Mozambican labor. It also declared that all Mozambicans working in South Africa would have to leave when their permits expired. However, three months later, the government modified its decision; the Mozambican labor force would be reduced instead of being completely phased out. The critical factor in this change of mind was pressure from the South African mining industry, which feared losing experienced miners, and from farmers in the eastern Transvaal who relied on seasonal Mozambican labor.

Differences within South Africa over this issue highlighted the question of "reverse dependency." The need of countries like Lesotho or Mozambique to send labor to South Africa was balanced by the dependency that many South African employers had on migrant labor. The mining industry, in particular, showed no signs of wanting to do away with the migrant labor connection.

Conclusion

In 1980 the economic battle lines seemed clearly drawn on the banks of the Limpopo, and some observers may have thought that the ensuing struggle would end in a clear win for one side or the other. In fact, such an outcome was never really a possibility. While it was true that the two sides had radically different visions of the region's political future, their economic connections were so deeply entrenched that, short of total war, neither side could afford a clean break.

In the decade that followed, both sides achieved some of their goals but not others. South Africa put its neighbors under enough pressure to deter them from providing cover for guerrilla operations. To that extent it succeeded in keeping them as a de facto buffer zone. It also dissuaded them from following up their calls for mandatory sanctions with any serious moves of their own. But it failed to defuse their political hostility as a group or to gain any acceptance of apartheid as a permanent institution.

The black states preserved a substantial degree of real as well as nominal independence, even though in some cases economic constraints forced them to undertake initiatives they might have wished to avoid—such as entering into nonaggression pacts. They finally laid to rest any lingering South African hopes that they could be made into the equivalent of the homelands as puppet states. And with the Southern African Development Coordination Conference they created a body that, whatever its limitations, established itself as a serious international presence with solid achievements to its credit.

From a broader perspective, SADCC can be seen as a strategy for the radical alteration of patterns of thought, of self-assessment, and of economic relations derived from centuries of history. The region's inhabitants had been conditioned for many generations to see themselves as the marginal hinterland of a greater South Africa. In creating SADCC, the political and intellectual leaders of the new black states, with a confidence born of their success in gaining political liberation, rejected the assumptions of a preordained design. They sought to present, to their own people and to the world at large, a conception of their countries as a cohesive group, not merely as an appendage of South Africa. The acceptance of that new concept would depend on changing the cast of thought bred into a population over a very long period.

After the first ten years it was possible to see results beyond the obvious ones of rehabilitating and maintaining transport routes. The SADCC countries were no longer looking to South Africa for the research and the new seeds on which their agriculture depends. Instead they were setting up their own research stations with programs related to their own ecologies and farming methods.

The region no longer looked south for vaccines and skills it needed to control animal illnesses such as foot-and-mouth disease. It had already become self-sufficient in these, through joint programs that were models of regional cooperation. To go by air from one SADCC country to another, it was no longer necessary to transit Johannesburg. The same was true of telecommunications. In the field of energy, electricity connections had been completed between Botswana and Zambia, between Botswana and Zimbabwe, and between Mozambique and Zimbabwe, with others on the way. For a group of countries with no background in cross-border cooperation, these and other initiatives must be reckoned substantial beginnings.

As the 1990s opened, new hope arose for resolving South Africa's political difficulties. Apartheid was finally being dismantled and, with the government talking to genuine black leaders about the country's future, South Africa became less of an international issue and less of a threat to its neighbors. With Namibia independent, the Cubans back home, the sixteen-year-old Angolan civil war ended by agreement between the warring parties, and the superpowers no longer competing for power and influence, the region found itself experiencing an unusual peaceful passage. The economies of the black states were inevitably affected by these changes. Instead of looking anxiously southward, South Africa's neighbors became more concerned about being pushed to the periphery of the world's attention at a time when they badly needed both emergency financial aid and investment capital for development.

When it was created, SADCC was a hybrid. It was both a political response to apartheid and a long-term undertaking to build an economic structure that would be needed whatever the complexion of the government in power in South Africa. SADCC's position on what would happen when majority rule came to South Africa was that the country would be welcome to join the group, as Namibia did after achieving majority rule and independence in 1990. In 1987 Simba Makoni, SADCC's executive secretary, pointed to the continuing importance of economic issues in the region. SADCC, he said, was not working "from a purely emotional or irrational political perspective," but also from "logical and rational economic realities. . . . We have made it clear that the relevance and validity of SADCC will not end the day that the people's flag is raised in Pretoria." As the 1990s get under way and majority rule in South Africa moves closer to becoming a reality, economics may well supplant politics as the region's primary concern.

THE SUPERPOWERS IN SOUTHERN AFRICA: FROM CONFRONTATION TO COOPERATION

Michael Clough

Introduction

On May 31, 1991, in Lisbon, Portugal, the final chapter in the troubled history of U.S.–Soviet competition in Africa was closed. With great fanfare, Angola's president, José Eduardo dos Santos, and Jonas Savimbi, the leader of the National Union for the Total Independence of Angola (UNITA), signed an agreement ending the Angolan civil war. U.S. Secretary of State James A. Baker, Soviet Foreign Minister Aleksandr A. Bessmertnykh, and UN Secretary-General Javier Pérez de Cuéllar all came to applaud the end of the sixteen-year conflict.

The Lisbon ceremony, however, was an anticlimax. The cold war had ended in southern Africa in 1988 when Havana, Moscow, Pretoria, and Washington decided, for different reasons, that it was no longer in their interest to be involved in a civil war in Angola. Having made this decision, the four parties were able to agree on a settlement, spelled out in the December 1988 Namibian-Angolan peace accords, providing for Namibia's independence and removing Cuban troops from the region (see Appendix D). The Angolan civil war should have ended then too. But the intransigence of the Angolan parties and American domestic politics kept it going for another two and a half years.

For much of the 1980s, the worst fears of those who had predicted that a Reagan presidency would intensify U.S.–Soviet competition and exacerbate conflict in southern Africa were confirmed. But something happened. The cycle that had become so familiar in the Third World—local conflict, external intervention, escalating violence—was broken. To understand how this came to pass, it is necessary to go back to the mid-1970s, when serious superpower competition for control of southern Africa first began.

The Early Stages of
Superpower Competition

The United States and the Soviet Union came into conflict over Angola suddenly and unexpectedly in the spring of 1975. Before the collapse of Portuguese colonial rule following the April 1974 coup in Lisbon, neither superpower had shown much interest in southern Africa. When they decided to support rival nationalist parties in Angola, neither superpower expected its actions to engulf it in a major international crisis. As they became aware of each other's involvement, however, the stakes changed. What began as low-cost efforts to provide limited support to regional allies became significant geopolitical gambits.

U.S. officials, with the exception of a handful of liberals and Africanists in the Kennedy administration, had long regarded southern Africa as a relatively secure and comparatively unimportant Western sphere of influence. This view was reinforced by a belief that the Brezhnev regime, in signing the May 1972 statement of "Basic Principles of Relations Between the United States and the Union of Soviet Socialist Republics," had committed itself to exercising restraint in the Third World. Based on this mistaken perception of Soviet policy and a belief that the white-dominated status quo in southern Africa was unlikely to be shaken, the Nixon administration adopted a policy of benign neglect in the region.[1] The Soviet Union and, just as important, Cuba had never accepted the view of southern Africa as a Western sphere of influence. Both countries had provided political and military support to liberation movements in the region since the early 1960s.[2] Throughout the 1960s and early

1970s, however, the relative weakness of their local allies and their own military limitations afforded them few opportunities to seriously challenge Western claims. In the mid-1970s, this equation was fundamentally altered by four developments: the collapse of Portuguese colonialism; the emergence of serious internal opposition to the apartheid state in South Africa; the increasingly anti-Western, anticapitalist orientation of the leading nationalist groupings in the region; and the Soviet Union's development of an effective military power projection capability.[3] The Angolan civil war in 1974–75 presented Moscow with irresistible opportunities for influence in the region. The most immediate was the possibility of assisting the accession to power of a socialist-oriented party—the Popular Movement for the Liberation of Angola (MPLA)—in a potentially rich and strategically positioned African country. Of probably greater importance was the prospect that a favorable outcome in Angola would put the Soviet Union in a position to make gains elsewhere in the region, especially South Africa. Finally, and most important, a successful demonstration of the newly developed reach of the Soviet military promised to validate the Brezhnev regime's claim to global superpower status and enhance its credibility as a reliable ally of socialist forces throughout the Third World. These attractions, combined with pressure from two Soviet allies with long historical ties to the MPLA—Cuba and the Portuguese Communist Party—and the probable assumption that the United States and other Western nations would not become significantly involved, tilted arguments inside the Kremlin in favor of intervention.[4]

In January 1975 the Ford administration approved a small amount of covert financial assistance ($300,000) for the Front for the National Liberation of Angola (FNLA). As the civil war in Angola escalated, Soviet-Cuban involvement became more apparent. U.S. Secretary of State Henry Kissinger tried to use the conflict in Angola to demonstrate to Moscow that the United States, although weakened by the collapse of the U.S.–backed government in Saigon, was still able to act as a great power.[5] But the U.S. Congress cut off aid to any of the warring groups in Angola with the Clark Amendment in January 1976, thus undermining Secretary of State Kissinger's policy. With the help of Soviet arms, Cuban troops, and African diplomatic recognition, the MPLA triumphed, and the United States was forced to develop a new regional strategy.

In a historic speech on April 27, 1976, in Lusaka, Zambia, Secretary of State Kissinger committed the United States to working actively to achieve three objectives: a negotiated settlement in Rhodesia that would ensure majority rule while protecting minority rights, an internationally supervised transition to independence in Namibia, and a peaceful end to "institutionalized inequality" in South Africa. By intervening diplomatically to hasten political change, the Ford administration hoped to prevent escalating violence, reduce the appeal and influence of "radicals," and hence eliminate opportunities for more Soviet successes in the region.

When the Carter administration took office in 1977, it quickly declared its intention to remain actively engaged in southern Africa. U.S. objectives continued to be those identified by Kissinger, but new emphases emerged. Human rights were given higher priority. Geopolitics was downplayed. More effort was made to work with the United Nations and other multilateral actors. The concerns of African governments and nationalist movements were given greater attention. Relations with Pretoria chilled.

Results came slowly. Throughout 1977–78 the regional tides continued to flow in Moscow's favor. The new governments in Luanda and Maputo declared their countries socialist states and embraced the notion of a "natural alliance" between the Soviet Union and "progressive" parties in the Third World. Both signed treaties of friendship and cooperation with Moscow. Liberation movements hostile to Western capitalism gained ground politically and militarily in Zimbabwe and Namibia. In South Africa, a race war with the West, which was entrapped by history on the side of the white minority, seemed increasingly likely.

By 1980, however, the regional environment had changed in ways that significantly reduced opportunities for Soviet gains. Several factors were at work. Efforts to negotiate settlements in Rhodesia and Namibia created a new basis of trust between regional leaders and Western officials. By brokering the settlement leading to the independence of Zimbabwe, accepting the election victory of Robert Mugabe—perceived as the most radical of the nationalist leaders—and providing substantial assistance to Mugabe's new government, the United States and Great Britain demonstrated to regional leaders that conflict with the West was not inevitable. This lesson came just as the revolutionary euphoria of 1975–76 had begun to wear off. Despite incessant chants about "natural alliances," the inability of the socialist bloc to provide the economic, political, and military support necessary to permit stable development in southern Africa was increasingly apparent to all but the most ideologically blinkered. In short, both the perceived need for and the attraction of close ties with Moscow and its allies was diminishing in the region.[6]

Constructive Engagement
and Regional Conflict

W hen the Reagan administration took office in 1981, it failed to appreciate that Soviet fortunes in southern Africa were already fading or to recognize the role its predecessors' policies had played in fostering and reinforcing this trend. Convinced that the Carter administration's policies had been naive and moralistic, President Reagan's Africa policy team, under the direction of Assistant Secretary of State for African Affairs Chester Crocker, attempted to project what it considered a tougher, more "realistic" image. Geopolitical considerations once again became the driving force behind policy; the assumption that South Africa could be an important strategic ally resurfaced; and multilateralism fell into disfavor.

In his first televised interview, President Reagan referred to South Africa as "a country that has stood beside us in every war we've ever fought."[7] More subtly, Assistant Secretary Crocker, in a May 1981 memo to Secretary of State Alexander Haig spelling out the basic assumptions of the strategy of "constructive engagement," argued:

> The political relationship between the United States and South Africa has now arrived at a crossroads of perhaps historic significance. After twenty years of generally increasing official U.S. Government coolness toward South Africa and concomitant South African intransigence, the possibility may exist for a more positive and reciprocal relationship between the two countries based upon shared strategic concerns in southern Africa, our recognition that the government of P. W. Botha

represents a unique opportunity for domestic change, and a willingness of the Reagan Administration to deal realistically with South Africa. The problem of Namibia, however, which complicates our relations with our European allies and with black Africa, is a primary obstacle to the development of a new relationship with South Africa. It also represents an opportunity to counter the Soviet threat in Africa. We thus need Pretoria's cooperation in working toward an internationally acceptable solution to Namibia which would, however, safeguard U.S. and South African essential interests and concerns.[8]

The Namibian negotiations, which had been started by Secretary of State Kissinger in 1976, thus became central to the Reagan administration's regional strategy. The major new policy twist linked Namibian independence with the withdrawal of Cuban troops from Angola. Two main rationales for linkage were given. Assistant Secretary Crocker believed that linkage, by reducing the Soviet-Cuban threat to South Africa, would provide a needed inducement for Pretoria to go along with the UN plan. More important, however, linkage offered Crocker a means of winning support from senior administration officials for continued U.S. diplomatic engagement in southern Africa. Without the promise of removing the Cuban-Soviet presence from Angola, President Reagan and Secretary of State Haig would have had little interest in promoting Namibian independence.[9]

If this strategy had succeeded relatively quickly (within two or three years), as Crocker evidently believed it would, U.S. credibility in the region would have received a significant boost and the Soviets would have been dealt a major political blow. But Crocker's strategy contained two basic problems. First, it failed to take into account the changing military situation inside Angola; and second, it assumed that South Africa was interested in a settlement.

The major problem was the growing strength of UNITA in Angola. The United States was prohibited from providing direct support to UNITA by the Clark Amendment, but South African assistance had increased, and other countries—for example, Morocco and Saudi Arabia—also reportedly began to aid UNITA. This assistance, and repeated incursions by the South African Defense Force (SADF) into southern Angola, helped to improve UNITA's military position, making it more and more difficult for the Angolan government to accede to U.S. demands for a Cuban withdrawal. At the same time, South Africa's destabilization campaign began to engulf the region in a widening spiral of violence, and officials in the Reagan administration were forced to rethink their initial premise that the United States and South Africa had a common set of regional interests. These problems became more and more evident, and by late 1982 the Namibian negotiations had stalemated.[10]

As hopes for a settlement in Namibia began to dim, constructive engagement entered a new phase. The first indication of a change in administration thinking came in a little-noticed speech by Frank Wisner, Crocker's top deputy, in September 1982:

> [W]e need to understand that Namibia is not the alpha and omega of U.S. policy interests in the region; there is a long agenda to which we need lend our efforts, including working toward a more productive relationship with Mozambique and Angola, supporting the development of a strong, stable, and pro-Western Zambia and Zimbabwe, and assisting in the stable and democratic development of Botswana, Lesotho, and Swaziland.[11]

Nine months later, this reformulation of regional strategy found its way into a speech by Undersecretary of State Lawrence Eagleburger billed as the most comprehensive and highest-level statement on southern Africa since the administration came into office. He spelled out a vision of "a framework of regional security" based on respect for international boundaries, renunciation of violence, and political coexistence. Significantly, he also observed: "A structure of regional stability is unlikely to take root in the absence of basic movement away from a system of legally entrenched rule by the white minority [in South Africa]."[12]

The clearest manifestation of a shift in regional strategy was the new importance attached to relations with Mozambique. Throughout 1983 Washington and Maputo engaged in discussions that led to the resumption of U.S. food aid and the reestablishment of normal diplomatic relations. In 1984, when South Africa signed agreements with Mozambique and Angola, which had been facilitated by the United States, the Crocker team credited constructive engagement and quickly predicted that peace in the region was at hand. Although these predictions proved premature, the United States' rapprochement with Mozambique did mark a significant watershed in the evolution of superpower competition in southern Africa.

Mozambique decided to turn to the West after it became clear that Moscow could not provide the levels of economic and military assistance Maputo required. Once the material limits of the "natural alliance" with the Soviet Union were revealed, the concept's appeal faded quickly. Without Soviet assistance, the Mozambican government had few options.[13]

In choosing not to provide the requisite levels of support for the survival of socialism in Mozambique, Soviet officials abandoned any hopes of achieving further strategic gains in the region. They did so for several reasons. Growing doubts about the prospects for socialist transformation in Third World regions such as southern Africa were reinforced by Moscow's increasing awareness of limits on its ability to influence the behavior of states that it befriended. Added to these concerns was the fact that a serious and sustained effort to assist Mozambique, much less other countries in the region, would have required far greater resources and commitment than the Soviet Union was able or willing to muster.

In short, by the early 1980s, Soviet officials realized that they had overestimated the benefits and underestimated the costs of expansion into southern Africa. As a result, they began to resist new commitments. Instead, they concentrated on avoiding regional defeats that might have ramifications beyond southern Africa. This meant, above all else, preventing the military defeat in Angola of the MPLA government.

According to the zero sum logic that shaped the Reagan administration's geopolitical calculations, Moscow's losses should have been Washington's gains. But something seemed to go wrong with the equation. Just as the Soviet threat in southern Africa receded, constructive engagement came under domestic attack.

The End of Constructive Engagement

As originally conceived by Assistant Secretary Crocker, constructive engagement had two strands. Through quiet diplomacy, he hoped to persuade Pretoria to give up Namibia and dismantle apartheid. At the same time, he hoped to establish pragmatic relationships with the region's black leaders aimed at producing a stable region resistant to Soviet advances. By late 1984, following the U.S. success in brokering pacts between South Africa and Mozambique and Angola, Crocker was being hailed by some commentators as a new diplomatic superman. He quickly lost this status, however, because of his inability to produce visible results in ending apartheid in South Africa itself.[14] Beginning in September 1984, political protest and violence in South Africa escalated and apartheid became a major domestic political issue in the United States. These developments overshadowed the administration's regional diplomacy and precipitated the collapse of constructive engagement. Responding to a growing public perception that the Reagan administration was "soft" on white rule in South Africa, Congress passed the Comprehensive Anti-Apartheid Act of 1986. This accelerated the transformation of Washington and Pretoria into adversaries.

During this period, the regional strand of constructive engagement came under serious attack from the right as support for the Reagan doctrine began to grow. Reagan, in one of his weekly radio broadcasts in early 1985, included UNITA on the administration's list of "freedom fighters." Such rhetoric contrasted sharply with Assistant Secretary Crocker's carefully worded statements. In early

1983, for example, Crocker had told a congressional hearing that Angola's internal problems were not an issue to be dealt with by the United States. While reiterating the view that "UNITA was an important and legitimate nationalist movement," he said: "Whether the Angolan government and others will conclude that in order for [the Cuban troop withdrawal issue] to be resolved there will need to be some kind of an agreement on the issue of UNITA, that is for them to say. We have no conditions on that issue."[15]

In mid-1985 conservatives in Congress began to push for repeal of the Clark Amendment, which barred U.S. aid to UNITA, thus placing Crocker in a difficult position. Given the president's personal preferences, he could not openly oppose repealing the amendment. Once the amendment was repealed, policy shifted quickly and Crocker's freedom to maneuver was greatly reduced.

Black unrest in South Africa and political developments in the United States were certainly important in the collapse of constructive engagement. More fundamentally, however, the strategy failed because it rested on a false set of assumptions about the underlying sources of regional conflict and the nature of South African regional interests and objectives. On March 22, 1982, Crocker had succinctly outlined the administration's early views on these issues:

> The Soviet Union alone has a vested interest in keeping the region in turmoil. It is to no one else's advantage, neither to that of the South Africans, the other southern Africans, nor certainly to the United States and the West.[16]

By 1985–86 it was clear that it was Pretoria, not Moscow, that believed that regional instability was in its interest. Slowly, over time, U.S. officials involved with southern African issues realized this.

Two actions had a particularly adverse effect on U.S. perceptions of South African regional policy. The first was Pretoria's failure to live up to the terms of the Nkomati Accord, a nonaggression treaty signed in 1984 by South Africa and Mozambique that required the end of assistance to the Mozambique National Resistance (RENAMO) (see Appendix C). As U.S. support for Maputo solidified, South Africa's continued aid to RENAMO increasingly placed the Reagan administration in direct conflict with the South African government. In June 1987 Crocker challenged Pretoria's repeated denials of its support to RENAMO by testifying at a congressional hearing that "there is credible evidence that South Africa remains a reliable supplier of high-priority items that RENAMO is not able to acquire on its own."[17]

A less discussed but extremely important cause for growing U.S.

hostility toward South Africa's regional policy was Pretoria's efforts to coerce Botswana into signing a nonaggression pact similar to the Nkomati Accord. Botswana had long enjoyed a positive reputation in the United States as one of Africa's few multiparty democracies. It should have come as no surprise to Pretoria, therefore, when a South African Defense Force raid on an alleged African National Congress facility in Gaborone on June 13, 1985, provoked a strong reaction in Washington. Declaring that the raid "comes against a background that raises the most serious questions about [the South African] government's recent conduct and policy," the Reagan administration recalled its ambassador to South Africa for consultations.[18]

The growing tension in U.S.–South African relations and the development of a surprisingly positive U.S.–Mozambican relationship had a dual effect on U.S.–Soviet relations. For one thing, these developments reduced the administration's tendency to view southern Africa through a geopolitical prism. U.S. officials continued to see the Soviet Union as a regional adversary, especially in Angola, but countering the Soviets became less important than ending regional destabilization. At the same time, Soviet views were altered by evidence of a split between Washington and Pretoria and a rapprochement between Washington and Maputo. The new set of regional realities, which could no longer be represented in the simplistic ideological terms on which Soviet officials had relied for so long, forced Moscow to develop a new way of perceiving and portraying conflict in southern Africa.[19] In a more positive sense, it permitted Soviet analysts who had already begun to engage in "new thinking" on the region to raise the possibility of a convergence of U.S.–Soviet policy toward southern Africa, and thus begin to explore possible formulas for cooperation.

The conceptual basis for a common U.S.–Soviet posture toward southern Africa was developed through a series of policy-oriented binational discussions involving academics, government officials, and other opinion-shapers over the period 1983–87. Implicit agreement developed on the need for a mutual acknowledgment that

- both the United States and the Soviet Union had important interests in southern Africa, but neither had vital interests there;
- neither superpower had the ability to shape the political and economic future of the region unilaterally;
- regional conflicts must ultimately be resolved through political—and not military—means; and

- both nations had an interest in seeing a more rapid, less violent, negotiated transition to majority rule in South Africa.

Those points of agreement had begun to take shape well before Soviet President Mikhail Gorbachev's rise to power. Regional realities would have forced changes in Soviet policy toward southern Africa no matter who emerged on top in Moscow. With Gorbachev in control, however, Soviet interest in a UN–supervised settlement in Namibia increased.

By 1987 these changes had created the potential for superpower cooperation on southern Africa but were not sufficient on their own to produce a diplomatic breakthrough in the negotiations on Angola-Namibia. That did not become possible until a dramatic series of military developments in southern Angola in late 1987 caused the main parties to the conflict—Luanda, Havana, and Pretoria—to reexamine their policies.

From Confrontation to Cooperation

I n early 1987 the Angolan government decided to launch a major military offensive against UNITA. After some initial successes, Angola's *Forças Armadas Populares de Libertação de Angola* (FAPLA) (People's Armed Forces for the Liberation of Angola) suffered a major defeat attempting to cross the Lomba River in southeastern Angola. As FAPLA retreated to Cuito Cuanavale, a key government staging base, it was pursued by UNITA and South African Defense Force units. By November these forces were threatening to overrun Cuito Cuanavale. This threat prompted an emergency meeting between Angola's president, José Eduardo dos Santos, and Cuba's president, Fidel Castro.

Cuba had opposed the decision to launch the offensive, believing that it would be costly and ineffective. However, in November, with the survival of the MPLA government jeopardized, Castro agreed to send more troops to Angola. The new units relieved Cuito Cuanavale and moved into position to threaten South African forces directly along the Namibian border. Had such a development occurred in the early years of the Reagan administration, alarm bells would have sounded in Washington. But in the winter of 1987–88, the United States remained calm as thousands of fresh Cuban troops arrived in Angola. Some U.S. officials, frustrated with Pretoria and convinced that Cuba and the Soviets were interested in a negotiated settlement, even hinted that Cuba's moves served U.S. interests.

South Africa's crackdown on domestic opposition and its continued regional belligerence had embarrassed and frustrated Assistant

Secretary Crocker. But the failure of constructive engagement, and the administration's refusal to consider economic sanctions as a means of pressure on Pretoria, left Washington with little leverage over the Botha government. In these circumstances, Cuba's military moves provided a timely warning to Pretoria that it was reaching the limits of its capabilities.

The battle of Cuito Cuanavale was not a clear defeat for South Africa, as many have claimed, but the country did experience heavier casualties than ever before. If South Africa had not abandoned its effort to take Cuito Cuanavale, it would have risked a potentially devastating defeat. President Botha and his advisers reassessed their Angolan policy and became more interested in exploring diplomatic options.[20] The Cuban military threat thus ironically became Crocker's best source of leverage over Pretoria.

Equally important in explaining Washington's low-key response to the emerging military situation in southern Angola was the fact that the Cuban build-up was accompanied by signals from Havana and Luanda of a willingness to return to the bargaining table and resolve the stalemate over linkage and timetables for Cuban troop withdrawal. In August 1987 Luanda had offered a compromise on the timetable for Cuban withdrawal from southern Angola, put forward in the "platform" presented to the United States in September 1984. Discussion of this offer was interrupted by the rapidly changing military situation. In January 1988, after the Cuban reinforcements had begun to arrive, the Angolan government informed Washington that it was ready to resume negotiations. These diplomatic gestures made it more difficult for conservatives to stir up fears that Cuba's moves signaled a commitment to a military resolution of regional conflicts.

A major breakthrough occurred in late January 1988, when the United States accepted the presence of Cuban representatives in the discussions, in exchange for Cuba's acknowledgment of the United States' role as the official mediator. Cuba accepted this "deal" for three reasons. First, it gave Havana some much desired diplomatic recognition. Second, it offered Castro an honorable way out of the military quagmire in Angola. Finally, the Cubans hoped a settlement would clear the way for an improvement in U.S.–Cuban relations. The Reagan administration was willing to allow the Cubans into the negotiations because it had become convinced that Havana was willing to pressure the MPLA to compromise. For this deal to work, each side had to make a concession on Angolan issues. Angola and Cuba dropped their demand for an immediate end to U.S. support for UNITA, and Crocker agreed to keep demands for national reconciliation in Angola off the formal agenda. However, all parties recognized that these issues would have to be addressed eventually.

In early May 1988, Crocker convened a meeting in London of negotiators from Angola, Cuba, and South Africa. Also present as an observer was a senior official from the Soviet Foreign Ministry. This meeting established the basic terms for subsequent negotiations. Significantly, all parties appeared to downplay differences on the UNITA issue in order to allow progress in discussions of South African and Cuban withdrawal and implementation of UN Resolution 435 on Namibia (see Appendix B).

After the London sessions, a period of intense maneuvering began. South Africa actively explored possibilities for a separate settlement with Angola that would not involve Namibian independence. When that gambit failed, it began to behave in ways, both diplomatic and military, that indicated it was having second thoughts about the negotiations. For example, officials in Pretoria began to suggest that national reconciliation in Angola would have to precede rather than follow Namibian independence. At the same time, UNITA and the Angolan government sent high-level delegations to the United States to test and influence U.S. opinion. Still, all of the principals, prompted by fears about the potential costs of responsibility for the breakdown of the talks, remained engaged in the negotiations.

A critical threshold was crossed in talks in New York in mid-July, when the parties agreed to a set of principles including a formal acknowledgment of the mediating role of the United States. From then on, Crocker's authority was not seriously challenged by any of the principals. Like the proverbial prophet, however, he remained without honor in his own country, where he was widely viewed as having been "soft" on apartheid.

In the final months of the negotiations, the greatest threat to a settlement came from conservatives in the United States who sought to block any agreement that might weaken UNITA or lend legitimacy to Cuba. Their political clout within Congress and the White House made it impossible for Crocker to use U.S. aid to Savimbi as a bargaining chip. The domestic constraints on Crocker's ability to maneuver were demonstrated clearly in mid-October, when the Senate voted to block the use of U.S. funds to support UN–supervised elections in Namibia until and unless the Angolan government agreed to national reconciliation with UNITA. Senate concerns were spelled out in a letter to President Reagan, signed by fifty-one senators, urging that UNITA be brought into the negotiations, that settlement of Namibian independence and Cuban troop withdrawal be linked to national reconciliation in Angola, and that U.S. aid to UNITA not be halted until all Cuban troops were withdrawn and the MPLA had agreed to a government of national reconciliation. An African-led initiative to bring the MPLA and UNITA together for preliminary talks finally provided all parties with the cover they needed to reach a settlement. On December 22, 1988, the Namibia-Angola peace accords were signed.

After the December 1988 accords were signed, neither superpower had any interest in seeing the Angolan civil war continue. In fact, both President Mikhail Gorbachev and newly elected President George Bush would have preferred to forget about southern Africa entirely. But they could not escape the legacy of their predecessors' policies.

In early 1989 neither the MPLA government nor UNITA was prepared to make the concessions necessary to end the war. Both were convinced that they had been favored by the changes in the Angolan equation brought about by the Namibian accords. The MPLA believed that the end of South African support for UNITA would make it possible for them to carry out a final offensive that would destroy Savimbi's stronghold in the southeast. Conversely, Savimbi believed that the withdrawal of Cuban troops would greatly weaken the government's armed forces and compel the MPLA leadership to agree to a settlement on terms favorable to UNITA. Both parties proceeded to do everything within their power to make it difficult for their erstwhile patrons to desert them.

UNITA's cause was greatly aided by its political allies in the United States. Just before President Bush took office, a UNITA lobbyist succeeded in getting the president-elect to sign a commitment not to cut off aid to UNITA.[21] Over the next three years, Savimbi and his supporters worked hard to ensure that the Bush administration did not renege on this commitment. As a result, covert U.S. aid to UNITA actually increased, even though the original rationale for the U.S. decision to back Savimbi had disappeared.

The MPLA had a more difficult time finding ways to keep Moscow from deserting it. By late 1989 it had become clear that Soviet aid to Angola would soon end, regardless of the consequences for the MPLA's political and military fortunes. When its "final offensive" stalled in December 1989, the MPLA leadership was forced to begin making major concessions.

In these circumstances, both of the rival Angolan parties

and the superpowers found it convenient to turn to Portugal as a mediator. The result was an agreement that could have been achieved in 1975 by an earlier generation of Portuguese mediators had it not been for the interjection of cold war rivalries into the region.

Conclusion

The ink on the 1988 Namibia-Angola accord had not dried before both superpowers began to lose interest in Namibia. In the period leading up to independence, they joined forces at the United Nations to force a reduction in the budget of the UN Transition Advisory Group (UNTAG). Neither has provided substantial financial assistance to Namibia since independence. Angola is likely to suffer a similar fate.

Neither Washington nor Moscow seemed particularly concerned about the ultimate outcome of the internal conflict. Each government remained involved for reasons that had little to do with Angola. For President Bush, it was a matter of domestic politics. Ending support for UNITA without achieving an acceptable settlement to Angola's civil war could anger conservatives at home. For the Soviet leader, it was concern about further damaging his government's international credibility by appearing to desert an erstwhile ally. As far as senior officials in Moscow and Washington are concerned, the Lisbon pact in May 1991, ending the civil war, was the end of the story.

U.S.–Soviet involvement in southern Africa thus came full circle. At the beginning of the 1990s, a situation existed not all that dissimilar from the one that prevailed in the early 1970s, when neither superpower was greatly interested in the region. Twenty years later, a significant difference existed, however. With the cold war over and the struggle for independence and majority rule in southern Africa in its final phase, little prospect existed that unanticipated events could spark a renewed phase of geopolitical competition. For better or worse, the era of the superpowers seemed over in southern Africa.

The Flowers Are Cut Down: The Human Costs of Regional Conflict

The late president of Mozambique, Samora Machel, repeatedly referred to his country's children as "the flowers that never wither." The reality is that war cut them down. During the 1980s twenty-five children died every hour from the effects of war in southern Africa. Although many of the countries in the region were affected, two stand out: Angola and Mozambique.

Between 1980 and 1989, an estimated 1.3 million people were killed either directly or indirectly by the conflicts in Mozambique and Angola—more than the total number of soldiers the United States lost in all its wars since 1776. A U.S. representative to the 1988 Emergency Conference, commenting on an independent report on human rights in Mozambique commissioned by his government and prepared by Robert Gersony, described the activities of rebels as "one of the most brutal holocausts against the human condition since World War II." As well as open warfare between governments and rebels, the Gersony report documents mass murder, rape, arson, and the use of enslaved labor by rebels. The report conservatively estimates that over 100,000 civilians were killed by rebel forces in Mozambique in the years 1986 and 1987 alone.

At least another 100,000 perished in the 1983–84 famine. That famine was not caused primarily by weather or agricultural policy. The basic causes were rebel disruption of rural life and food production in southern Mozambique, the destruction of Mozambique's ability to raise export earnings to purchase food and distribute it, and the tardiness of the international community in formulating an effective response. The situation in Angola was similar, where it appears that during 1980–85 at least 100,000 deaths occurred due to war-related famine and its effects.

A high proportion of those victims were children. By 1988 the number of Angolan and Mozambican children under the age of five whose lives were lost as a consequence of war and destabilization totaled more people than were killed by atomic bombs in Hiroshima and Nagasaki. Most of these deaths were not caused by bullets or beatings, but by malnutrition and diarrhea, untreated diseases and lack of immunization, and lack of access to clean water, to child-care clinics, and to adequate health education. To calculate the numbers precisely is impossible. But for Angola and Mozambique, the most ravaged countries, reasoned estimates are possible.

Infants and children were the most vulnerable to the loss of adequate nutrition and health care, as well as to the effects of forced migration; about 850,000 infants and young children perished who could have lived. Infant and child mortality rates in Mozambique and Angola are estimated to be the highest in the world. The underlying cause is underdevelopment, but this was massively compounded by war, economic destabilization, and the resulting dislocations.

From 1977 to 1980 both Angola and Mozambique were implementing policies which, by 1985, could have been expected to lower their infant and child mortality levels to those of Tanzania. Like the Tanzanian government, these countries were stressing primary health care, clean water supply, immunization, and mother-and-child clinics. Similarly, they were focusing attention on the availability of food. Indeed, these programs, especially in Angola, had stronger financial backing than in Tanzania. Tragically, they were overwhelmed by the direct and indirect effects of war.

In the absence of war, Angola and Mozambique could have attained by 1985 a child mortality rate comparable to that of Tanzania, which similarly had low levels of per capita income but high government commitment to health and social welfare policies. But instead of an under-five mortality rate in the range of 185 per 1,000, Angola and Mozambique can be conservatively estimated to have a child mortality rate of 325 and possibly as high as 375 per 1,000. In other words, in these countries one child in three will die before the age of five.

Trauma among children was widespread, although very incompletely documented and even less generally treated. In Mozambique, estimates of children traumatized, orphaned, or abandoned run from 150,000 to 500,000. Most of these children had seen relatives and friends butchered and their homes destroyed. Many were injured themselves. Some were forced to undergo military training and obliged to wound or kill.

It also must be borne in mind that throughout Africa women are responsible not only for domestic chores and child care, but also for a large part of agricultural food production at the family level. During the conflict in southern Africa, many mothers were unable to fulfill their role as providers of food security. The interruption of food production was just one of the traumas that assailed the mother-centered family, the basic social unit on which children depend for their physical and psychological development.

Internal and External Refugees

Over eleven million Angolans and Mozambicans were driven from their homes at least once—some 1.5 million into refuge in neighboring states and over 9 million into rural or urban refuge at home. A further 3 to 5 million people cannot be located. In all, about half of the rural population in these two countries was made internal or international refugees by war.

> *"My name is Patricio Nthupuela. I am from Zambezia. I came to Maputo to try to find prosthesis for my maimed arm. Early in 1983 I decided to continue with my studies at a district located 100 kilometres from Marrun, my motherland. There were no good living conditions in Marrun because of what armed bandits did. One day the car I was traveling in blew up due to a land mine laid by the bandits. In the explosion I lost both my arms. It was very hard to be without my upper limbs as they are very important to a human being. However, I learned to write by using my mouth. I passed the 4th and 5th degrees and now I am attending standard 6 in spite of my disability. Nobody believed I would succeed. I have tried very hard to get a prosthesis but unfortunately I never had a chance. I can put my clothes on although I can't fasten the buttons. When I was in Quelimane my friends were always ready to help me. The bandits killed my parents and other people and they created a lot of destruction. On 19 December 1986 they kidnapped my sister and my nephews. Only I managed to escape. Now I have no relatives. The state is the only relative I have. My government has taken care of me for all these years."*

Again, children and women were the principal victims. Almost half were under fifteen, and about three-quarters were women and children. By late 1988 Malawi was host to over 600,000 Mozambicans, Zimbabwe to about 165,000, Tanzania to 75,000, and Swaziland to 20,000. Substantial numbers also fled into South Africa to escape the fighting in southern Mozambique. The refugee influx was especially disrupting for Malawi, which suffers from severe land shortages in areas along the Mozambique border as well as from a weak social service infrastructure. In 1987 Malawi's net food self-sufficiency was eliminated by a combination of drought and refugee-related problems. The marked increase in Mozambican refugee outflow after 1986 was offset to some degree by a modest but growing return flow—perhaps as many as 90,000 in 1988—partly attributable to the improved security situation in certain districts.

> "My name is Luis Engenheiro. I am seven years old and I am from Mkocuba, Zambezia Province. I came here running from armed bandits who destroyed everything in my house. We had ducks and chickens which were stolen by the bandits. We were at home when the bandits arrived. When they started shooting we dodged them and escaped away to the bush. After their departure we returned home but we found nothing. They had stolen everything. We became poor forever. My father and I decided to leave the place before they could kill us. We came here in Quelimane. I do not like war because it has already ravished us. Someone without anything is a nobody. When the war ends I will have good clothing, a watch and shoes."

About 200,000 Angolans fled to neighboring Zambia. Because most of them settled among related peoples and were at least partially self-sufficient, this estimate is even more uncertain than most. The pattern of terror and invasion in Angola shifted geographically over time. Therefore, many refugees of the early 1980s returned, while many others, particularly those from the north-central and northeastern areas, were forced to flee into exile.

The more stable environment brought about by the peace initiatives that began at the end of the 1980s will probably cause a substantial reduction in the number of refugees flowing out of affected countries. However, the number of people displaced internally may actually rise for a time due to the return of displaced populations to their home areas.

"My name's Ann Paula. I live here in Montize in a CFM house [Mozambique Railways]. The house is a wagon surrounded by a small backyard. At Mutarara I used to go to school. I was attending Grade 3 in a primary school. I am twelve years old. I was living in a very big house in Mutarara. We had orange, tangerine, and mango trees and a farm. I used to play Ker-Kerr *with my friends there. I came here because one day some bandits came while we were asleep. They shot and attacked repeatedly. Many people were killed by the bazookas. I was afraid. I saw a lady dying. She was shot on the chest. She was bleeding all over. She died. Another lady was shot on the arm but she managed to escape. They were all crying. Children were crying. I was so terrified that I only wanted to run and run. I ran away and escaped to Malawi. When we arrived there, we were given food and water. At night I couldn't sleep because I kept thinking of that lady with blood coming out of a burnt wound. I slept very late and when I woke up in the morning they gave me some blankets. This way of killing people indiscriminately should be put to an end. What I would like is to go to school and have clean exercise books, a pen, a pencil and a good eraser. Only that."*

The Region's Infrastructure

The links between war and child health, malnutrition, and mortality can be seen in broad terms but not yet in fine detail. The destruction of health, educational, and social facilities is easier to quantify. Again, the physical destruction of the economic and social infrastructure and the ambushing of food and medical transport were concentrated in Angola and Mozambique. However, the economies of all nine Southern African Development Coordination Conference (SADCC) countries suffered from economic destabilization by

South Africa, armed attack, and the necessity to maintain abnormally high levels of expenditures on security.

Health workers, schoolteachers, pupils, foreign aid personnel, vehicles transporting health and relief supplies, schools, and health facilities were deliberately chosen as targets in order to bring about a breakdown in civil administration and make large areas of Angola and Mozambique ungovernable and uninhabitable.

In Mozambique, 822 health posts and centers were destroyed or forced to close permanently or temporarily between 1982 and 1989 (over 50 percent of the total that existed in 1982). By 1985 over 2 million people had been deprived of access to health care. The distribution of essential supplies was almost impossible, due to the destruction of vehicles and roads by land-mine explosions. More than 500,000 primary-school children lost their places because some 36 percent of rural schools were destroyed or abandoned as insecure. The problem of school facilities would have been far worse had it not been for the efforts made by Mozambican communities and government agencies to reconstruct the facilities. At the end of the decade, 3.3 million rural residents in Mozambique were estimated to be at risk of famine, largely because of the destruction of food crops and transport capacity, and the loss of export earnings to pay for replacement food imports.

Many of the rural vaccination programs in Angola and Mozambique were halted because of the security situation. The destruction of health care facilities and the killing and maiming of health workers meant that easily preventable diseases and curable illnesses took a rising toll on infants and children under five. An estimate of physical damage and its consequences, prepared by the Angolan government in conjunction with the United Nations, totals U.S. $17 billion for Angola between 1975 and 1985. The country's war losses during that decade could have financed three times over a worldwide vaccination program that could have reached almost every child in every developing country, saving 3 million young lives a year and preventing 230,000 cases of polio every year. The losses for Mozambique total approximately U.S. $15 billion, and the losses for the other seven states of SADCC total about U.S. $15 billion in all.

In 1988 both Angola and Mozambique lost about half of their potential GDP in the conflict. For the other states, losses ranged from under 5 percent in Botswana, Lesotho, and Swaziland to 10 percent for Tanzania, 20 percent for Zambia, 25 percent for Zimbabwe and 40 percent for Malawi. For very poor countries like Malawi and Tanzania, these losses matter desperately in human and economic development terms. For Zambia they make the task of debt management and structural dependence on the declining copper sector almost insuperable. For Zimbabwe, the conflict held per capita growth to an average of less than half of what might have been expected in conditions of peace and security.

The largest portion of the war burden for Botswana, Tanzania, Zambia, and Zimbabwe was for excess military spending. Zimbabwe, for instance, spent considerable sums to defend the Beira corridor through Mozambique—a vital link to the sea for the landlocked states that are otherwise largely dependent on South African transport. Without war, Zimbabwe would have had both recurrent and capital budget surpluses. Due to war conditions the deficit is about 10 percent of GDP.

The Victims

The nine countries of SADCC—Angola, Botswana, Lesotho, Malawi, Mozambique, Swaziland, Tanzania, Zambia, and Zimbabwe— have a population of some 70 million. Out of approximately 3.5 million annual births, some 750,000 children died before the age of five during the decade of the eighties. A fifth of these deaths were traceable to the conflicts that changed the environment of the region.

Drought, floods, lack of access to hard currency, falling terms of trade, rising debt service, the legacy of past mistakes in domestic policy—all these played a role in undermining the health and welfare of the children of southern Africa. But the main culprits were economic pressure and war, whose targets were not only economic and military but also the very social fabric of nations. The deaths stemmed from the destruction of health and education facilities, the dislocation of communities, the loss of food production, and the constriction of government health and water budgets—all resulting from the war.

One of the deadliest weapons of the war was mass terrorism. Rebels, bandits, and foreign-led forces burned crops and farmhouses; pillaged and destroyed schools, clinics, churches, mosques, stores, and villages; poisoned wells by throwing bodies down them; and attacked the transport system, which is a vital part of a country's life. Members of religious orders, mainly Catholics, were murdered and kidnapped. So, too, were foreign aid workers from both the West and the East. In Angola and Mozambique, hundreds of citizens, teachers, nurses, agricultural technicians, engineers, and geologists were kidnapped, maimed, mutilated, and murdered. The main victims were the children.

Adapted from Children on the Frontline: The Impact of Apartheid, Destabilization and Warfare on Children in Southern and South Africa *(New York: United Nations Children's Fund, 1989).*

APPENDICES

APPENDIX A
Lusaka Manifesto, April 16, 1969

LUSAKA MANIFESTO ON SOUTHERN AFRICA

Africa's ultimate statement on racism and colonialism—the Lusaka Manifesto—was issued as the final communiqué of the fifth conference of Heads of State and Government of East and Central African States, held in Lusaka, Zambia, in April, 1969. Fourteen nations, six represented by their heads of state, attended the conference, and all but Malawi joined in support of the Manifesto. . . . It was subsequently approved by the Heads of State and Government of the Organization of African Unity in September, 1969, and then endorsed by the UN General Assembly in November of the same year in resolution 2505 (XXIV).

1. When the purpose and the basis of States' international policies are misunderstood, there is introduced into the world a new and unnecessary disharmony, disagreements, conflicts of interest, or different assessments of human priorities, which provoke an excess of tension in the world, and disastrously divide mankind, at a time when united action is necessary to control modern technology and put it to the service of man. It is for this reason that, discovering widespread misapprehension of our attitudes and purposes in relation to Southern Africa, we, the leaders of East and Central African States meeting at Lusaka, on 16 April 1969, have agreed to issue this Manifesto.

2. By this Manifesto, we wish to make clear, beyond all shadow of doubt, our acceptance of the belief that all men are equal, and have equal rights to human dignity and respect, regardless of colour,

race, religion, or sex. We believe that all men have the right and duty to participate, as equal members of the society, in their own Government. We do not accept that any individual or group has any right to govern any other group of sane adults, without their consent, and we affirm that only the people of a society, acting together as equals, can determine what is, for them, a good society and a good social, economic, or political organization.

3. On the basis of these beliefs we do not accept that any one group within a society has the right to rule any society without the continuing consent of all the citizens. We recognize that at any one time there will be, within every society, failures in the implementation of these ideals. We recognize that for the sake of order in human affairs, there may be transitional arrangements while a transformation from group inequalities to individual equality is being effected. But we affirm that without an acceptance of these ideals—without a commitment to these principles of human equality and self-determination—there can be no basis for peace and justice in the world.

4. None of us would claim that within our own States we have achieved that perfect social, economic and political organization which would ensure a reasonable standard of living for all our people and establish individual security against avoidable hardship or miscarriage of justice. On the contrary, we acknowledge that within our own States the struggle towards human brotherhood and unchallenged human dignity is only beginning. It is on the basis of our commitment to human equality and human dignity, not on the basis of achieved perfection, that we take our stand of hostility towards the colonialism and racial discrimination which is being practised in southern Africa. It is on the basis of their commitment to these universal principles that we appeal to other members of the human race for support.

5. If the commitment to these principles existed among the States holding power in southern Africa, any disagreements we might have about the rate of implementation, or about isolated acts of policy, would be matters affecting only our individual relationships with the States concerned. If these commitments existed, our States would not be justified in the expressed and active hostility towards the régimes of southern Africa such as we have proclaimed and continue to propagate.

6. The truth is, however, that in Mozambique, Angola, Rhodesia, Namibia and the Republic of South Africa, there is an open and continued denial of the principles of human equality and national self-determination. This is not a matter of failure in the

implementation of accepted human principles. The effective administrations in all these territories are not struggling towards these difficult goals. They are fighting the principles; they are deliberately organizing their societies so as to try to destroy the hold of these principles in the minds of men. It is for this reason that we believe the rest of the world must be interested. For the principle of human equality, and all that flows from it, is either universal or it does not exist. The dignity of all men is destroyed when the manhood of any human being is denied.

7. Our objectives in southern Africa stem from our commitment to this principle of human equality. We are not hostile to the administrations of these States because they are manned and controlled by white people. We are hostile to them because they are systems of minority control which exist as a result of, and in the pursuance of, doctrines of human inequality. What we are working for is the right of self-determination for the people of those territories. We are working for a rule in those countries which is based on the will of all the people and an acceptance of the equality of every citizen.

8. Our stand towards southern Africa thus involves a rejection of racialism, not a reversal of the existing racial domination. We believe that all the peoples who have made their homes in the countries of southern Africa are Africans, regardless of the colour of their skins; and we would oppose a racialist majority government which adopted a philosophy of deliberate and permanent discrimination between its citizens on grounds of racial origin. We are not talking racialism when we reject the colonialism and apartheid policies now operating in those areas; we are demanding an opportunity for all the people of these States, working together as equal individual citizens, to work out for themselves the institutions and the system of government under which they will, by general consent, live together and work together to build a harmonious society.

9. As an aftermath of the present policies, it is likely that different groups within these societies will be self-conscious and fearful. The initial political and economic organizations may well take account of these fears, and this group self-consciousness. But how this is to be done must be a matter exclusively for the peoples of the country concerned, working together. No other nation will have a right to interfere in such affairs. All that the rest of the world has a right to demand is just what we are now asserting, that the arrangements within any State which wishes to be accepted into the community of nations must be based on an acceptance of the principles of human dignity and equality.

10. To talk of the liberation of Africa is thus to say two things. First, that the peoples in the territories still under colonial rule shall be free to determine for themselves their own institutions of self-government. Secondly, that the individuals in southern Africa shall be freed from an environment poisoned by the propaganda of racialism, and given an opportunity to be men, not white men, brown men, yellow men, or black men.

11. Thus the liberation of Africa for which we are struggling does not mean a reverse racialism. Nor is it an aspect of African imperialism. As far as we are concerned the present boundaries of the States of southern Africa are the boundaries of what will be free and independent African States. There is no question of our seeking or accepting any alterations to our own boundaries at the expense of these future free African nations.

12. On the objective of liberation as thus defined, we can neither surrender nor compromise. We have always preferred, and we still prefer, to achieve it without physical violence. We would prefer to negotiate rather than destroy, to talk rather than kill. We do not advocate violence, we advocate an end to the violence against human dignity which is now being perpetrated by the oppressors of Africa. If peaceful progress to emancipation were possible, or if changed circumstances were to make it possible in the future, we would urge our brothers in the resistance movements to use peaceful methods of struggle even at the cost of some compromise on the timing of change. But while peaceful progress is blocked by actions of those at present in power in the States of southern Africa, we have no choice but to give to the peoples of those territories all the support of which we are capable in their struggle against their oppressors. This is why the signatory States participate in the movement for the liberation of Africa under the aegis of the Organization of African Unity. However, the obstacle to change is not the same in all the countries of southern Africa, and it follows therefore that the possibility of continuing the struggle through peaceful means varies from one country to another.

13. In Mozambique and Angola, and in so-called Portuguese Guinea, the basic problem is not racialism but a pretence that Portugal exists in Africa. Portugal is situated in Europe; the fact that it is a dictatorship is a matter for the Portuguese to settle. But no decree of the Portuguese dictator, nor legislation passed by any Parliament in Portugal, can make Africa part of Europe. The only thing which could convert a part of Africa into a constituent unit in a union which also includes a European State would be the freely expressed will of the people of that part of Africa. There is no such popular will

in the Portuguese colonies. On the contrary, in the absence of any opportunity to negotiate a road to freedom, the people of all three territories have taken up arms against the colonial Power. They have done this despite the heavy odds against them, and despite the great suffering they know to be involved.

14. Portugal, as a European State, has naturally its own allies in the context of ideological conflict between West and East. However, in our context, the effect of this is that Portugal is enabled to use her resources to pursue the most heinous war and degradation of man in Africa. The present Manifesto must, therefore, lay bare the fact that the inhuman commitment of Portugal in Africa and her ruthless subjugation of the people of Mozambique, Angola and so-called Portuguese Guinea are not only irrelevant to the ideological conflict of power-politics, but also diametrically opposed to the politics, the philosophies and the doctrines practised by her Allies in the conduct of their own affairs at home. The peoples of Mozambique, Angola, and Portuguese Guinea are not interested in communism or capitalism; they are interested in their freedom. They are demanding an acceptance of the principles of independence on the basis of majority rule, and for many years they called for discussions on this issue. Only when their demands for talks were continually ignored did they begin to fight. Even now, if Portugal should change her policy and accept the principle of self-determination, we would urge the liberation movements to desist from their armed struggle and to co-operate in the mechanics of a peaceful transfer of power from Portugal to the peoples of the African territories.

15. The fact that many Portuguese citizens have immigrated to these African countries does not affect this issue. Future immigration policy will be a matter for the independent Governments when these are established. In the meantime we would urge the liberation movements to reiterate their statements that all those Portuguese people who have made their homes in Mozambique, Angola or Portuguese Guinea, and who are willing to give their future loyalty to those States, will be accepted as citizens. An independent Mozambique, Angola or Portuguese Guinea may choose to be as friendly with Portugal as Brazil is. That would be the free choice of a free people.

16. In Rhodesia that situation is different in so far as the metropolitan Power has acknowledged the colonial status of the territory. Unfortunately, however, it has failed to take adequate measures to reassert its authority against the minority which has seized power with the declared intention of maintaining white domination. The matter cannot rest there. Rhodesia, like the rest of Africa, must be

free, and its independence must be on the basis of majority rule. If the colonial Power is unwilling or unable to effect such a transfer of power to the people, then the people themselves will have no alternative but to capture it as and when they can. Africa has no alternative but to support them. The question which remains in Rhodesia is therefore whether Great Britain will reassert her authority in Rhodesia and then negotiate the peaceful progress to majority rule before independence. In so far as Britain is willing to make this second commitment, Africa will co-operate in her attempts to reassert her authority. This is the method of progress which we would prefer; it could involve less suffering for all the peoples of Rhodesia, both black and white. But until there is some firm evidence that Britain accepts the principle of independence on the basis of majority rule and is prepared to take whatever steps are necessary to make it a reality, Africa has no choice but to support the struggle for the people's freedom by whatever means are open.

17. Just as a settlement of the Rhodesian problem with a minimum of violence is a British responsibility, so a settlement in Namibia with a minimum of violence is a United Nations responsibility. By every canon of international law and by every precedent, Namibia should by now have been a sovereign, independent State with a government based on majority rule. South West Africa was a German colony until 1919, just as Tanganyika, Rwanda and Burundi, Togoland and Cameroon were German colonies. It was a matter of European politics that when the mandatory system was established after Germany had been defeated, the administration of South West Africa was given to the white minority Government of South Africa, while the other ex-German colonies in Africa were put into the hands of the British, Belgian or French Governments. After the Second World War every mandated territory except South West Africa was converted into a Trust Territory and has subsequently gained independence. South Africa, on the other hand, has persistently refused to honour even the international obligation it accepted in 1919 and has increasingly applied to South West Africa the inhuman doctrines and organization of apartheid.

18. The United Nations General Assembly has ruled against this action, and in 1966 terminated the Mandate under which South Africa had a legal basis for its occupation and domination of South West Africa. The General Assembly declared that the territory is now the direct responsibility of the United Nations, and set up an ad hoc committee to recommend practical means by which South West Africa would be administered, and the people enabled to exercise self-determination and to achieve independence.

19. Nothing could be clearer than this decision, which no permanent member of the Security Council voted against. Yet, since that time no effective measures have been taken to enforce it. Namibia remains in the clutches of the most ruthless minority Government in Africa. Its people continue to be oppressed, and those who advocate even peaceful progress to independence continue to be persecuted. The world has an obligation to use its strength to enforce the decision which all the countries co-operated in making. If they do this there is hope that the change can be effected without great violence. If they fail, then sooner or later the people of Namibia will take the law into their own hands. The people have been patient beyond belief but one day their patience will be exhausted. Africa, at least, will then be unable to deny their call for help.

20. South Africa is itself an independent sovereign State and a member of the United Nations. It is more highly developed and richer than any other nation in Africa. On every legal basis its internal affairs are a matter exclusively for the people of South Africa. Yet, the purpose of law is people and we assert that the actions of the South African Government are such that the rest of the world has a responsibility to take some action in defense of humanity.

21. There is one thing about South African oppression which distinguishes it from other oppressive régimes. The apartheid policy adopted by its Government, and supported to a greater or lesser extent by almost all its white citizens, is based on a rejection of man's humanity. A position of privilege or the experience of oppression in the South African society depends on the one thing which is beyond the power of any man to change. It depends upon a man's colour, his parentage and his ancestors. If you are black you cannot escape this categorization, nor can you escape it if you are white. If you are a black millionaire and a brilliant political scientist, you are still subject to the pass laws and still excluded from political activity. If you are white, even protests against the system and an attempt to reject segregation will lead you only to the segregation and the comparative comfort of a white jail. Beliefs, abilities, and behaviour are all irrelevant to a man's status; everything depends upon race. Manhood is irrelevant. The whole system of government and society in South Africa is based on the denial of human equality. The system is maintained by a ruthless denial of the human rights of the majority of the population and thus, inevitably, of all.

22. These things are known and are regularly condemned in the United Nations and elsewhere. But it appears that for many countries international law takes precedence over humanity; there-

fore no action follows the words. Yet even if international law is held to exclude active assistance to the South African opponents of apartheid, it does not demand that the comfort and support of human and commercial intercourse should be given to a Government which rejects the manhood of most of humanity. South Africa should be excluded from the United Nations agencies, and even from the United Nations itself. It should be ostracized by the world community. It should be isolated from world trade patterns and left to be self-sufficient if it can. The South African Government cannot be allowed both to reject the very concept of mankind's unity and to benefit by the strength given through friendly international relations. Certainly Africa cannot acquiesce in the maintenance of the present policies against people of African descent.

23. The signatories of this Manifesto assert that the validity of the principles of human equality and dignity extend to South Africa just as they extend to the colonial territories of southern Africa. Before a basis for peaceful development can be established on this continent, these principles must be acknowledged by every nation and in every State there must be a deliberate attempt to implement them.

24. We reaffirm our commitment to these principles of human equality and human dignity and to the doctrines of self-determination and non-racialism. We shall work for their extension within our own nations and throughout the continent of Africa.

Source: Human Rights Sourcebook, ed. Albert P. Blaustein, Roger S. Clark, and Jay A. Sigler (New York: Paragon House Publishers, 1987), 910–17.

APPENDIX B
UN Security Council Resolution 435,
September 29, 1978

RESOLUTION 435 (1978)
Adopted by the Security Council at its 2087th meeting on
29 September 1978

The Security Council,

Recalling its resolutions 385 (1976) and 431 (1978), and 432 (1978),

Having considered the report submitted by the Secretary-General pursuant to paragraph 2 of resolution in the Security Council on 29 September 1978 (S/12869),

Taking note of the relevant communications from the Government of South Africa addressed to the Secretary-General,

Taking note also of the letter dated 8 September 1978 from the President of the South West Africa People's Organization (SWAPO) addressed to the Secretary General (S/12841),

Reaffirming the legal responsibility of the United Nations over Namibia,

1. *Approves* the report of the Secretary-General (S/12827) for the implementation of the proposal for a settlement of the Namibian situation (S/12636) and his explanatory statement (S/12869);

2. *Reiterates* that its objective is the withdrawal of South Africa's illegal administration of Namibia and the transfer of power to the people of Namibia with the assistance of the United Nations in accordance with resolution 385 (1976);

3. *Decides* to establish under its authority a United Nations

Transition Assistance report of the Secretary-General for a period of up to 12 months in order to assist his Special Representative to carry out the mandate conferred upon him by paragraph 1 of Security Council resolution 431 (1978), namely, to ensure the early independence of Namibia through free and fair elections under the supervision and control of the United Nations;

4. *Welcomes* SWAPO's preparedness to co-operate in the implementation of the Secretary-General's report, including its expressed readiness to sign and observe the cease-fire provisions as manifested in the letter from the President of SWAPO dated 8 September 1978 (S/12841);

5. *Calls* on South Africa forthwith to co-operate with the Secretary-General in the implementation of this resolution;

6. *Declares* that all unilateral measures taken by the illegal administration in Namibia in relation to the electoral process, including unilateral registration of voters, or transfer of power, in contravention of Security Council resolutions 285 (1976), 431 (1978) and this resolution are null and void;

7. *Requests* the Secretary-General to report to the Security Council no later than 23 October 1978 on the implementation of this resolution.

DOCUMENT S/12636
(Referred to in Resolution 435 [1978], item 1.)

Letter dated 10 April 1978 from the representatives of Canada, the Federal Republic of Germany, France, the United Kingdom of Great Britain and Northern Ireland, and the United States of America to the President of the Security Council

On instructions from our Governments we have the honour to transmit to you a proposal for the settlement of the Namibian situation and to request that it should be circulated as a document of the Security Council.

The objective of our proposal is the independence of Namibia in accordance with resolution 385 (1976), adopted unanimously by the Security Council on 30 January 1976. We are continuing to work towards the implementation of the proposal.

(Signed) William H. BARTON
Permanent Representative of Canada
to the United Nations

(Signed) Rüdiger VON WECHMAR
Permanent Representative
of the Federal Republic of Germany
to the United Nations

(Signed) M. Jacques LEPRETTE
Permanent Representative of France
to the United Nations

[Original: English]
[10 April 1978]
(Signed) James MURRAY
Deputy Permanent Representative
of the United Kingdom of Great Britain
and Northern Ireland to the United Nations

(Signed) Andrew YOUNG
Permanent Representative
of the United States of America
to the United Nations

PROPOSAL FOR A SETTLEMENT OF
THE NAMIBIAN SITUATION

I. *Introduction*

1. Bearing in mind their responsibilities as members of the Security Council the Governments of Canada, the Federal Republic of Germany, France, the United Kingdom and the United States have consulted the various parties involved in the Namibian situation with a view to encouraging agreement on the transfer of authority in Namibia to an independent government in accordance with resolution 385 (1976), adopted unanimously by the Security Council on 30 January 1976.

2. To this end, our Governments have drawn up a proposal for the settlement of the Namibian question designed to bring about a transition to independence during 1978 within a framework acceptable to the people of Namibia and thus to the international community. While the proposal addresses itself to all elements of resolution 385 (1976), the key to an internationally acceptable transition to independence is free elections for the whole of Namibia as one political entity with an appropriate United Nations role in accordance with resolution 385 (1976). A resolution will be required in the Security Council requesting the Secretary-General to appoint a United Nations special representative whose central task will be to make sure that conditions are established which will allow free and

fair elections and an impartial electoral process. The Special Representative will be assisted by a United Nations transition assistance group.

3. The purpose of the electoral process is to elect representatives to a Namibian Constituent Assembly which will draw up and adopt the Constitution for an independent and sovereign Namibia. Authority would then be assumed during 1978 by the Government of Namibia.

4. A more detailed description of the proposal is contained below. Our Governments believe that this proposal provides an effective basis for implementing resolution 385 (1976) while taking adequate account of the interests of all parties involved. In carrying out his responsibilities, the Special Representative will work together with the official appointed by South Africa (the Administrator-General) to ensure the orderly transition to independence. This working arrangement shall in no way constitute recognition of the legality of the South African presence in and administration of Namibia.

II. *The electoral process*

5. In accordance with resolution 385 (1976), free elections will be held, for the whole of Namibia as one political entity, to enable the people of Namibia freely and fairly to determine their own future. The elections will be under the supervision and control of the United Nations in that, as a condition to the conduct of the electoral process, the elections themselves and the certification of their results, the United Nations Special Representative will have to satisfy himself at each stage as to the fairness and appropriateness of all measures affecting the political process at all levels of administration before such measures take effect. Moreover the Special Representative may himself make proposals in regard to any aspect of the political process. He will have at his disposal a substantial civilian section of the United Nations Transition Assistance Group (UNTAG), sufficient to carry out his duties satisfactorily. He will report to the Secretary-General, keeping him informed and making such recommendations as he considers necessary with respect to the discharge of his responsibilities. The Secretary-General, in accordance with the mandate entrusted to him by the Security Council, will keep the Council informed.

6. Elections will be held to select a Constituent Assembly which will adopt a Constitution for an independent Namibia. The Constitution will determine the organization and powers of all levels of government. Every adult Namibian will be eligible, without discrimi-

nation or fear of intimidation from any source, to vote, campaign and stand for election to the Constituent Assembly. Voting will be by secret ballot, with provisions made for those who cannot read or write. The date for the beginning of the electoral campaign, the date of elections, the electoral system, the preparation of voters rolls and other aspects of electoral procedures will be promptly decided upon so as to give all political parties and interested persons, without regard to their political views, a full and fair opportunity to organize and participate in the electoral process. Full freedom of speech, assembly, movement and press shall be guaranteed. The official electoral campaign shall commence only after the United Nations Special Representative has satisfied himself as to the fairness and appropriateness of the electoral procedures. The implementation of the electoral process, including the proper registration of voters and the proper and timely tabulation and publication of voting results, will also have to be conducted to the satisfaction of the Special Representative.

7. The following requirements will be fulfilled to the satisfaction of the United Nations Special Representative in order to meet the objective of free and fair elections:

(a) Prior to the beginning of the electoral campaign, the Administrator-General will repeal all remaining discriminatory or restrictive laws, regulations, or administrative measures which might abridge or inhibit that objective.

(b) The Administrator-General will make arrangements for the release, prior to the beginning of the electoral campaign, of all Namibian political prisoners or political detainees held by the South African authorities so that they can participate fully and freely in that process, without risk of arrest, detention, intimidation or imprisonment. Any disputes concerning the release of political prisoners or political detainees will be resolved to the satisfaction of the Special Representative acting on the independent advice of a jurist of international standing who will be designated by the Secretary-General to be legal adviser to the Special Representative.

(c) All Namibian refugees or Namibians detained or otherwise outside the Territory of Namibia will be permitted to return peacefully and participate fully and freely in the electoral process without risk of arrest, detention, intimidation or imprisonment. Suitable entry points will be designated for these purposes.

(d) The Special Representative, with the assistance of the United Nations High Commissioner for Refugees and of other appropriate international bodies, will ensure that Namibians remaining outside of Namibia will be given a free and voluntary choice whether to

return. Provision will be made to attest to the voluntary nature of decisions made by Namibians who elect not to return to Namibia.

8. A comprehensive cessation of all hostile acts will be observed by all parties in order to ensure that the electoral process will be free from interference and intimidation. The annex [see pages 154–58] describes provisions for the implementation of the cessation of all hostile acts, military arrangements concerning the UNTAG, the withdrawal of South African forces, and arrangements with respect to other organized forces in Namibia, and with respect to the forces of SWAPO. These provisions call for:

(a) A cessation of all hostile acts by all parties and the restriction of South African and SWAPO armed forces to base.

(b) Thereafter, a phased withdrawal from Namibia of all but 1500 South African troops within 12 weeks and prior to the official start of the political campaign. The remaining South African force would be restricted to Grootfontein or Oshivello or both and would be withdrawn after the certification of the election.

(c) The demobilization of the citizen forces, commandos and ethnic forces, and the dismantling of their command structures.

(d) Provision will be made for SWAPO personnel outside the Territory to return peacefully to Namibia through designated entry points to participate freely in the political process.

(e) A military section of UNTAG to ensure that the provisions of the agreed solution will be observed by all parties. In establishing the military section of UNTAG, the Secretary-General will keep in mind functional and logistical requirements. The five Governments, as members of the Security Council, will support the Secretary-General's judgement in his discharge of this responsibility. The Secretary-General will, in the normal manner, include in his consultations all those concerned with the implementaion of the agreement. The United Nations Special Representative will be required to satisfy himself as to the implementation of all these arrangements and will keep the Secretary-General informed of developments in this regard.

9. Primary responsibility for maintaining law and order in Namibia during the transition period will rest with the existing police forces. The Administrator-General will ensure the good conduct of the police forces to the satisfaction of the United Nations Special Representative and take the necessary action to ensure their suitability for continued employment during the transition period. The Special Representative will make arrangements, when appropriate, for United Nations personnel to accompany the police forces in the

discharge of their duties. The police forces would be limited to the carrying of small arms in the normal performance of their duties.

10. The United Nations Special Representative will take steps to guarantee against the possibility of intimidation or interference with the electoral process from whatever quarter.

11. Immediately after the certification of election results, the Constituent Assembly will meet to draw up and adopt a Constitution for an independent Namibia. It will conclude its work as soon as possible so as to permit whatever additional steps may be necessary prior to the installation of an independent Government of Namibia during 1978.

12. Neighbouring countries will be requested to ensure to the best of their abilities that the provisions of the transitional arrangements, and the outcome of the election, will be respected. They will also be requested to afford the necessary facilities to the United Nations Special Representative and all United Nations personnel to carry out their assigned functions and to facilitate such measures as may be desirable for ensuring tranquility in the border areas.

ANNEX to Document S/12636

Timing	SAG*	SWAPO*	UN	Other Action
1. At date unspecified . . .			SC* passes resolution authorizing SG* to appoint UNSR* and requesting him to submit plan for UN involvement. SG appoints UNSR and dispatches UN contingency planning group to Namibia. SG begins consultations with potential participants in UNTAG.*	
2. As soon as possible, preferably within one week of Security Council action . . .			SG reports back to SC. SC passes further resolution adopting plan for UN involvement. Provision is made for financing.	
3. Transitional period formally begins on date of SC passage of resolution adopting SG's plan . . .	General cessation of hostile acts comes under UN supervision. Restriction to base of all South African forces including ethnic forces.	General cessation of hostile acts comes under UN supervision. Restriction to base.	As soon as possible: UNSR and staff (UNTAG) arrive in Namibia to assume duties. UN military personnel commence monitoring of cessation of hostile acts and commence monitoring of both South African and SWAPO troop restrictions. Begin infiltration prevention and border sur-	Release of political prisoners/detainees wherever held begins and is to be completed as soon as possible.

ANNEX to Document S/12636 (continued)

Timing	SAG	SWAPO	UN	Other Action
3. Transitional period formally begins . . . (cont'd)			veillance. Begin monitoring of police forces. Begin monitoring of citizen forces, ethnic forces, and military personnel performing civilian functions. UNSR makes necessary arrangements for co-ordination with neighbouring countries concerning the provisions of the transitional arrangements.	
4. Within six weeks . . .	Restriction to base continues. Force levels reduced to 12,000 men.	Restriction to base continues.	Appropriate action by UN High Commissioner for Refugees outside Namibia to assist in return of exiles. All UN activity continues.	Establishment in Namibia of provisions to facilitate return of exiles. Establishment and publication of general rules for elections. Completion of repeal of discriminatory laws and restrictive legislation. Dismantlement of command structures of citizen forces, commandos and ethnic forces, including the withdrawal of all South African soldiers

ANNEX to Document S/12636 (continued)

Timing	SAG	SWAPO	UN	Other Action
4. Within six weeks . . . (cont'd)				attached to these units. All arms, military equipment, and ammunition of citizen forces and commandos confined to drill halls under UN supervision. AG* to ensure that none of these forces will drill or constitute an organized force during the transitional period except under order of the AG with the concurrence of UNSR. AG with concurrence of UNSR determines whether and under what circumstances those military personnel performing civilian functions will continue those functions.
5. Within nine weeks . . .	Restriction to base continues. Force levels reduced to 8,000 men.	Restriction to base continues. Peaceful repatriation under UN supervision starts for return through designated entry points.	All UN activity continues.	Completion of release of political prisoners/detainees wherever held.

ANNEX to Document S/12636 (continued)

Timing	SAG	SWAPO	UN	Other Action
6. Within twelve weeks . . .	Force levels reduced to 1,500 men, restricted to Grootfontein or Oshivello or both. All military installations along northern border would by now either be deactivated or put under civilian control under UN supervision. Facilities which depend on them (e.g., hospitals, power stations) would be protected where necessary by the UN.	Restriction to base continues.	All UN activity continues. Military Section of UNTAG at maximum deployment.	
7. Start of the thirteenth week . . .				Official start of election campaign of about four months' duration.

ANNEX to Document S/12636 (continued)

Timing	SAG	SWAPO	UN	Other Action
8. On date established by AG to satisfaction of UNSR . . .				Election to Constituent Assembly.
9. One week after date of certification of election . . .	Completion of withdrawal.	Closure of all bases.		Convening of Constituent Assembly.
10. At date unspecified . . .				Conclusion of Constituent Assembly and whatever additional steps may be necessary prior to installation of new government.
11. By 31 December 1978 at the latest . . .				Independence.

* AG = Administrator-General; SAG = South African Government; SC = Security Council; SG = Secretary-General; SWAPO = South West Africa People's Organization; UNSR = United Nations Special Representative; UNTAG = United Nations Transition Assistance Group.

Source: UN Security Council, 1978.

APPENDIX C
The Accord of Nkomati, March 16, 1984

AGREEMENT ON NON–AGGRESSION AND
GOOD NEIGHBOURLINESS
*between the Government of the People's Republic
of Mozambique and the Government of the
Republic of South Africa*

The Government of the People's Republic of Mozambique and the Government of the Republic of South Africa, hereinafter referred to as the High Contracting Parties;

RECOGNISING the principles of strict respect for sovereignty and territorial integrity, sovereign equality, political independence and the inviolability of the borders of all states;

REAFFIRMING the principle of non-interference in the internal affairs of other states;

CONSIDERING the internationally recognised principle of the right of peoples to self-determination and independence and the principle of equal rights of all peoples;

CONSIDERING the obligation of all states to refrain, in their international relations, from the threat or use of force against the territorial integrity or political independence of any state;

CONSIDERING the obligation of states to settle conflicts by peaceful means, and thus safeguard international peace and security and justice;

RECOGNISING the responsibility of states not to allow their territory to be used for acts of war, aggression or violence against other states;

CONSCIOUS of the need to promote relations of good neighbourliness based on the principles of equality of rights and mutual advantage;

CONVINCED that relations of good neighbourliness between the High Contracting Parties will contribute to peace, security, stability and progress in Southern Africa, the Continent and the World;

Have solemnly agreed to the following:

ARTICLE ONE

The High Contracting Parties undertake to respect each other's sovereignty and independence and, in fulfillment of this fundamental obligation, to refrain from interfering in the internal affairs of the other.

ARTICLE TWO

1) The High Contracting Parties shall resolve differences and disputes that may arise between them and that may or are likely to endanger mutual peace and security or peace and security in the region, by means of negotiation, enquiry, mediation, conciliation, arbitration or other peaceful means, and undertake not to resort, individually or collectively, to the threat or use of force against each other's sovereignty, territorial integrity or political independence.

2) For the purposes of this article, the use of force shall include *inter alia*—
   a) attacks by land, air or sea forces;
   b) sabotage;
   c) unwarranted concentration of such forces at or near the international boundaries of the High Contracting Parties;
   d) violation of the international land, air or sea boundaries of either of the High Contracting Parties.

3) The High Contracting Parties shall not in any way assist the armed forces of any state or group of states deployed against the territorial sovereignty or political independence of the other.

ARTICLE THREE

1) The High Contracting parties shall not allow their respective territories, territorial waters or air space to be used as a base, thoroughfare, or in any other way by another state, government, foreign military forces, organisations or individuals which plan or prepare to commit acts of violence, terrorism or aggression

against the territorial integrity or political independence of the other or may threaten the security of its inhabitants.

2) The High Contracting Parties, in order to prevent or eliminate the acts or the preparation of acts mentioned in paragraph (1) of this article, undertake in particular to—

a) forbid and prevent in their respective territories the organisation of irregular forces or armed bands, including mercenaries, whose objective is to carry out the acts contemplated in paragraph (1) of this article;

b) eliminate from their respective territories bases, training centres, places of shelter, accommodation and transit for elements who intend to carry out acts contemplated in paragraph (1) of this article;

c) eliminate from their respective territories centres or depots containing armaments of whatever nature, destined to be used by the elements contemplated in paragraph (1) of this article;

d) eliminate from their respective territories command posts or other places for the command, direction and co-ordination of the elements contemplated in paragraph (1) of this article;

e) eliminate from their respective territories communication and telecommunication facilities between the command and the elements contemplated in paragraph (1) of this article;

f) eliminate and prohibit the installation in their respective territories of radio broadcasting stations, including unofficial or clandestine broadcasts, for the elements that carry out the acts contemplated in paragraph (1) of this article;

g) exercise strict control, in their respective territories, over elements which intend to carry out or plan the acts contemplated in paragraph (1) of this article;

h) prevent the transit of elements who intend to plan to commit the acts contemplated in paragraph (1) of this article, from a place in the territory of either to a place in the territory of the other or to a place in the territory of any third state which has a common boundary with the High Contracting Party against which such elements intend or plan to commit the said acts;

i) take appropriate steps in their respective territories to prevent the recruitment of elements of whatever nationality for the purpose of carrying out the acts contemplated in paragraph (1) of this article;

j) prevent the elements contemplated in paragraph (1) of this article from carrying out from their respective territories by any means, acts of abduction or other acts, aimed at taking citizens of any nationality hostage in the territory of the other High Contracting Party; and

   k) prohibit the provision on their respective territories of any logistic facilities for carrying out the acts contemplated in paragraph (1) of this article.

3) The High Contracting Parties will not use the territory of third states to carry out or support the acts contemplated in paragraphs (1) and (2) of this article.

ARTICLE FOUR

The High Contracting Parties shall take steps, individually and collectively, to ensure that the international boundary between their respective territories is effectively patrolled and that the border posts are efficiently administered to prevent illegal crossings from the territory of a High Contracting Party to the territory of the other, and in particular, by elements contemplated in Article Three of this Agreement.

ARTICLE FIVE

The High Contracting Parties shall prohibit within their territory acts of propaganda that incite a war of aggression against the other High Contracting Party and shall also prohibit acts of propaganda aimed at inciting acts of terrorism and civil war in the territory of the other High Contracting Party.

ARTICLE SIX

The High Contracting Parties declare that there is no conflict between their commitments in treaties and international obligations and the commitment undertaken in this Agreement.

ARTICLE SEVEN

The High Contracting Parties are committed to interpreting this Agreement in good faith and will maintain periodic contact to ensure the effective application of what has been agreed.

ARTICLE EIGHT

Nothing in this Agreement shall be construed as detracting from the High Contracting Parties' right to self-defense in the event of armed attacks, as provided for in the Charter of the United Nations.

ARTICLE NINE

1) Each of the High Contracting Parties shall appoint high-ranking representatives to serve on a Joint Security Commission with the aim of supervising and monitoring the application of this Agreement.
2) The Commission shall determine its own working procedure.
3) The Commission shall meet on a regular basis and may be specially convened whenever circumstances so require.
4) The Commission shall—
   a) Consider all allegations of infringements of the provisions of this Agreement;
   b) advise the High Contracting Parties of its conclusions; and
   c) make recommendations to the High Contracting Parties concerning measures for the effective application of this Agreement and the settlement of disputes over infringements or alleged infringements.
5) The High Contracting Parties shall determine the mandate of their respective representatives in order to enable interim measures to be taken in cases of duly recognised emergency.
6) The High Contracting Parties shall make available all the facilities necessary for the effective functioning of the Commission and will jointly consider its conclusions and recommendations.

ARTICLE TEN

This Agreement will also be known as "The Accord of Nkomati."

ARTICLE ELEVEN

1) The agreement shall enter into force on the date of the signature thereof.
2) Any amendment to this Agreement agreed to by the High Contracting Parties shall be affected by the Exchange of Notes between them.

IN WITNESS WHEREOF, the signatories, in the name of their respective governments, have signed and sealed this Agreement, in quadruplicate in the Portuguese and English languages, both texts being equally authentic.

THUS DONE AND SIGNED AT the common border on the banks of the Nkomati River, on this the sixteenth day of March 1984.

SAMORA MOISÉS MACHEL
   Marshal of the Republic
   President of the People's Republic of Mozambique
   President of the Council of Ministers
FOR THE GOVERNMENT OF THE PEOPLE'S REPUBLIC OF MOZAMBIQUE

PIETER WILLEM BOTHA
   Prime Minister of the Republic of South Africa
FOR THE GOVERNMENT OF THE REPUBLIC OF SOUTH AFRICA

Source: Frontline Southern Africa: Destructive Engagement, ed. Phyllis Johnson and David Martin (New York: Four Walls Eight Windows, 1988).

APPENDIX D

Agreements for Peace in Southwestern Africa,
December 22, 1988

Selected Documents
No. 32

December 1988

United States Department of State
Bureau of Public Affairs
Washington, D.C.

TRIPARTITE AGREEMENT, DECEMBER 22, 1988

*AGREEMENT AMONG THE PEOPLE'S REPUBLIC OF ANGOLA, THE
REPUBLIC OF CUBA, AND THE REPUBLIC OF SOUTH AFRICA*

The Governments of the People's Republic of Angola, the Republic
of Cuba, and the Republic of South Africa, hereinafter designated as
"the Parties,"

Taking into account the "Principles for a Peaceful Settlement in
Southwestern Africa," approved by the Parties on 20 July 1988, and
the subsequent negotiations with respect to the implementation of
these Principles, each of which is indispensable to a comprehensive
settlement,

Considering the acceptance by the Parties of the implementation of United Nations Security Council Resolution 435 (1978),
adopted on 29 September 1978, hereinafter designated as "UNSCR
435/78,"

Considering the conclusion of the bilateral agreement between the People's Republic of Angola and the Republic of Cuba providing for the redeployment toward the North and the staged and total withdrawal of Cuban troops from the territory of the People's Republic of Angola,

Recognizing the role of the United Nations Security Council in implementing UNSCR 435/78 and in supporting the implementation of the present agreement,

Affirming the sovereignty, sovereign equality, and independence of all states of southwestern Africa,

Affirming the principle of non-interference in the internal affairs of states,

Affirming the principle of abstention from the threat or use of force against the territorial integrity or political independence of states,

Reaffirming the right of the peoples of the southwestern region of Africa to self-determination, independence, and equality of rights, and of the states of southwestern Africa to peace, development, and social progress,

Urging African and international cooperation for the settlement of the problems of the development of the southwestern region of Africa,

Expressing their appreciation for the mediating role of the Government of the United States of America,

Desiring to contribute to the establishment of peace and security in southwestern Africa,

Agree to the provisions set forth below:

(1) The Parties shall immediately request the Secretary-General of the United Nations to seek authority from the Security Council to commence implementation of UNSCR 435/78 on 1 April 1989.

(2) All military forces of the Republic of South Africa shall depart Namibia in accordance with UNSCR 435/78.

(3) Consistent with the provisions of UNSCR 435/78, the Republic of South Africa and People's Republic of Angola shall cooperate with the Secretary-General to ensure the independence of Namibia through free and fair elections and shall abstain from any action that could prevent the execution of UNSCR 435/78. The Parties shall respect the territorial integrity and inviolability of borders of Namibia and shall ensure that their territories are not used by any state, organization, or person in connection with acts of war, aggression, or violence against the territorial integrity or inviolability of borders of Namibia or any other action which could prevent the execution of UNSCR 435/78.

(4) The People's Republic of Angola and the Republic of Cuba shall implement the bilateral agreement, signed on the date of signature of this agreement, providing for the redeployment toward the North and the staged and total withdrawal of Cuban troops from the territory of the People's Republic of Angola, and the arrangements made with the Security Council of the United Nations for the on-site verification of that withdrawal.

(5) Consistent with their obligations under the Charter of the United Nations, the Parties shall refrain from the threat or use of force, and shall ensure that their respective territories are not used by any state, organization, or person in connection with any acts of war, aggression, or violence, against the territorial integrity, inviolability of borders, or independence of any state of southwestern Africa.

(6) The Parties shall respect the principle of non-interference in the internal affairs of the states of southwestern Africa.

(7) The Parties shall comply in good faith with all obligations undertaken in this agreement and shall resolve through negotiation and in a spirit of cooperation any disputes with respect to the interpretation or implementation thereof.

(8) This agreement shall enter into force upon signature.

Signed at New York in triplicate in the Portuguese, Spanish and English languages, each language being equally authentic, this 22nd day of December 1988.

FOR THE PEOPLE'S REPUBLIC OF ANGOLA
Afonso Van Dunem
FOR THE REPUBLIC OF CUBA
Isidoro Octavio Malmierca
FOR THE REPUBLIC OF SOUTH AFRICA
Roelof F. Botha

BILATERAL AGREEMENT, DECEMBER 22, 1988

Following is the unofficial U.S. translation of the original Portuguese and Spanish texts of the agreement, with annex.

AGREEMENT BETWEEN THE GOVERNMENTS OF THE PEOPLE'S REPUBLIC OF ANGOLA AND THE REPUBLIC OF CUBA FOR THE TERMINATION OF THE INTERNATIONALIST MISSION OF THE CUBAN MILITARY CONTINGENT

The Government of the People's Republic of Angola and the Republic of Cuba, hereinafter designated as the Parties,

Considering,

That the implementation of Resolution 435 of the Security Council of the United Nations for the independence of Namibia shall commence on the 1st of April,

That the question of the independence of Namibia and the safeguarding of the sovereignty, independence and territorial integrity of the People's Republic of Angola are closely interrelated with each other and with peace and security in the region of southwestern Africa,

That on the date of signature of this agreement a tripartite agreement among the Governments of the People's Republic of Angola, the Republic of Cuba and the Republic of South Africa shall be signed, containing the essential elements for the achievement of peace in the region of southwestern Africa,

That acceptance of and strict compliance with the foregoing will bring to an end the reasons which compelled the Government of the People's Rebublic of Angola to request, in the legitimate exercise of its rights under Article 51 of the United Nations Charter, the deployment to Angolan territory of a Cuban internationalist military contingent to guarantee, in cooperation with the FAPLA [the Angolan Government army], its territorial integrity and sovereignty in view of the invasion and occupation of part of its territory,

Noting,

The agreements signed by the Governments of the People's Republic of Angola and the Republic of Cuba on 4 February 1982 and 19 March 1984, the platform of the Government of the People's Republic of Angola approved in November 1984, and the Protocol of Brazzaville signed by the Governments of the People's Republic of Angola, the Republic of Cuba and the Republic of South Africa on December 13, 1988,

Taking into account,

That conditions now exist which make possible the repatriation of the Cuban military contingent currently in Angolan territory and the successful accomplishment of their internationalist mission,

The parties agree as follows:

Article 1

To commence the redeployment by stages to the 15th and 13th parallels and the total withdrawal to Cuba of the 50,000 men who constitute the Cuban troops contingent stationed in the People's Republic of Angola, in accordance with the pace and timeframe established in the attached calendar, which is an integral part of this agreement. The total withdrawal shall be completed by the 1st of July, 1991.

Article 2

The Governments of the People's Republic of Angola and the Republic of Cuba reserve the right to modify or alter their obligations deriving from Article 1 of this Agreement in the event that flagrant violations of the Tripartite Agreement are verified.

Article 3

The Parties, through the Secretary General of the United Nations Organization, hereby request that the Security Council verify the redeployment and phased and total withdrawal of Cuban troops from the territory of the People's Republic of Angola, and to this end shall agree on a matching protocol.

Article 4

This agreement shall enter into force upon signature of the tripartite agreement among the People's Republic of Angola, the Republic of Cuba, and the Republic of South Africa.

Signed on 22 December 1988, at the Headquarters of the United Nations Organization, in two copies, in the Portuguese and Spanish languages, each being equally authentic.

FOR THE PEOPLE'S REPUBLIC OF ANGOLA
Afonso Van Dunem
FOR THE REPUBLIC OF CUBA
Isidoro Octavio Malmierca

Annex on Troop Withdrawal Schedule

Calendar

In compliance with Article 1 of the agreement between the Government of the Republic of Cuba and the Government of the People's Republic of Angola for the termination of the mission of the Cuban internationalist military contingent stationed in Angolan territory, the parties establish the following calendar for the withdrawal:

Time Frames

Prior to the first of April, 1989 (date of the beginning of implementation of Resolution 435)	3,000 men
Total duration of the calendar Starting from the 1st of April, 1989	27 months
Redeployment to the north:	
to the 15th parallel	by 1 August 1989
to the 13th parallel	by 31 Oct. 1989
Total men to be withdrawn:	
by 1 November 1989	25,000 men (50%)
by 1 April 1990	33,000 (66%)
by 1 October 1990	38,000 (76%); 12,000 men remaining
by July 1991	50,000 (100%)

Taking as its base a Cuban force of 50,000 men.

PROVISIONS OF UN RESOLUTION 435

Following an agreement on a date to implement UN Resolution 435 and establishment of a formal cease-fire, a UN representative and a UN planning group would administer Namibia during the transition to independence in conjunction with the South African-appointed Administrator General. A UN Transitional Assistance

Group (UNTAG) would supervise the cease-fire and monitor South African and South-West Africa People's Organization (SWAPO) forces.

Within three months of a cease-fire, South African forces would be reduced to 1,500 men, confined to one or two bases in northern Namibia. SWAPO forces would be restricted to specified locations in Angola under UN supervision. All political prisoners held by both sides would be released.

Seven months after the implementation date, elections would be held under UN auspices for a new constituent assembly. The remaining South African troops would depart within a few months, once elections were certified by the UN and independence granted. Unarmed SWAPO members and Namibian refugees would be permitted to return to participate in the election process.

APPENDIX E
Harare Declaration, August 1989

DECLARATION ON THE QUESTION OF SOUTH AFRICA
by
THE AD HOC COMMITTEE ON SOUTHERN AFRICA OF
THE ORGANIZATION OF AFRICAN UNITY

The following declaration and programme of action on South Africa were adopted by the Ad Hoc Committee on Southern Africa of the Organization of African Unity at its meeting held in Harare, Zimbabwe, on 21 August 1989.

I. PREAMBLE

The people of Africa, singly, collectively and acting through the Organization of African Unity (OAU), are engaged in serious efforts to establish peace throughout the continent by ending all conflicts through negotiations based on the principle of justice and peace for all.

We affirm our conviction, which history confirms, that where colonial, racial and *apartheid* domination exist, there can neither be peace nor justice.

Accordingly, we reiterate that while the *apartheid* system in South Africa persists, the peoples of our continent as a whole cannot achieve the fundamental objectives of justice, human dignity and peace, which are both crucial in themselves and fundamental to the stability and development of Africa.

With regard to the region of southern Africa, the entire continent is vitally interested that the processes in which it is involved, leading to the complete and genuine independence of Namibia, as well as peace in Angola and Mozambique, should succeed in the shortest possible time. Equally, Africa is deeply concerned that the destabilization of all the countries in the region by South Africa, whether through direct aggression, sponsorship of surrogates, economic subversion and other means, should end immediately.

We recognize the reality that permanent peace and stability in southern Africa can only be achieved when the system of *apartheid* in South Africa has been liquidated and South Africa has been transformed into a united, democratic and non-racial country. We therefore reiterate that all the necessary measures should be adopted now, to bring a speedy end to the *apartheid* system, in the interest of all the people of southern Africa, our continent and the world at large.

We believe that, as a result of the liberation struggle and international pressure against *apartheid*, as well as global efforts to liquidate regional conflicts, possibilities exist for further movement towards the resolution of the problems facing the people of South Africa. For these possibilities to lead to fundamental change in South Africa, the Pretoria régime must abandon its abhorrent concepts and practices of racial domination and its record of failure to honour agreements, all of which have already resulted in the loss of so many lives and the destruction of much property in the countries of southern Africa.

We reaffirm our recognition of the right of all peoples, including those of South Africa, to determine their own destiny, and to work out for themselves the institutions and the system of government under which they will, by general consent, live and work together to build a harmonious society. OAU remains committed to do everything possible and necessary to assist the people of South Africa, in such ways as the representatives of the oppressed may determine, to achieve this objective. We are certain that, arising from its duty to help end the criminal *apartheid* system, the rest of the world community is ready to extend similar assistance to the people of South Africa.

We make these commitments because we believe that all people are equal and have equal rights to human dignity and respect, regardless of colour, race, sex or creed. We believe that all men and women have the right and duty to participate in their own government, as equal members of society. No individual or group of individuals has any right to govern others without their consent. The *apartheid* system violates all those fundamental and universal principles. Correctly characterized as a crime against humanity, it is responsible for the death of countless numbers of people in South Africa. It has sought to dehumanize entire peoples. It has imposed a brutal war on the whole region of southern Africa, resulting in untold loss of life, destruction of property and massive displacement of innocent men, women and children. This scourge and affront to humanity must be fought and eradicated in its totality.

We have therefore supported and continue to support all those in South Africa who pursue this noble objective through political, armed and other forms of struggle. We believe this to be our duty, carried out in the interest of all humanity.

While extending this support to those who strive for a non-racial and democratic society in South Africa, a point on which no compromise is possible, we have repeatedly expressed our preference for a solution arrived at by peaceful means. We know that the majority of the people of South Africa and their liberation movement who have been compelled to take up arms have also upheld this position for many decades and continue to do so.

The positions contained in this Declaration are consistent with and are a continuation of those elaborated in the Lusaka Manifesto two decades ago. They take into account the changes that have taken place in southern Africa since that Manifesto was adopted by OAU and by the rest of the international community. They constitute a new challenge to the Pretoria régime to join in the noble effort to end the *apartheid* system, an objective to which OAU has been committed from its very birth.

Consequently, we shall continue to do everything in our power to help intensify the liberation struggle and international pressure against the system of *apartheid* until this system is ended and South Africa is transformed into a united, democratic and non-racial country, with justice and security for all its citizens.

In keeping with this solemn resolve, and responding directly to the wishes of the representatives of the majority of the people of South Africa, we publicly pledge ourselves to the positions contained hereunder. We are convinced that their implementation will lead to a speedy end of the *apartheid* system and therefore to the opening of a new dawn of peace for all the peoples of Africa, in which racism, colonial domination and white minority rule on our continent would be abolished forever.

II. STATEMENT OF PRINCIPLES

We believe that a conjuncture of circumstances exists which, if there is demonstrable readiness on the part of the Pretoria régime to engage in negotiations genuinely and seriously, could create the possibility to end *apartheid* through negotiations. Such an eventuality would be an expression of the long-standing preference of the majority of the people of South Africa to arrive at a political settlement.

We would therefore encourage the people of South Africa, as part of their overall struggle, to get together to negotiate an end to the *apartheid* system and agree on all the measures that are necessary to transform their country into a non-racial democracy. We support the position held by the majority of the people of South Africa that these objectives, and not the amendment or reform of the *apartheid* system, should be the aims of the negotiations.

We are at one with them that the outcome of such a process should be a new constitutional order based on the following principles, among others:

    a) South Africa shall become a united, democratic and non-racial State;

    b) All its people shall enjoy common and equal citizenship and nationality, regardless of race, colour, sex or creed;

    c) All its people shall have the right to participate in the government and administration of the country on the basis of a universal suffrage, exercised through the one-person, one-vote system, under a common voters' roll;

    d) All shall have the right to form and join any political party of their choice, provided that this is not furtherance of racism;

    e) All shall enjoy universally recognized human rights, freedoms and civil liberties, protected under an entrenched Bill of Rights;

    f) South Africa shall have a new legal system which shall guarantee equality of all before the law;

    g) South Africa shall have an independent and non-racial judiciary;

    h) There shall be created an economic order which shall promote and advance the well-being of all South Africans;

    i) A democratic South Africa shall respect the rights, sovereignty and territorial integrity of all countries and pursue a policy of peace, friendship, and mutually beneficial cooperation with all peoples.

We believe that agreement on the above principles shall constitute the foundation for an internationally acceptable solution which shall enable South Africa to take its rightful place as an equal partner among the African and world community of nations.

III. CLIMATE FOR NEGOTIATIONS

Together with the rest of the world, we believe that it is essential before any negotiations can take place, that the necessary climate for negotiations be created. The *apartheid* régime has the urgent responsibility to respond positively to this universally acclaimed demand and thus create this climate.

Accordingly, the present régime should, at the very least:

a) Release all political prisoners and detainees unconditionally and refrain from imposing any restrictions on them;

b) Lift all bans and restrictions on all proscribed and restricted organizations and persons;

c) Remove all troops from the townships;

d) End the state of emergency and repeal all legislation, such as and including the Internal Security Act, designed to circumscribe political activity; and,

e) Cease all political trials and political executions.

These measures are necessary to produce the conditions in which free political discussion can take place—an essential condition to ensure that the people themselves participate in the process of remaking their country. The measures listed above should therefore precede negotiations.

IV. GUIDELINES TO THE PROCESS OF NEGOTIATION

We support the view of the South African liberation movement that upon the creation of this climate, the process of negotiations should commence along the following lines:

a) Discussions should take place between the liberation movement and the South African régime to achieve the suspension of hostilities on both sides by agreeing to a mutually binding cease-fire;

b) Negotiations should then proceed to establish the basis for the adoption of a new constitution by agreeing on, among others, the principles enunciated above;

c) Having agreed to these principles, the parties should then negotiate the necessary mechanism for drawing up the new constitution;

d) The parties shall define and agree on the role to be played by the international community in ensuring a successful transition to a democratic order;

e) The parties shall agree on the formation of an interim Government to supervise the process of the drawing up and adoption of a new constitution, govern and administer the country, as well as effect the transition to a democratic order, including the holding of elections.

After the adoption of the new constitution, all armed hostilities will be deemed to have formally terminated.

For its part, the international community would lift the sanctions that have been imposed against *apartheid* South Africa.

The new South Africa shall qualify for membership of OAU.

V. PROGRAMME OF ACTION

In pursuance of the objectives stated in this document, OAU hereby commits itself:

a) To inform Governments and intergovernmental organizations throughout the world, including the Movement of Non-aligned Countries, the United Nations General Assembly, the Security Council, the Commonwealth and others of these perspectives, and solicit their support;

b) To mandate the OAU *Ad Hoc* Committee on Southern Africa, acting as the representative of OAU and assisted by the front-line States, to remain seized of the issue of a political resolution of the South African question;

c) To step up all-round support for the South African liberation movement and campaign in the rest of the world in pursuance of this objective;

d) To intensify the campaign for mandatory and comprehensive sanctions against *apartheid* South Africa: in this regard, immediately mobilize against the rescheduling of Pretoria's foreign debt; work for the imposition of a mandatory oil embargo; and the full observance by all countries of the arms embargo;

e) To ensure that the African continent does not relax existing measures for the total isolation of *apartheid* South Africa;

f) To continue to monitor the situation in Namibia and extend all necessary support to the South West Africa People's Organization (SWAPO) in its struggle for a genuinely independent Namibia;

g) To extend such assistance as the Governments of Angola and Mozambique may request in order to secure peace for their peoples;

h) To render all possible assistance to the front-line States to enable them to withstand Pretoria's campaign of aggression and destabilization and enable them to continue to give their all-round support to the people of Namibia and South Africa.

We appeal to all people of good will throughout the world to support this programme of action as a necessary measure to secure the earliest liquidation of the *apartheid* system and the transformation of South Africa into a united, democratic and non-racial country.

Source: United Nations Center Against Apartheid, *Notes and Documents*, New York, October 1989.

Notes

WAR AND DIPLOMACY
(Robert S. Jaster)

EVOLUTION OF A REGIONAL CONFLICT

1. The Frontline States, designated by the Organization of African Unity in 1976 to coordinate support for the Rhodesian nationalist movements, included Angola, Botswana, Mozambique, Tanzania, and Zambia. Zimbabwe became the sixth member on its independence in 1980.

ESCALATING WARFARE: 1978–88

2. Speech of 2 June 1978, in *P. W. Botha: A Political Backgrounder* (London: South African Embassy, September 1978), 57.

3. *House of Assembly Debates*, 21 March 1980, cols. 3316–24.

4. New Year's Message of 1 January 1977, in *P. W. Botha: A Political Backgrounder*, 33.

5. Deon Geldenhuys, *The Diplomacy of Isolation* (Johannesburg: Macmillan South Africa Publishers Pty., 1984), 92.

6. Robert S. Jaster, *The Defence of White Power: South African Foreign Policy Under Pressure* (New York: St. Martin's Press, 1989), 82–88.

7. *House of Assembly Debates*, vol. 86, 1 May 1980, col. 5295.

8. For a detailed analysis of the destabilization campaign, see Richard Leonard, *South Africa at War* (Craighall: Ad. Donker Pty. Ltd, 1985), ch. 2, and Jaster, *The Defence of White Power*, ch. 8.

9. "Mozambique: What's In It For Us?" *The Economist*, 2 June 1984.

10. See Phyllis Johnson and David Martin, eds., *Frontline Southern Africa: Destructive Engagement* (New York: Four Walls Eight Windows, 1988), 32–36, for a detailed account of the "Gorongosa Documents."

11. Robert S. Jaster, "The Security Outlook in Mozambique," *Survival* 27, no. 6 (London: International Institute for Strategic Studies, November/December 1985), 258–64.

12. Ibid.

13. See Pauline H. Baker, *The United States and South Africa: The Reagan Years* (New York: Ford Foundation and Foreign Policy Association, 1989), 58.

14. Alan Cowell, *New York Times*, 5 August 1986.

15. For an incisive analysis of changing ANC strategy and tactics, see Tom Lodge, "The Second Consultative Congress of the African National Congress," *South Africa International* (Johannesburg: The South Africa Foundation, November 1985).

16. *Weekly Mail* (Johannesburg), 9–14 June 1989.

17. *New York Times*, 21 August 1988.

18. *Die Transvaaler*, 25 March 1981.

19. *Covert Action Information Bulletin*, no. 13 (Washington, D.C.: Covert Action Publications, Inc., July/August 1981), 38.

20. *House of Assembly Debates,* vol. 87, 19 May 1980, col. 6627.

21. Major-General Meiring [SADF commander in Namibia], *Star* (Johannesburg), 10 January 1987.

22. André du Pisani, "Namibia: A New Transitional Government," *South Africa International* (Johannesburg), October 1985.

23. For a detailed analysis of South Africa's Namibian diplomacy, see Robert S. Jaster, *South Africa in Namibia: The Botha Strategy* (Lanham: University Press of America and Center for International Affairs, Harvard University, 1985), 74–95.

24. *Christian Science Monitor*, 8 June 1984; *Weekly Star* (Johannesburg), 28 May 1984.

25. See, for example, *Covert Action Information Bulletin*, no. 13.

26. *Strategic Survey 1985–1986* (London: International Institute for Strategic Studies, Spring 1986), 188–89.

27. "Angola: SAAF Air Superiority Is Lost," *Star*, 11 November, and *Star*, 9 December 1985, citing interview in *Afrique-Asie*.

28. Speech by President Fidel Castro of Cuba to the 8th Non-Aligned Summit in Harare, 2 September 1986.

29. *Strategic Survey 1986–1987*, Spring 1987.

30. Lt. Gen. D. J. Earp, "The Role of Air Power in Southern Africa," *ISSUP Review* (April 1986): 34.

31. Castro's "Address to the Nation," *FBIS Latin America*, 28 July 1988.

32. John Battersby, "Afrikaner Church Questions South Africa's Angola Role," *New York Times*, 8 July 1988.

33. *House of Assembly Debates*, 29 March 1962, cols. 3444–57.

34. See Robert S. Jaster, *South Africa's Narrowing Security Options*, Adelphi Paper No. 159 (London: International Institute for Strategic Studies, Spring 1980), 14–16.

35. *House of Assembly Debates*, 22 April 1975.

36. *Financial Mail* (South Africa), 11 September 1982.

37. *South Africa Digest*, 17 September 1982.

38. André Brink, "Weapons Promoted at International Arms Show," *Die Volksblad*, 3 May 1989.

39. See, for example, Christopher Coker, *South Africa's Security Dilemmas*, The Washington Papers No. 126 (Washington, D.C.: Center for Strategic and International Studies, 1987), ch. 4.

40. Ibid.

41. Thomas Friedman, "Israelis Reassess Supplying Arms to South Africa," *New York Times*, 28 January 1987; Coker, *South Africa's Security Dilemmas*, 52.

42. *Star*, 29 November 1986; *Christian Science Monitor*, 12 December 1986.

43. *Star*, 28 May 1984.

44. Thomas Friedman, *New York Times*, 18 March and 2 April 1987.

45. David Ottoway, "State Department Sees No Israel–South Africa Transfer," *Washington Post*, 31 October 1989.

46. Carol Giacomo, "South African Connection Stalls US Computers for Israel," *Washington Times*, 9 November 1989.

47. See Kenneth W. Grundy, *The Militarization of South African Politics* (Bloomington: Indiana University Press, 1986), ch. 2.

48. John D. Battersby, *New York Times*, 22 August 1988.

49. Kenneth W. Grundy, *Soldiers Without Politics* (Berkeley: University of California Press, 1983), 167.

50. Robert S. Jaster, "The South African Military Reassesses Its Priorities," *CSIS Africa Notes*, 30 September 1989, 4.

51. John Battersby, "Pretoria Ousts 47 Black Troops," *New York Times*, 22 November 1987; *Weekly Star*, 24 November 1987.

52. Christopher S. Wren, *New York Times*, 8 December 1989.

53. Quoted in *Business Day* (South Africa), 21 April 1989.

54. Robert S. Jaster, "Politics and the 'Afrikaner Bomb,'" *Orbis* (Winter 1984): 842–44.

55. Ibid., 832.

56. Leonard Spector, *The Nuclear Nations* (New York: The Carnegie Endowment and Random House, 1985), 218.

57. Jaster, "Politics and the 'Afrikaner Bomb'," 846–47.

58. *White Paper on Defence and Armaments Supply 1984* (Republic of South Africa, Department of Defense, April 1984).

59. *White Paper on Defence and Armaments Supply 1986* (Republic of South Africa, Department of Defense, April 1986).

60. See Coker, *South Africa's Security Dilemmas*, 88; Jaster, "Politics and the 'Afrikaner Bomb'," 848–49.

REGIONAL PEACEMAKING: 1988–90

61. David Ottoway, "Angola Offers Removal of All Cuban Troops," *Washington Post*, 14 February 1988.

62. Arnaud de Borchgrave, "Botha Vows to Remain in Angola Until Cuba Withdraws Its Troops," *Washington Times*, 14 March 1988.

63. From Robert S. Jaster, *The 1988 Peace Accords and the Future of Southwestern Africa*, Adelphi Paper No. 253 (London: International Institute for Strategic Studies, Autumn 1990).

64. Bertrand Rosenthal in *Washington Times*, 6 June 1988.

65. From Jaster, *The 1988 Peace Accords and the Future of South-western Africa*.

66. James Brooke, *New York Times*, 1 March 1989.

67. See Grundy, *The Militarization of South African Politics*, ch. 3, and Jaster, *The Defence of White Power*, 31–41.

68. Peter Fabricius, "Congo Safari Filled With Irony," *Star*, 18 May 1988.

69. Nicholas Woodsworth, *Financial Times*, 5 October 1988.

70. Christopher S. Wren, *New York Times*, 26 August 1989.

71. "Statement by Representatives of Botswana, Kenya, and Uganda to the United Nations," *New York Times*, 13 October 1988.

ECONOMIC RIVALRY AND INTERDEPENDENCE IN SOUTHERN AFRICA
(Moeletsi Mbeki and Morley Nkosi)

RIVAL STRATEGIES: THE CONSTELLATION VS. SADCC

1. Roy Laishley, "SADCC's Second Ten Years," *Africa Recovery* 4, no. 1 (April–June 1990): 26.

2. "What is SACU?" *Africa Research Bulletin, Economic Series* 23, no. 7 (31 August 1986): 831.

PRESSURE ON THE ECONOMIC ARTERIES

3. Graham Leach, *South Africa* (London: Routledge and Kegan Paul, 1987), 218.

4. "Background Brief: Southern African Transport Routes" (London: Foreign and Commonwealth Office, March 1987).

5. "Tanzania-Zambia—Hopes for Great Uhuru Railway," *Africa Research Bulletin, Economic Series* 24, no. 5 (30 June 1987): 86–96.

6. Comments by E. C. Cross, managing director, Beira Corridor Group Limited, and Dennis Norman, former Zimbabwe minister of agriculture, at a meeting on "The Strategic and Economic Importance of the Beira Corridor Project," sponsored by the African Studies Program of the Center for Strategic and International Studies (CSIS), Washington, D.C., 12 May 1988. (Henceforth referred to as Cross and Norman, CSIS meeting.)

7. Deon Geldenhuys, *The Diplomacy of Isolation: South African Foreign Policy Making* (Johannesburg: Macmillan, South Africa, 1984), 154.

8. *African Economic Digest* (London), 17 December 1982.

9. Joseph Hanlon, *Beggar Your Neighbours: Apartheid Power in Southern Africa* (Bloomington: Indiana University Press, 1986), 70.

10. Ibid., 188–90.

11. Gillian Gunn, "The Nonaligned Summit: Behind the Rhetoric," *CSIS Africa Notes*, no. 63 (25 October 1986): 4.

12. Anon., "The Impact of Economic Sanctions Against South Africa on the SADCC States," draft report prepared for the Canadian Embassy in Harare, Zimbabwe (Harare, 17 February 1986), 18.

13. Hanlon, *Beggar Your Neighbours*, 135.

14. Ibid., 150.

15. Ibid., 159.

16. Ibid., 138.

17. Ibid., 138.

18. Anon., "The Impact of Economic Sanctions," 18.

19. Stephen R. Lewis, Jr., *The Economics of Apartheid* (New York: Council on Foreign Relations Press, 1990), 85.

20. Cross and Norman, CSIS meeting.

21. Ibid.

22. Anon., "The Impact of Economic Sanctions," 16.

23. Allister Sparks, "If Sanctions Come, South Africa Looks to Swaziland As 'Back Door,'" *International Herald Tribune*, 10 July 1986, 5.

24. Hanlon, *Beggar Your Neighbours*, 185.

25. Lewis, *The Economics of Apartheid*, 89.

26. Ibid., 13.

27. Hanlon, *Beggar Your Neighbours*, 115.

CONCLUSION

28. Sam Kongwa, "South Africa and the SADCC Countries in the 1990s," *South Africa Foundation Review* 16, no. 4 (April 1990): 3.

THE SUPERPOWERS IN SOUTHERN AFRICA: FROM CONFRONTATION TO COOPERATION (Michael Clough)

THE EARLY STAGES OF SUPERPOWER COMPETITION

1. Anthony Lake, *The "Tar Baby" Option: American Policy Toward Southern Rhodesia* (New York: Columbia University Press, 1976); Roger Morris, *Uncertain Greatness: Henry Kissinger and American Foreign Policy* (New York: Harper & Row, 1977).

2. On Soviet policy toward southern Africa see Seth Singleton, "The Natural Ally: Soviet Policy in Southern Africa," in *Changing Realities in Southern Africa*, ed. Michael Clough (Berkeley: Institute of International Studies, 1982). On Cuban policy see William Durch, "The Cuban Military in Africa and the Middle East: From Algeria to Angola," *Studies in Comparative Communism* 11, no. 1 (Spring-Summer 1978): 34–74.

3. On the changes in Southern Africa, see John Marcum, *The Angolan Revolution*, Volume II (Cambridge: MIT Press, 1978). On changes in Soviet military capabilities, see Bruce Porter, *The USSR in Third World Conflicts* (Cambridge: Cambridge University Press, 1984).

4. See Raymond Garthoff, *Détente and Confrontation: American-Soviet Relations from Nixon to Reagan* (Washington, D.C.: Brookings Institution, 1985), 502–37.

5. On the U.S. intervention in Angola, see Nathaniel Davis, "The Angola Decision of 1975," *Foreign Affairs* 57, no. 1 (Fall 1978): 109–24; and William Hyland, *Mortal Rivals* (New York: Random House, 1987), 130–47.

CONSTRUCTIVE ENGAGEMENT AND REGIONAL CONFLICT

6. See Michael Clough, ed., *Reassessing the Soviet Challenge in Africa* (Berkeley: Institute of International Studies, 1986).

7. Office of the Historian, Bureau of Public Affairs, *The United States and South Africa: U.S. Public Statements and Related Documents, 1977–1985* (Washington, D.C.: U.S. Department of State, September 1985), 58.

8. This document was published in *Counterspy* (August–October, 1981): 54.

9. See Michael Clough, "United States Policy in Southern Africa," *Current History* 83, no. 491 (March 1984): 97–100.

10. See Robert S. Jaster, "War and Diplomacy" in *Changing Fortunes: War, Diplomacy, and Economics in Southern Africa* by Robert S. Jaster et al. (New York: Ford Foundation and Foreign Policy Association, 1992).

11. *The United States and South Africa*, 122.

12. Ibid., 192.

13. See Winrich Kuhne, "What the Mozambique Case Tells Us About Soviet Ambivalence Toward Africa," *CSIS Africa Notes*, no. 46 (August 1985); and Gillian Gunn, "Post-Nkomati Mozambique," *CSIS Africa Notes*, no. 38 (January 1986).

THE END OF CONSTRUCTIVE ENGAGEMENT

14. For a more detailed account, see Michael Clough, "Beyond Constructive Engagement," *Foreign Policy*, no. 61 (Winter 1985–86): 3–24.

15. *The United States and South Africa*, 172.

16. Ibid., 106.

17. Chester Crocker, "U.S. Policy Toward Mozambique," *Department of State Bulletin* 87, no. 2126 (September 1987): 21.

18. *The United States and South Africa*, 337.

19. See Neil MacFarlane, "The Soviet Union and Southern Africa Security," *Problems of Communism* 38 (March–June 1989): 71–89.

FROM CONFRONTATION TO COOPERATION

20. See Michael Clough and Jeffrey Herbst, *South Africa's Changing Regional Strategy* (New York: Council on Foreign Relations, 1989).

21. Lionel Barber, "The Selling of an African Conflict," *Financial Times*, 16 March 1990.

Selected Bibliography: War, Diplomacy, and Economics in Southern Africa

---

WAR AND DIPLOMACY
(Robert S. Jaster)

COCK, Jacklyn, and NATHAN, Laurie, eds. *War and Society: the Militarization of South Africa.* Cape Town and Johannesburg: David Philip, 1989.

CLOUGH, Michael. *Changing Realities in Southern Africa.* Berkeley: Institute for Strategic Studies, 1982.

COKER, Christopher. *South Africa's Security Dilemmas.* Washington Papers 3126. Washington, D.C.: Center for Strategic and International Studies, 1987.

GELDENHUYS, Deon. *The Constellation of Southern African States and the Southern African Development Coordination Council* [sic]*: Towards a New Regional Stalemate?* Braamfontein: South African Institute of International Affairs, January 1981.

———. *The Diplomacy of Isolation: South African Foreign Policy Making.* Braamfontein: South African Institute of International Affairs, 1984.

GRUNDY, Kenneth W. *The Militarization of South African Politics.* Bloomington: Indiana University Press, 1986.

———. *Soldiers Without Politics: Blacks in the South African Armed Forces.* Berkeley: University of California Press, 1983.

JASTER, Robert S. *The Defence of White Power: South African Foreign Policy Under Pressure.* New York: St. Martin's Press, and London: the International Institute for Strategic Studies, 1988.

———. *A Regional Security Role for Africa's Front-Line States.* Adelphi Paper No. 180. London: International Institute for Strategic Studies, 1983.

———. *South Africa in Namibia: The Botha Strategy.* Boston: Center for International Affairs, Harvard University, 1985.

LEONARD, Richard. *South Africa at War: White Power and the Crisis in Southern Africa.* Westport, Conn.: Lawrence Hill & Company, 1983.

Southern Africa: Prospects for Peace and Security. IPA Report No. 25. New York: International Peace Academy, 1987.

ECONOMIC RIVALRY AND INTERDEPENDENCE IN SOUTHERN AFRICA
(Moeletsi Mbeki and Morley Nkosi)

ARNOLD, Millard W. "Southern Africa in the Year 2000: An Optimistic Scenario," *CSIS Africa Notes,* no. 122 (March 1991).

Canadian High Commission. *The Impact of Economic Sanctions Against South Africa on the SADCC States.* Harare, Zimbabwe: Canadian High Commission, 1986.

LEWIS, Stephen R., Jr. "Southern Africa Interdependence," *CSIS Africa Notes,* no. 56 (March 1986).

MARTIN, David, and JOHNSON, Phyllis, eds. *Frontline Southern Africa: Destructive Engagement.* New York: Four Walls Eight Windows, 1988.

MULAISHO, Dominic. "SADCC Faces Up to New Challenges." *Africa Recovery* 4, no. 1. New York: UN Department of Public Information, April–June 1990.

U.S. General Accounting Office. *South Africa: Trends in Trade, Lending, and Investment.* Washington, D.C., April 1988.

THE SUPERPOWERS IN SOUTHERN AFRICA: FROM CONFRONTATION TO COOPERATION
(Michael Clough)

ALBRIGHT, David. *Communism in Africa.* Bloomington: Indiana University Press, 1980.

CLOUGH, Michael. *Free at Last?: U.S. Policy Toward Africa and the End of the Cold War.* New York: Council on Foreign Relations, 1991.

———, ed. *Reassessing the Soviet Challenge in Africa.* Berkeley: Institute of International Studies, 1986.

JACKSON, Henry. *From the Congo to Soweto: U.S. Foreign Policy Toward Africa Since 1960.* New York: Columbia University Press, 1977.

LAKE, Anthony. *The "Tar Baby" Option: American Policy Toward Southern Rhodesia.* New York: Columbia University Press, 1976.

SOMERVILLE, Keith. *Foreign Military Intervention in Africa.* New York: St. Martin's Press, 1990.

Selected Annotated Bibliography: South Africa

The books below, most of which were written for a general audience, provide an introduction to South African history, politics, and society. Most have been published in the last decade and are available in libraries and college bookstores in the United States, except for the annual surveys of the South African Institute of Race Relations. Books issued by South African publishers have been omitted, although they are an essential resource for readers who intend to study South Africa in depth.

ADAM, Heribert, and GILIOMEE, Hermann. *Ethnic Power Mobilized: Can South Africa Change?* New Haven: Yale University Press, 1979.
> A collection of essays about Afrikaner history and politics through the Vorster era.

BAKER, Pauline. *The United States and South Africa: The Reagan Years.* New York: Ford Foundation and Foreign Policy Association, 1989.
> A concise analysis of the forces that produced the rise and fall of constructive engagement.

BARBER, James, and BARRATT, John. *South Africa's Foreign Policy: The Search for Status and Security 1945–1988.* New York: Cambridge University Press, 1990.
> This useful and highly readable account of South Africa's diplomacy stops a year short of the De Klerk era. The authors chart four distinct phases, each resulting in the progressive isolation of Pretoria in Africa and the world. They show how persistent opposition from blacks and their allies eventually doomed the efforts of the Western powers to separate economic from political relations with South Africa.

BENSON, Mary. *Nelson Mandela: The Man and the Movement.* New York: W. W. Norton and Company, 1986.
> A sympathetic biography of the African National Congress leader imprisoned from 1962 to 1990, describing his early life and political career, his nationalist beliefs, and his central role within the ANC.

BERGER, Peter L., and GODSELL, Bobby, eds. *A Future South Africa: Visions, Strategies and Realities.* Boulder, Colo.: Westview Press, 1988.
> Eight chapters by liberal analysts survey the contemporary array of political protagonists in South Africa. A conclusion by the editors predicts a slow, painful evolutionary transition to a post-apartheid society.

BIKO, Steve. *I Write What I Like.* San Francisco: Harper & Row, 1986. (First edition: London: Bowerdean Press, 1978.)
> The collected writings of the martyred founder of the black consciousness movement, who was South Africa's most influential black leader in the post-Sharpeville era.

BRINK, André. *A Dry White Season.* New York: Morrow, 1980.
> A powerful story by South Africa's leading Afrikaner novelist about an apolitical Afrikaner teacher drawn by the death of a black friend into a web of state repression and social isolation.

BUNDY, Colin, and SAUNDERS, Christopher, principal consultants. *Illustrated History of South Africa: The Real Story.* Pleasantville, N.Y., and Montreal: The Reader's Digest Association, 1989.
> Excellent general history directed at nonspecialist readers, extensively illustrated and incorporating the most recent scholarship.

BUTLER, Jeffrey; ELPHICK, Richard; and WELSH, David, eds. *Democratic Liberalism in South Africa: Its History and Prospect.* Middletown, Conn.: Wesleyan University Press, 1987.
> This book brings together twenty-four essays by white liberals who critically review the principles, policies, history, and historiography of liberalism in South Africa and argue for the continuing relevance of liberal beliefs.

DAVIS, Stephen M. *Apartheid's Rebels: Inside South Africa's Hidden War.* New Haven: Yale University Press, 1987.
> Focusing on the African National Congress in its exile years, this book offers the fullest portrait to date of the ANC's guerrilla campaign.

DUGARD, John. *Human Rights and the South African Legal Order.* Princeton: Princeton University Press, 1978.
> An introduction to what the author, a prominent South African jurist, calls "the pursuit of justice within an unjust legal order." Covers the laws involving civil rights and liberties, state security laws, judicial procedures in political trials, and the South African judiciary.

FINNEGAN, William. *Crossing the Line: A Year in the Land of Apartheid.* New York: Harper & Row, 1986.
> An appealing memoir by a young American writer who discovers South Africa through teaching at a Coloured high school in Cape Town.

FREDRICKSON, George M. *White Supremacy: A Comparative Study in American and South African History.* New York: Oxford University Press, 1981.
   An interpretive work by an American historian on the causes, character, and consequences of white supremacist ideology and practice.

GERHART, Gail M. *Black Power in South Africa: The Evolution of an Ideology.* Berkeley: University of California Press, 1978.
   Explores the historical strain of African nationalism, still popular today, which eschews white participation in black liberation movements.

GORDIMER, Nadine. *Burger's Daughter.* New York: Viking Press, 1979.
   This, the most political of Gordimer's novels, is loosely based on the life and legacy of Abram Fischer, a distinguished Afrikaner lawyer sentenced to life imprisonment for his role in South Africa's underground Communist Party.

GRUNDY, Kenneth W. *The Militarization of South African Politics.* Bloomington: Indiana University Press, 1986.
   An examination of the influence of the military establishment in fashioning both foreign and domestic security policy under the Botha government.

HANLON, Joseph. *Beggar Your Neighbours: Apartheid Power in South Africa.* Bloomington: Indiana University Press, 1986.
   A comprehensive assessment of political, military, and economic relationships between South Africa and the Frontline States by a journalist critical of South Africa's policies.

HANLON, Joseph, and OMOND, Roger. *The Sanctions Handbook.* New York: Viking Penguin, 1987.
   A summary of the evidence, the arguments, and the politics surrounding the sanctions debate in the United States and Britain.

HARRISON, David. *The White Tribe of Africa: South Africa in Perspective.* Berkeley and Los Angeles: University of California Press, 1981.
   Engaging and informative sketches of personalities and episodes in Afrikaner history.

JOUBERT, Elsa. *Poppie.* London: Hodder and Stoughton, 1980.
   A novel that movingly portrays the needless human suffering caused by the apartheid system and the forbearance of its victims.

KANE-BERMAN, John. *South Africa: A Method in the Madness.* London: Pluto Press, 1979. [Published in South Africa under the title: *Soweto — Black Revolt, White Reaction.* Johannesburg: Ravan Press, 1978.]
   An informative account of the causes and circumstances surrounding the Soweto revolt of 1976–77, written by a journalist who later became director of the South African Institute of Race Relations.

KARIS, Thomas, and CARTER, Gwendolen, eds. *From Protest to Challenge: A Documentary History of African Politics in South Africa 1882–1964* (four volumes). Stanford: Hoover Institution Press, 1972–77.

A comprehensive survey of the history of extraparliamentary black and allied opposition groups. Volumes 1–3 contain primary source documents explained in their historical context, and Volume 4 presents biographical profiles of over three hundred political leaders.

LELYVELD, Joseph. *Move Your Shadow: South Africa, Black and White*. New York: Times Books, 1985.

A Pulitzer Prize–winning book by a *New York Times* correspondent. Sensitively chronicles the tragedy and absurdity of apartheid.

LEWIS, Stephen R., Jr. *The Economics of Apartheid*. New York: Council on Foreign Relations Press, 1990.

A nontechnical overview of South Africa's economy, focusing on historical evolution, pressures for fundamental policy change, and alternative strategies for future development.

LIPTON, Merle. *Capitalism and Apartheid: South Africa, 1910–1984*. Totowa, N.J.: Rowman and Allanheld, 1985.

A lucid contribution to the debate about the historic and possible future role of capitalism in fostering racial inequality. The author, a South African–born economist, comes down on the side of nonracial capitalism.

LODGE, Tom. *Black Politics in South Africa Since 1945*. New York: Longman, 1983.

A well-documented interpretation of key events, issues, and personalities in the African nationalist struggle.

MACSHANE, Denis; PLAUT, Martin; and WARD, David. *Power! Black Workers, Their Unions and the Struggle for Freedom in South Africa*. Boston: South End Press, 1984.

An introduction to the South African trade union movement; less authoritative than Steven Friedman's *Building Tomorrow Today: African Workers in Trade Unions 1970–1984*, published in South Africa by the Ravan Press in 1987.

MATHABANE, Mark. *Kaffir Boy: The True Story of a Black Youth's Coming of Age in Apartheid South Africa*. New York: Macmillan, 1986.

An autobiographical account of life in Alexandra, long one of South Africa's poorest and most neglected black townships. The author describes his struggle to obtain an education and to escape the straitjacket of apartheid.

MERMELSTEIN, David, ed. *The Anti-Apartheid Reader: South Africa and the Struggle Against White Racist Rule*. New York: Grove Press, 1987.

A wide-ranging anthology of eighty pieces excerpted from the writings of scholars, journalists, and activists. Provides a thought-provoking excursion through the complexities of the current South African scene.

MINTER, William. *King Solomon's Mines Revisited: Western Interests and the Burdened History of South Africa.* New York: Basic Books, 1986.
>One of America's leading anti-apartheid activists reviews the history of U.S. and British involvement in the economic exploitation of southern Africa and makes the case for sanctions.

MUFSON, Steven. *Fighting Years: Black Resistance and the Struggle for a New South Africa.* Boston: Beacon Press, 1990.
>Focusing entirely on the underreported black resistance, this lively and intelligent contribution to the history of South Africa's transformation in the 1980s is written by a former correspondent of the *Wall Street Journal.* Enough of the larger national scene is sketched in to add context to the mass of detail.

MUTLOATSE, Mothobi, ed. *Africa South: Contemporary Writings.* Exeter, N.H.: Heinemann Educational Books, 1981.
>An anthology of short stories and other pieces by South Africa's current generation of black writers.

OMOND, Roger. *The Apartheid Handbook: A Guide to South Africa's Everyday Racial Policies.* New York: Viking Penguin, 1985.
>Arranged in simple question-and-answer form, this is a detailed factual guide to the racial laws and practices of South Africa in the mid-1980s.

RUSSELL, Diana E. H. *Lives of Courage: Women for a New South Africa.* New York: Basic Books, 1989.
>Interviews with twenty-four South African women active in opposition politics, on topics ranging from experiences in prison and exile to sexism in the African National Congress and the labor movement.

SAMPSON, Anthony. *Black and Gold: Tycoons, Revolutionaries and Apartheid.* New York: Pantheon Books, 1987.
>A highly readable analysis of the relationship between international business and black nationalism in the modern era, by a British writer and journalist with long South African experience.

SAUL, John, and GELB, Stephen. *The Crisis in South Africa,* revised edition. New York: Monthly Review Press, 1986.
>An influential Marxist analysis of what the authors perceive as an "organic crisis" in the South African system that will lead to its ultimate demise.

SECRETARY OF STATE'S ADVISORY COMMITTEE ON SOUTH AFRICA. *A U.S. Policy Toward South Africa.* Washington, D.C.: U.S. Department of State, January 1987.
>A post–U.S. sanctions assessment of the situation in South Africa and

an incisive critique of the Reagan administration's policy of constructive engagement.

SMITH, David M., ed. *Living Under Apartheid: Aspects of Urbanization and Social Change in South Africa.* Boston: George Allen & Unwin, 1982.
    A collection of twelve essays on housing, land use, migration, unemployment, and other contemporary social issues.

SOUTH AFRICAN INSTITUTE OF RACE RELATIONS. *Race Relations Survey.* Johannesburg. Annual publication.
    This yearly compendium of facts, events, and statistics, published in South Africa, is an invaluable resource for research on social and political developments.

SPARKS, Allister. *The Mind of South Africa.* New York: Alfred A. Knopf, 1990.
    An engaging and perceptive interpretation of South African history and society by a former editor of the defunct *Rand Daily Mail.*

STUDY COMMISSION ON U.S. POLICY TOWARD SOUTHERN AFRICA. *South Africa: Time Running Out.* Berkeley: University of California Press and Foreign Policy Study Foundation, 1981.
    One of the most comprehensive introductions to South Africa and to U.S. interests and policy options; a useful reference work.

THOMPSON, Leonard. *A History of South Africa.* New Haven: Yale University Press, 1990.
    Covers South African history from precolonial times to the present; written for the general reader but synthesizes the best of modern scholarship.

VILLA-VICENCIO, Charles, and DE GRUCHY, John W., eds. *Resistance and Hope: South African Essays in Honour of Beyers Naudé.* Grand Rapids: Wm. B. Eerdmans Publishing Co., 1985.
    Tutu, Boesak, Chikane, Tlhagale, and other prominent church leaders have contributed chapters to this collection of essays on religion in contemporary South Africa.

WILSON, Francis, and RAMPHELE, Mamphela. *Uprooting Poverty: The South African Challenge. Report for the Second Carnegie Inquiry into Poverty and Development in Southern Africa.* New York: W. W. Norton and Company, 1989.
    A vivid and extensively documented landmark study of socioeconomic conditions affecting South Africa's impoverished majority. The authors draw on the work of dozens of researchers in the fields of health, employment, literacy, and housing and present recommendations for transforming South African society.

This bibliography was prepared by Gail M. Gerhart, Ph.D., currently at the City University of New York.

Chronology: Southern Africa

1884

Germany establishes colony in South-West Africa (later Namibia).

1910

Southern African Customs Union (SACU) formed to link the three British territories of Bechuanaland (later Botswana), Swaziland, and Basutoland (later Lesotho) with South Africa.

1915

South Africa conquers German colony of South-West Africa.

1920

League of Nations grants South Africa trusteeship to govern South-West Africa.

1928

Portuguese ruler, Antonio Salazar, reorganizes colonial empire, making African colonies (Angola, Mozambique, Guinea-Bissau, Sao Tomé and Príncipe, and Cape Verde) effective provinces of Portugal.

1946

South Africa resists United Nations' attempt to take over South-West Africa mandate, claiming UN trusteeship system not legal successor to League of Nations; South Africa increases colonial control over South-West Africa.

1951

Portugal officially incorporates five African territories into the Portuguese state.

1953

Britain creates Central African Federation consisting of Northern Rhodesia (later Zambia), Nyasaland (later Malawi), and Southern Rhodesia (later Zimbabwe).

1959

Ovamboland People's Organization formed to oppose South African rule in South-West Africa; becomes South West Africa People's Organization (SWAPO) in 1966.

1961

Tanganyika, later renamed Tanzania after union with Zanzibar, becomes independent.

1963

Organization of African Unity (OAU) founded with its headquarters in Addis Ababa. Malawi, formerly Nyasaland, becomes independent. United Nations passes resolution for voluntary arms embargo against South Africa.

1964

Zambia, formerly Northern Rhodesia, becomes independent.

1965

November 11: British colony of Southern Rhodesia issues Unilateral Declaration of Independence; diplomatic and economic reprisals from Britain and eventually mandatory UN sanctions follow. South Africa supports Rhodesian government.

1966

SWAPO launches low-level guerrilla campaign against South African–controlled South-West Africa. UN General Assembly strips South Africa of mandate in the territory. Lesotho (formerly Basutoland) and Botswana (formerly Bechuanaland) become independent.

1967

May 19: United Nations establishes council to administer South-West Africa and secure independence; South Africa continues rule, in defiance of United Nations. **August**: Twenty key SWAPO officials, including leader Herman Toivo Ja Toivo, sentenced to life imprisonment. South Africa and Malawi establish diplomatic relations.

1968

September: Swaziland becomes independent.

1969

April: Lusaka Manifesto adopted by thirteen African states under leadership of Presidents Kenneth Kaunda of Zambia and Julius Nyerere of Tanzania. Botswana, Lesotho, and Swaziland sign agreement with South Africa continuing trade links through SACU.

1970

South African prime minister, B. J. Vorster, pays official visit to Malawi, and in 1971, Malawi president, Hastings Banda, visits Pretoria.

1971

Byrd Amendment allows United States to import strategic materials, including Rhodesian chrome, in contravention of UN economic embargo against Rhodesia. **June 21:** International Court of Justice's advisory opinion declares South Africa's occupation of South-West Africa illegal and calls for withdrawal. **December:** United Nations endorses court's decision.

1974

April 25: Young army officers in Lisbon overthrow Portuguese government.

1975

June 25: Mozambique becomes independent. **September:** Outbreak of Angolan civil war; South Africa intervenes in Angola on side of National Front for the Liberation of Angola (FNLA) and National Union for the Total Liberation of Angola (UNITA). **October:** Large numbers of Cuban troops arrive in Angola to assist Popular Movement for the Liberation of Angola (MPLA). **November 11:** Angola becomes independent under MPLA.

1976

Mozambique National Resistance (RENAMO) set up by Rhodesians as fifth column in Mozambique; RENAMO taken over by South Africa after Zimbabwe becomes independent in 1980. **January:** Clark Amendment bars U.S. aid to any of the factions in Angola (repealed in 1985); South Africa withdraws its forces from Angola. UN Security Council passes resolution 385, calling for free elections in Namibia under the supervision and control of the United Nations; UN General Assembly gives observer status to SWAPO. **April:** Key speech by Henry Kissinger, U.S. secretary of state, in Lusaka, Zambia, lays out U.S. priorities in southern Africa, focusing on Rhodesia. OAU approves creation of informal grouping of "Frontline States" to support and coordinate liberation struggle in Rhodesia. Group consists of Angola, Botswana, Mozambique, Tanzania, and Zambia; joined by Zimbabwe in 1980.

1977

January: Byrd Amendment, allowing U.S. imports of Rhodesian chrome, repealed. **August:** United States condemns South Africa for allegedly planning atomic test in Kalahari Desert. **November 4:** UN Security Council makes 1963 voluntary arms embargo against South Africa mandatory.

1978

South Africa begins series of military incursions into Angolan territory, targeting SWAPO guerrillas seeking to end Pretoria's control over Namibia. **March 26:** South Africa's choice for South-West African president, Clemens Kapuuo of South African–created Democratic Turnhalle Alliance, assassinated. **May 4:** South Africa agrees in principle to plans for UN–monitored independence for South-West Africa. **September 29:** UN Security Council Resolution 435 endorses plan, brokered by Western "Contact Group," for UN–supervised elections leading to South-West African independence in 1979 (finally implemented in 1990).

1979

March: South African government proposes "constellation of states" as a loose confederation of "independent" homelands, Botswana, Lesotho, Swaziland, Malawi, Namibia, and Rhodesia. **December:** Conference in London of rival Rhodesian groups, chaired by Britain, produces Lancaster House agreement paving way for free elections and independence of Rhodesia as Zimbabwe.

1980

March 4: Robert Mugabe, leader of Zimbabwe African National Union (ZANU) wins preindependence election under British supervision. **April 1:** The six Frontline States (now including Zimbabwe), plus Lesotho, Malawi, and Swaziland form Southern African Development Coordination Conference (SADCC). **April 18:** Zimbabwe becomes independent. **June 1:** Resurgence of African National Congress (ANC) marked by sabotage attacks on South Africa's oil-from-coal installations at Sasolburg.

1981

January: At conference on Namibia in Geneva, South Africa rejects implementation of UN plan for territory's independence; South Africa attacks ANC headquarters in Maputo, Mozambique. **March:** South Africa imposes two-week railway embargo on Maputo-bound traffic. **March 5:** Mozambique expels four U.S. diplomats; United States cuts off aid to Mozambique. **April 4:** South African Railways demands return of twenty-four leased diesel locomotives after Zimbabwe votes in favor of sanctions against South Africa in United Nations. **May 31:** Reagan administration links Namibia's independence to withdrawal of Cuban forces from Angola. **August 25–31:** In "Operation Protea," South Africa sends more than eleven thousand troops into Angola in largest military invasion since 1976.

1982

South Africa expels twelve thousand Mozambican migrant workers from eastern Transvaal farms. **December 9:** South African commandos attack Maseru, Lesotho. **December 19:** ANC sabotages South Africa's nuclear power complex at Koeberg. South African forces blow up fuel depots in Beira, Mozambique.

1983

May 20: ANC car bomb outside military headquarters in Pretoria kills nineteen people. South African planes attack ANC sanctuaries in Mozambique. **December 26:** South African Defense Force (SADF) advances into Angola in "Operation Askari," capturing Cassinga and bombing Lubango and other towns; retreats after losses and Soviet warning against escalation of conflict.

1984

February 16: Lusaka Accord signed by South Africa and Angola agreeing to separation of forces and joint patrols in southern Angola. **February 16:** Representatives of Angolan and South African governments, meeting under chairmanship of Zambia's President Kenneth Kaunda, sign U.S.–brokered "Lusaka Accord." **March 16:** Nkomati Accord, a "non-aggression and good neighborliness" pact, signed by South Africa and Mozambique. Similar pact between South Africa and Swaziland disclosed, signed in 1982. **June 12:** United States lifts ban on aid to Mozambique. **July 1:** UN Economic Commission for Africa launches Preferential Trade Area (PTA), comprising fifteen east and southern African states.

1985

May 21: U.S.–owned oil installations in Cabinda, northern Angola, attacked by South African special forces. **June 13:** SADF attacks alleged ANC facility in Gaberone, Botswana; U.S. recalls ambassador to Pretoria in protest. **July 10:** U.S. Congress repeals Clark Amendment. **August:** Documents recovered by Mozambican government forces after raid on RENAMO base at Gorongosa reveal continuing South African support for RENAMO. **September:** Major offensive launched by Angolan government against UNITA in southeastern Angola; repulsed with South African assistance; Mozambican President Samora Machel meets President Reagan in Washington.

1986

January 1–25: South Africa blockades Lesotho's border; Prime Minister Leabua Jonathan overthrown in military coup led by Major General Justin Lekhanya; sixty ANC members deported and blockade lifted. **January 30:** UNITA leader Jonas Savimbi meets President Reagan in Washington, D.C. **February 18:** Reagan administration gives $15 million in covert military aid to UNITA. **May 19:** South Africa attacks alleged ANC bases in capitals of Botswana, Zambia, and Zimbabwe, all Commonwealth countries. Commonwealth Eminent Persons Group (EPG) abandons attempt to mediate between Pretoria and its opponents. United States recalls military attaché from South Africa and expels South African counterpart. **September:** Zimbabwe and Tanzania send troops into Mozambique to protect transport routes against RENAMO. **October 2:** U.S. Congress overrides presidential veto and passes Comprehensive Anti-Apartheid Act. **October 8:** South Africa moves to phase out all migrant labor from Mozambique; later, under pressure from mining industry and white farmers, allows half of Mozambican labor force to remain. **October 19:** Mozambican President Samora Machel killed in plane crash in South Africa near Mozambican border. Joaquim Chissano becomes president.

1987

January 28: Oliver Tambo, head of exiled ANC, meets with U.S. Secretary of State George Shultz in Washington, D.C. **April 25:** SADF raids Livingstone, Zambia. **June 10:** Reagan administration announces second grant of $15 million in military aid to UNITA. **July 18:** Nearly four hundred people, mostly civilians, killed in ambush on village of Homoine in Mozambique in worst attack by RENAMO. **August 6:** Mozambique and South Africa agree to reactivate Nkomati Accord. **August–September:** Angola launches new offensive against UNITA; routed by combined UNITA–South African forces; protracted siege of Cuito Cuanavale, held by Angolans, follows. **November 18:** South Africa acknowledges for first time that its troops are fighting in Angola. **November 20:** Four hundred black troops in South-West Africa Territorial Force mutiny. **December:** First phase of Beira port rehabilitation finished. RENAMO attacks on Beira corridor average twice a week during year. Large contingent of fresh Cuban troops begins arriving in Angola; Cubans move south to Cuito Cuanavale and Namibian border.

1988

March: SADF raids Gaberone, Botswana. **April:** South Africa announces withdrawal from Angola after heavy losses in clashes with Angolan and Cuban troops; several thousand South African troops remain outside Cuito Cuanavale. **April 19:** U.S. State Department releases independent report strongly condemning RENAMO. **May 3–4:** Negotiations over Namibia's independence and removal of Cuban troops from Angola begin among Angola, Cuba, and South Africa, with United States as mediator and Soviet Union as observer. **June 27:** Serious clashes between South African and Cuban forces at Calueque near Angolan-Namibian border. **August 8:** Cuba, Angola, and South Africa meet in Geneva and agree to a cease-fire in Angola and Namibia. South African troops leave Angola. **September:** President P. W. Botha visits Mozambique; two countries reaffirm their adherence to Nkomati Accord. **December 22:** Angola, Cuba, and South Africa sign two interlocking accords providing for independence of Namibia and withdrawal of fifty thousand Cuban troops from Angola.

1989

January 10: Cuban troops begin withdrawal from Angola. **April 1:** UN Transitional Assistance Group (UNTAG) begins preparing Namibia for elections and independence; fighting between returning SWAPO and South African security forces breaks out soon afterward. **April 26:** Soviet Union sends diplomatic mission to South Africa, for first time since countries broke off relations in 1956, to discuss implementation of Namibian peace agreement. **June 22:** Angolan President José Eduardo dos Santos and UNITA leader Jonas Savimbi meet in Zaire and agree to a cease-fire in Angola, to go into effect June 24. **July:** President Joaquim Chissano appoints President Daniel arap Moi of Kenya as mediator in efforts to end war between Mozambican government and RENAMO. **July 19:** F. W. de Klerk meets President Joaquim Chissano in Mozambique; first visit to black state since De Klerk became National Party leader. **August 21:** OAU Ad Hoc Committee on Southern Africa issues Harare Declaration, approving ANC's conditions for negotiating with South African government. **August 22:** Leaders of eight African countries meet in Zimbabwe to discuss alleged violations of cease-fire in Angola. **August 24:** UNITA leader Jonas Savimbi declares that truce in Angola has broken down and urges his followers to resume firing. **August 28:** F. W. de Klerk visits President Kenneth Kaunda of Zambia in Lusaka. **September 14:** SWAPO leader Sam Nujoma returns to Namibia after thirty years in exile. **October 15:** South Africa, United States, and UNITA try to revive Angolan peace process after collapse of cease-fire. **November 14:** SWAPO wins 57 percent of vote in Namibia's election for a constituent assembly to write new constitution. **December 7:** Period of military service for white South African conscripts reduced from two years to one year.

1990

March 21: Namibia becomes independent under SWAPO government led by Sam Nujoma, after seventy-five years of colonial rule. **November:** U.S. Secretary of State James Baker and Soviet Foreign Minister Eduard Shevardnadze agree to help further Portuguese mediation efforts on Angola. **December 10:** MPLA votes to revise Angolan constitution to allow for a two-phase (rather than an immediate) transition to a multiparty system, falling short of UNITA's demand for endorsement of a multiparty system.

1991

April 15: European Community lifts the 1986 bans on import of South African iron, steel, and gold coins. **April 28:** In Angola, MPLA party congress rejects Marxism-Leninism in favor of social democracy and accepts plan for elections. **April 29:** Lesotho Major General Lekhanya ousted by rebel army officers in bloodless coup. **May 1:** Peace accord initialed by representatives of Angolan government and UNITA in Portugal calls for cease-fire and elections in second half of 1992. **May 15:** De facto cease-fire between UNITA and MPLA begins. **May 25:** Cuba withdraws last of 50,000 troops from Angola. **May 31:** Agreement initialed on May 1 is formally signed in Lisbon by Jonas Savimbi and President José Eduardo dos Santos. **July 10:** U.S. lifts economic sanctions against South Africa.

Key Events in South African History

B.C.–1902

B.C.: San ("Bushmen") and Khoikhoi ("Hottentots") reside in area now known as South Africa. **A.D. 200–300**: Bantu-speaking African farmers cross Limpopo River and move southward into the eastern part of present-day South Africa. **1488**: Portuguese explorers circumnavigate Cape of Good Hope. **1500–1600**: Africans settle in Transvaal, Orange Free State, Natal, and Eastern Cape. **1652–1795**: Dutch East India Company establishes a station in Cape Peninsula. Dutch, German, and French Huguenot immigrants settle in the Cape and merge to become "Afrikaners" (called "Boers" by the British); slaves are imported from East Indies, Madagascar, and other parts of Africa; indigenous San and Khoikhoi die off or are assimilated. **1760**: First "pass laws" introduced; all slaves in the Cape required to carry documents designed to control movement of population.

1795–1806: British capture Cape Colony from Dutch in 1795; conquest legalized by treaty in 1806. **1811–78**: Xhosa and British fight frontier wars in Eastern Cape; Xhosa defeated. **1816–28**: Zulu kingdom rises under Shaka. **1820**: Several thousand English immigrants arrive; most settle in Eastern Cape. **1834**: Britain abolishes slavery throughout empire.

1836–40: Afrikaner farmers, rejecting British rule, make "Great Trek" into interior. **1838**: Afrikaners defeat Zulus at battle of Blood River in Natal; event celebrated by Afrikaners annually on December 16 as "Day of the Covenant." **1841**: Lovedale Missionary Institution established in Eastern Cape, first African secondary school. **1843**: Britain annexes Natal. **1852–54**: Britain recognizes South African Republic (Transvaal) and Orange Free State as independent Afrikaner states. **1853**: Nonracial, qualified franchise established in Cape Colony through British influence. In later decades, Cape legislature redefines property qualifications to curb the expansion of the African electorate; but African voters, around 1900, hold balance of power in a handful of districts. **1860–1911**: Indentured laborers brought from India by British to work on Natal sugar plantations; most settle permanently.

1867: Diamonds discovered north of Cape Colony, near Kimberley. **1877**: Britain annexes Transvaal. **1879**: Zulus defeat British at Isandhlwana; British crush Zulu military power at Ulundi and later annex Zululand. **1880–81**: First Anglo-Boer War; Transvaal Afrikaners regain their independence. **1884**: First African-edited newspaper started. **1886**: Gold discovered on the Witwatersrand. **1894**: Natal Indian Congress (NIC) formed under Mohandas K. Gandhi, who lived in South Africa from 1893 until 1914. **1898**: Afrikaners defeat Venda, the last independent African kingdom. **1899–1902**: Second Anglo-Boer War ends with Afrikaner defeat; Transvaal and Orange Free State become self-governing crown colonies.

1902

Cape Coloureds form African Political Organization.

1906

Rebellion led by Chief Bambatha against imposition of poll tax in Natal; thirty whites and three thousand Zulus killed.

1909

Africans hold South African Native Convention to protest racial segregation in proposed constitution.

1910

Union of South Africa formed as self-governing British dominion; Parliament limited to whites; General Louis Botha, leader of Afrikaner-English coalition and supported by General Jan C. Smuts, becomes first prime minister.

1912

South African Native National Congress, first national African political movement, founded to overcome ethnic divisions and oppose racial segregation; renamed African National Congress (ANC) in 1923.

1913

Native Land Act limits land purchases by Africans, 70 percent of population, to reserves, which equal 7 percent of the land. African reserves form basis of today's tribal homelands.

1914

Afrikaners form National Party under General J. B. M. Hertzog to oppose Botha and Smuts. South African armed forces fight in World War I on side of Britain; Afrikaner nationalists oppose decision.

1915

South Africa conquers German colony of South-West Africa (Namibia).

1916

South African Native College opens at Fort Hare, Eastern Cape.

1919

Smuts becomes prime minister. South African Native National Congress campaigns against pass laws; hundreds arrested.

1920

Industrial and Commercial Workers' Union formed, the first nationwide mass movement for Africans. League of Nations grants South Africa trusteeship to govern South-West Africa.

1921

South African Communist Party (SACP) formed.

1924

General Hertzog, leader of National Party, becomes prime minister in coalition with English-speaking Labor Party.

1925

Afrikaans recognized as second official language after English.

1930

White women enfranchised.

1931

All property and literacy tests removed for white voters. Britain recognizes South Africa's legal sovereignty within the Commonwealth.

1934

Hertzog and Smuts, during worldwide depression, join forces to form the United Party under Hertzog's leadership. Afrikaner nationalists, under Dr. Daniel F. Malan, break away to establish "purified" National Party.

1936

Native Land and Trust Act provides for eventual increase of African reserves from 7 percent to 13.7 percent of all land; companion legislation removes Africans from common voters' roll in Cape Province, places them on separate roll to elect seven whites to Parliament, and creates national advisory Natives' Representative Council; in protest, All-African Convention held.

1939

Parliament by a small margin votes to enter World War II. Smuts succeeds Hertzog and becomes prominent Allied leader. South African volunteer forces, including Africans as labor auxiliaries, join Allies; some Afrikaner leaders advocate neutrality or support for Nazi Germany.

1940s

During World War II, pass laws suspended in all major towns.

1943

ANC adopts "African Claims," based on 1941 Atlantic Charter, and bill of rights calling for nonracial franchise; authorizes formation of Youth League, later led by Nelson Mandela and Oliver Tambo. Non-European Unity Movement formed, primarily in Western Cape, and advocates non-collaboration with all segregated bodies.

1946

NIC and Transvaal Indian Congress (TIC) begin two-year passive resistance campaign, the first since Gandhi, to protest policies on land and representation. About seventy thousand African mine workers stop work; strike broken by government forces. Natives' Representative Council adjourns indefinitely.

1947

Declaration of Cooperation by leaders of ANC, NIC, and TIC.

1948

National Party, led by Malan, wins narrow surprise victory; introduces "apartheid," which codifies and expands racial segregation.

1949

Prohibition of marriage between Africans and whites extended to Coloureds and whites. ANC adopts Program of Action calling for boycotts, strikes, and (for the first time) nonviolent civil disobedience. Legislation abolishes remaining Indian and Coloured voting rights in Natal province.

1950

Population Registration Act requires racial classification of all South Africans. Group Areas Act requires segregated residential and business areas for whites, Coloureds, and Asians. Prohibition of sexual relations between whites and Africans extended to whites and Coloureds. SACP dissolves before enactment of Suppression of Communism Act, later used against all forms of dissent. **June 26:** National stay-at-home; date becomes ANC commemorative day.

1951

Bantu Authorities Act abolishes Natives' Representative Council and establishes basis for ethnic government in African reserves or "homelands." Bill to remove Coloureds from common voters' roll by simple legislative majority provokes five-year constitutional crisis. ANC and South African Indian Congress form Joint Planning Council.

1952

June 26: ANC and allied groups begin nonviolent Defiance Campaign against discriminatory laws that lasts all year; about eighty-five hundred protesters are jailed. **December:** Albert Lutuli, deposed as chief by government, is elected ANC president.

1953

Public Safety Act empowers government to declare stringent states of emergency. Companion legislation authorizes severe penalties for protesters, virtually eliminating passive resistance as a tactic. In opposition to mission-run schools, Bantu Education Act imposes government control over African schools. Government legislation enacted designed to undermine African unions. Reservation of Separate Amenities Act overturns judicial precedent of "separate but equal." **May 9:** United Party dissidents form Liberal Party, favoring nonracial but qualified franchise for blacks. **October 10:** Leftwing whites form Congress of Democrats in sympathy with ANC.

1954

December: J. G. Strijdom succeeds Malan as prime minister.

1955

ANC defies Bantu Education Act, keeping thousands of children out of school. Government packs Senate and the highest court in order to remove Coloureds from common voters' roll. **March 5–6:** Formation of South African Congress of Trade Unions links African and multiracial trade unions to ANC. **June 25–26:** ANC, in alliance with Indian, Coloured, and white organizations, endorses Freedom Charter at Congress of the People; adopts it officially in 1956.

1956

Coloureds removed from common voters' roll and placed on separate roll to elect four whites to represent them in Parliament. Government systematically begins to issue passes to African women. Twenty thousand women of all races, organized by the Federation of South African Women, march in Pretoria to protest issuance of passes to African women. Albert Lutuli, Nelson Mandela, and 154 others arrested on charges of treason; those not yet discharged found not guilty in March 1961. Legislation prohibits formation of racially mixed unions and requires existing mixed unions to split into segregated unions or form segregated branches under an all-white executive. Enactment of Riotous Assemblies Act provides for control of public meetings of twelve or more persons.

1957

January: Africans in Johannesburg wage bus boycott against fare increase; ends successfully after three months. **May:** Parliament approves bill to bar blacks from white church services. Thousands demonstrate in Cape Town.

1958

September: Dr. Hendrik Verwoerd, theoretician of apartheid, becomes prime minister. **November:** "Africanists," who oppose inclusion of non-Africans, break away from ANC.

1959

Promotion of Bantu Self-Government Act provides for an end to African representation by whites in Parliament and envisages that all Africans will belong to one of eight ethnic "national units" that will eventually become independent. Apartheid and increased government control extended to higher education. Africanists form Pan Africanist Congress of Azania (PAC) under the leadership of Robert Sobukwe. Ovamboland People's Organization is formed to oppose South African rule in South-West Africa (Namibia); becomes the South West Africa People's Organization (SWAPO) in 1966. Former United Party members form Progressive Party (later the Progressive Federal Party) favoring high but nonracial qualifications for the franchise.

1960

March 21: In Sharpeville, police kill 69 unarmed Africans and wound 186 during demonstration against pass laws organized by PAC. Lutuli burns his pass and urges Africans to follow his example. Government declares state of emergency (ends August 31), detains nearly two thousand activists of all races, and outlaws ANC and PAC. **October 5:** Majority of whites vote yes in whites-only referendum on South Africa becoming a republic within the Commonwealth.

1961

May 31: South Africa leaves Commonwealth. ANC abandons nonviolence. **October 23:** Lutuli awarded Nobel Peace Prize. **December 16:** *Umkhonto* *we Sizwe* (Spear of the Nation), armed wing of ANC, launches sabotage campaign.

1962

Sabotage Act provides for prolonged detention without trial. **November 7:** Mandela sentenced to five years in prison for inciting workers and leaving country without passport. **November 21–22:** *Poqo* (Africans Alone), armed offshoot of PAC, attacks whites.

1963

"90-Day Act" virtually abrogates habeas corpus. **July 11:** *Umkhonto* leaders arrested in Rivonia, a white Johannesburg suburb.

1964

June 12: Eight *Umkhonto* leaders, including Nelson Mandela, Walter Sisulu, and Govan Mbeki, sentenced to life imprisonment after admitting sabotage and preparation for guerrilla warfare.

1966

September 6: Prime Minister Verwoerd assassinated; succeeded by B. J. Vorster.

1967

Terrorism Act broadens the definition of terrorism and provides for indefinite detention.

1968

Legislation outlaws multiracial political parties; Liberal Party disbands. Parliamentary representation of Coloureds by whites ended. Coloured Persons' Representative Council and South African Indian Council established. **December:** South African Students' Organization, formed under leadership of Steve Biko, is precursor to various black consciousness organizations.

1969

April: ANC conference in Tanzania invites non-Africans to join while stressing African "national consciousness."

1971

NIC revived.

1972

July: Black People's Convention formed to advance black consciousness outside schools and colleges.

1973

January: Wave of strikes by black workers in Durban leads to growth of independent nonracial (but mainly African) trade union movement. **March:** Steve Biko and seven other leaders of black consciousness movement banned.

1974

April 25: Young army officers in Lisbon overthrow Portuguese government. **November:** UN General Assembly suspends credentials of South African delegation; first time UN member denied participation. UN General Assembly invites ANC and PAC (both recognized by the Organization of African Unity) to participate as observers.

1975

June 25: Mozambique becomes independent. **August:** South African Defense Force invades Angola. **November 11:** Angola becomes independent.

1976

June 16: Soweto students, protesting inferior education and use of Afrikaans as medium of instruction, fired on by police; countrywide protest results in deaths of estimated one thousand protesters during following months. Internal Security Act supersedes Suppression of Communism Act, broadening government's power to crush dissent. **October 26:** Transkei becomes first homeland given "independence" (Bophuthatswana follows in 1977, Venda in 1979, and Ciskei in 1981).

1977

May 19: Winnie Mandela, wife of Nelson Mandela, banished to Brandfort in Orange Free State; one in a series of restrictive and harassing actions. **September 12:** Steve Biko dies after police beatings while in detention. **October 19:** Black consciousness groups, Christian Institute, and the *World*, a major black newspaper, outlawed; black consciousness leaders and others detained. **November 4:** UN Security Council makes 1963 voluntary arms embargo against South Africa mandatory.

1978

September 20: Prime Minister Vorster resigns after "Muldergate affair," a major scandal in the National Party involving misappropriation of public funds; P. W. Botha becomes prime minister. **September 29:** UN Security Council Resolution 435 endorses plan, brokered by Western "Contact Group," for UN–supervised elections leading to Namibian independence in 1979 (finally implemented in 1990).

1979

Industrial Relations Act officially recognizes African trade unions. **April:**

Federation of South African Trade Unions (FOSATU) organized. **April 6:** Solomon Mahlangu is first guerrilla to be executed. ANC school in Tanzania later named after him. **September:** Azanian People's Organization holds inaugural conference. **November:** Azanian Students' Organization (AZASO) formed for college students; Congress of South African Students (COSAS) formed for high school students. Western Cape hit by a wave of stayaways with broad community support and focusing on a wide range of issues.

1980

March: Thousands of black high school and university students begin prolonged boycott of schools. **April 18:** Zimbabwe becomes independent. **June 1:** Resurgence of ANC marked by sabotage attacks on South Africa's oil-from-coal installations at Sasolburg. **June 26:** ANC publicly breaks with Zulu Chief Mangosuthu Gatsha Buthelezi. Countrywide protests erupt over wages, rents, bus fares, and education.

1981

April: National Party wins election with reduced majority. **May:** Widespread opposition to twentieth anniversary of the Republic. Burning of South African flag becomes an offense.

1982

February: Rightwing breaks away from National Party over proposed constitution providing a tricameral Parliament with separate chambers for whites, Coloureds, and Indians, but excluding Africans; forms Conservative Party. **December 19:** ANC sabotages South Africa's nuclear power complex at Koeberg.

1983

January 3: Coloured Labor Party votes to support proposed constitution. **May 20:** ANC car bomb outside military headquarters in Pretoria kills nineteen people. South African planes attack ANC sanctuaries in Mozambique. **June 11–12:** National Forum, organized primarily by black consciousness leaders, attended by representatives of nearly two hundred anti-apartheid organizations. **August 20–21:** United Democratic Front (UDF), a coalition of anti-apartheid organizations sympathetic to the Freedom Charter, launched nationally. **November 2:** Whites-only referendum approves proposed constitution.

1984

March 16: Nkomati Accord, a "nonaggression and good neighborliness" pact, signed by South Africa and Mozambique. **August:** Labor Party wins seventy-six of eighty seats in Coloured chamber of new tricameral Parliament. National People's Party wins in Indian chamber. Less than one-fifth of

Coloured and Indian voters participate. **September 3:** New constitution goes into effect. Most widespread and prolonged black uprising since 1976 erupts in Vaal Triangle. **October 16:** Anglican Bishop Desmond Tutu awarded Nobel Peace Prize for nonviolent opposition to apartheid. **October 23:** Some seven thousand soldiers, in unprecedented action, enter Sebokeng township to join police in house-to-house raids. **November 5–6:** Transvaal stayaway, largest yet, organized by COSAS and FOSATU, signals student-worker alliance.

1985

February 19: Thirteen top leaders of UDF arrested; six charged with high treason. **March 21:** On twenty-fifth anniversary of Sharpeville shootings, police in Langa township kill nineteen African funeral mourners. **July 20:** State of emergency imposed in parts of the country following nearly five hundred deaths in township violence since September 1984. **August 15:** President Botha, in the "Rubicon" speech, rejects foreign and domestic calls for fundamental change. **August 28:** COSAS banned. **September 4:** Foreign banks suspend credit following Chase Manhattan's July 31 refusal to roll over loans; action sets off financial crisis. **September 9:** U.S. President Reagan imposes limited sanctions against South Africa to preempt stronger measures by Congress. **September 13:** White South African businessmen and newspaper editors hold talks in Zambia with ANC leaders. **November 2:** Government announces media restrictions in locations covered by emergency decree. **November 30:** Congress of South African Trade Unions (COSATU) formed, creating largest mainly African labor federation.

1986

February 7: Frederik Van Zyl Slabbert resigns as leader of the Progressive Federal Party, rejecting white political structure. **March 7:** Partial state of emergency lifted. **May 1:** Some 1.5 million blacks stage largest stayaway in South Africa's history. Buthelezi's Inkatha launches United Workers' Union of South Africa. **May 19:** South Africa attacks alleged ANC bases in capitals of Botswana, Zambia, and Zimbabwe, all Commonwealth countries. Commonwealth Eminent Persons Group abandons attempt to mediate between Pretoria and its opponents. **June 12:** Nationwide state of emergency imposed. **July 1:** Pass laws repealed; indirect controls on movement remain. **July 7:** Winnie Mandela freed from government restrictions after twenty-four years. **September 7:** Reverend Desmond Tutu becomes first black archbishop of the Anglican Church in southern Africa. **October 2:** U.S. Congress overrides presidential veto to pass Comprehensive Anti-Apartheid Act imposing economic sanctions against South Africa. **December 11:** Almost total censorship imposed on media reports of political protest.

1987

January 28: Oliver Tambo, head of exiled ANC, meets with U.S. Secretary of State George Shultz in Washington, D.C. **May 6:** Conservative Party displaces Progressive Federal Party as official opposition to National Party in

Parliament. **June 12**: State of emergency extended for a second year. **July 9**: Delegation of sixty whites, led by Frederik Van Zyl Slabbert, head of Institute for a Democratic Alternative in South Africa, arrive in Dakar, Senegal, for talks with members of ANC. **August 9**: Estimated two hundred thousand members of black National Union of Mineworkers begin three-week strike—longest legal strike in South African history. **November**: Violence escalates around Pietermaritzburg, Natal, between supporters of Inkatha and supporters of UDF; by end of year, 230 persons killed. **November 3**: Natal province and KwaZulu announce formation of Natal-KwaZulu Joint Executive Authority, first multiracial administrative body. **November 4**: Govan Mbeki released from Robben Island prison. **December 30**: Transkei prime minister ousted in coup led by Major General Bantu Holomisa. South African Youth Congress organized semiclandestinely; claims over one million followers.

1988

February 10: Troops put down attempted coup against Lucas Mangope, president of Bophuthatswana. **February 24**: Activities of seventeen anti-apartheid organizations, including UDF, effectively banned; COSATU prohibited from engaging in political activities. **May 3–4**: Negotiations over Namibia's independence and removal of Cuban troops from Angola begin among Angola, Cuba, and South Africa, with United States as mediator and Soviet Union as observer. **June 8**: Estimated three million black workers end three-day nationwide strike to protest antilabor legislation and government action of February 24. **June 9**: State of emergency extended for third year. **August 8**: ANC issues Constitutional Guidelines for a Democratic South Africa in Lusaka, Zambia. **August 31**: Bombs destroy headquarters of South African Council of Churches and several leading anti-apartheid groups in Johannesburg; twenty-three wounded. **September 2**: Inkatha and UDF/COSATU sign accord to end twenty months of fighting in Natal. Violence continues. **November 18**: Popo Molefe, Patrick Lekota, and others in Delmas treason trial are convicted. Convictions reversed on December 15, 1989. **November 26**: Zephania Mothopeng, PAC president, and Harry Gwala, senior ANC and SACP member, released from prison. **December 2**: Pro–ANC newspaper editor Zwelakhe Sisulu released after nearly two years of detention. **December 22**: Angola, Cuba, and South Africa sign two interlocking accords providing for independence of Namibia and withdrawal of fifty thousand Cuban troops from Angola.

1989

February 2: P. W. Botha, following a stroke, resigns as leader of National Party; retains post of president. Frederik W. de Klerk elected to succeed Botha as National Party leader. **February 9**: Prison hunger strike increases pressure on government to formally charge political detainees. **April**: Progressive Federal Party and two other smaller white-led parties form multiracial Democratic Party. **April 24**: "Alexandra Five," black anti-apartheid activists, acquitted by Supreme Court of charges of subversion and sedition. **April 26**: Soviet Union sends diplomatic mission to South Africa, for first time since countries broke off relations in 1956, to discuss implementation of Namibian peace agreement. **May 18**: Anglican Archbishop Desmond Tutu, the Reverend Allan Boesak, and the Reverend Beyers Naudé meet with U.S. President George Bush. **June 9**: Nationwide state of emergency extended for fourth year. **June 30**: Albertina Sisulu and other UDF leaders meet with President Bush. **July 5**: Nelson Mandela and President Botha have unprecedented meeting in Cape Town. **August 2**: Black South Africans present themselves at white hospitals and are treated despite apartheid regulations. **August 14**: Botha resigns as president. De Klerk becomes acting president and on September 14 is elected president for five-year term. **August 21**: Organization of African Unity Ad Hoc Committee on Southern Africa issues the Harare Declaration, approving ANC's position for negotiating with South African government. **September 5**: Beginning of two-day strike to protest exclusion of blacks from next day's parliamentary elections; hundreds of thousands boycott work and schools. **September 6**: National Party suffers major setback but retains control; Conservative and Democratic parties gain seats. **September 15**: Anti-apartheid demonstrations in Johannesburg, Pretoria, and Port Elizabeth permitted by government. **October 15**: Walter Sisulu, former ANC secretary-general, and seven others released from long-term imprisonment. **November 16**: All public beaches are desegregated. **November 28**: Pan Africanist Movement, surrogate for PAC, launched.

1990

February 2: President De Klerk announces unbanning of ANC, SACP, and PAC; lifting of restrictions on UDF, COSATU, and thirty-one other organizations; release of political prisoners; and suspension of death penalty. **February 11**: Nelson Mandela released from jail after twenty-seven years of imprisonment. **March 2**: Nelson Mandela named deputy president of ANC, making him effective leader; ANC president Oliver Tambo had been partially disabled by a stroke in 1989. **March 4**: Lennox Sebe, leader of "independent" homeland of Ciskei, overthrown by military. **March 21**: Namibia becomes independent under SWAPO government led by Sam Nujoma, after seventy-five years of colonial rule. **April 5**: Venda government overthrown by military coup. **May 2–4**: First formal talks between ANC and South African government produce progress on release of political prisoners and return of exiles; Groote Schuur Minute signed. **June 7**: South African government lifts nationwide state of emergency in all provinces except Natal. **June 9**: Nelson Mandela begins world tour that includes eleven-day visit to United States, where he meets President George Bush; also addresses joint session of Congress. **June 19**: Repeal of Separate Amenities Act. **July 14**: Inkatha leader Chief Buthelezi announces that his movement, renamed Inkatha Freedom Party, will be open to all races. **July 22**: Fighting between Inkatha and UDF/ANC supporters spreads from Natal to townships around Johannesburg. **July 28**: SACP holds first public rally in forty years. **August 6–7**: Second round of talks between ANC and South African government results in Pretoria Minute; ANC announces ceasefire, ending thirty-year-old armed struggle; government pledges to release political prisoners, beginning September 1, and to allow political exiles to return beginning October 1. **September 23–25:** President De Klerk visits United States and meets President George Bush and members of Congress. **September 24:** Soweto municipal councillors, Transvaal Provincial Authority, and Soweto People's Delegation sign accord ending four-year rent boycott and laying foundations for unified metropolitan area embracing Johannesburg, Soweto, and other white towns and black townships. **October 18:** Government ends emergency rule in Natal. **October 19:** National Party opens membership to all races. **October 23:** Zephania Mothopeng, president of PAC, dies; Clarence Makwetu succeeds him. **November 7:** Dutch Reformed church joins other churches in condemning apartheid as a sin. **December 3:** Renewed clashes between Inkatha and UDF/ANC supporters around Johannesburg claim more than one hundred lives. **December 13:** ANC president Oliver Tambo returns to South Africa after thirty-one years in exile. **December 16:** Ending its first legal meeting inside South Africa in thirty years, ANC threatens suspension of talks with government if a number of conditions are not met.

1991

January: Fighting between rival political groups continues in many townships. **January 29:** Nelson Mandela and Chief Buthelezi meet, for first time since Mandela's release, in Durban; they agree to end Inkatha–ANC rivalry. **February 1:** President De Klerk announces that government will repeal remaining apartheid laws affecting land, residence, and racial classification in forthcoming parliamentary session. **March 4:** UDF announces that it will disband on August 20, the eighth anniversary of its founding. **April:** ANC and PAC announce intention to form a common front after unity talks in Harare, Zimbabwe. ANC's Constitutional Proposals for a Democratic South Africa published. **April 28:** In Angola MPLA party congress rejects Marxism-Leninism in favor of social democracy and accepts plan for elections. **April 29:** Lesotho military leader Major General Justin Lekhanya ousted by rebel army officers in bloodless coup. **May 1:** Peace accord signed by Angolan government, and UNITA in Portugal calls for cease-fire and elections in second half of 1992. President De Klerk announces plans to end preventive detention and other repressive provisions of the Internal Security Act of 1982. **May 4:** Winnie Mandela found guilty of kidnapping and accessory to assault of four Soweto youths; sentenced to six years in prison; appeals sentence. **June 5:** Native Land and Trust Act of 1936 and Group Areas Act repealed. **June 17:** Population Registration Act repealed. **July 5:** ANC holds first legal national conference in South Africa since banning in 1960; elects Nelson Mandela president, Oliver Tambo national chairman, Walter Sisulu deputy president, and Cyril Ramaphosa secretary-general. **July 10:** United States lifts economic sanctions against South Africa. **July 19:** *Weekly Mail* exposes secret government funding of Inkatha and its allied labor movement, the United Workers' Union of South Africa (UWUSA). **July 20–31:** "Inkathagate" scandal becomes major crisis for government, leading to demotion of Minister of Police Adriaan Vlok and Minister of Defense Magnus Malan and review of all legislation affecting secret funds. Nelson Mandela demands establishment of interim government. **August 9**: Three members of a white extremist paramilitary group killed by police during political meeting held by President De Klerk in Ventersdorp, Transvaal. **August 10:** Government appoints first black judge (Ismail Mahomed) to Transvaal Provincial Division of Supreme Court. **August 16:** South African government declares broad amnesty for political exiles, removing major barrier to negotiations and making it possible for UN High Commissioner for Refugees to establish South African office to help with repatriation. **September 4:** De Klerk presents National Party's constitutional proposals that feature proportional representation for a lower house, veto powers for an upper one, and a collective presidency; rejected by ANC and allies. **September 14:** National Peace Accord aimed at ending violence and regulating conduct of political activity signed by government, ANC/SACP, Inkatha, and other smaller groups; radical parties on right and left reject pact.

Abbreviations

ANC African National Congress
ECA Economic Commission for Africa
ECC End Conscription Campaign
FAPLA People's Armed Forces for the Liberation of Angola (*Forças Armadas Populares de Libertação de Angola*)
FNLA National Front for the Liberation of Angola (*Frente Nacional de Libertação de Angola*)
FRELIMO Front for the Liberation of Mozambique (*Frente de Libertação de Moçambique*)
MPC Multi-Party Coalition
MPLA Popular Movement for the Liberation of Angola (*Movimento Popular de Libertação de Angola*)
OAU Organization of African Unity
OPEC Organization of Petroleum Exporting Countries
PAC Pan Africanist Congress
PTA Preferential Trade Association
RENAMO or MNR Mozambique National Resistance (*Resistência Nacional Moçambicana*)
RMA Rand Monetary Agreement
SACU Southern African Customs Union
SADCC Southern African Development Coordination Conference
SADF South African Defense Force
SATCC Southern African Transport and Communication Commission
SATS South African Transport Services
SOEKOR Southern Oil Exploration Corporation
SWAPO South West Africa People's Organization
SWATF South West Africa Territorial Force

UDF	United Democratic Front
UNITA	National Union for the Total Independence of Angola (*União Nacional para a Independência Total de Angola*)
UNTAG	United Nations Transitional Assistance Group
ZANU	Zimbabwe African National Union
ZAPU	Zimbabwe African People's Union

INDEX

Kissinger, Henry, 13, 114–15, 117

Labor force, South African, 45, 49,
  50, 52
  migrant labor, 71, 72, 102–4
Lancaster House agreement, 14
Lesotho
  ANC sanctuary in, 26, 30, 31
  dissident forces in, 30
  economy of, 31, 78–79, 103, 136
  independence of, 6
  migrant labor from, 103
  South African attacks against, 27
  South African relations with, 8
Lewis, Stephen R., 98
Linkage, Namibian settlement and,
  36–37, 55–57, 117, 121, 125
Loubser, J. G. H., 94–95
Lusaka Manifesto, 8–9
  text of 141–48

Machel, Samora, 60, 86
Macmillan, Harold, 4
Makoni, Simba, 107
Malan, Magnus, 33, 50, 56
Malawi, 6, 60
  agriculture in, 88, 89
  defense against RENAMO in, 29
  economy of, 88–90, 136–37
  refugees in, 134
  South Africa's diplomatic efforts in,
    61
  trade and, 5
Malnutrition, 132
Mandela, Nelson, 62
Migrant labor, 71, 72, 102–4
Military, South African, 43–53
  arms embargo and, 9, 24, 43, 47–
    48
  arms industry and, 43, 45–48
  attacks on guerrilla bases, 20, 27–
    29, 32–35, 46, 122
  black volunteers in, 25, 45, 49–50
  conscripts in, 48
  diminished importance of, 64
  End Conscription Campaign (ECC)
    and, 49
  ethnic battalions, 49–50
  Frontline States' forces compared
    to, 43, 44
  growth of, 43

lack of recruits, 45
in Namibia, 49–50
nuclear weapons and, 51–53
Permanent Force, 48, 49
personnel and, 48–50
total national strategy and, 24–25
vulnerabilities of, 45
Walvis Bay base and, 33–34
Mining industry, migrant labor and,
  103, 104
Mmusi, Peter, 96
Money figures, viii
Mother-centered family, 132–33
Mozambique. See also Mozambique
  National Resistance
  (RENAMO)
  ANC sanctuary in, 13, 14, 26, 27–
    29, 87, 88, 96
  Cahora Bassa hydroelectric dam,
    12, 87
  casualties in, 131–38
    children, 131–38
    infrastructure and, 135–37
    refugees and, 133–35
  colonial, 4, 6, 7, 9
  dependence on South Africa of,
    87, 88, 96, 104
  dissident forces in, 65
  economic profile of, 86–88
  as Frontline State, 13
  health care in, 132
  independence of, 11–13, 19
  migrant labor from, 104
  nationalist movements in, 8
  Nkomati Accord and, 28–30, 87,
    121
    text of, 161–66
  peacemaking process in, 59
  refugees from, 89
  Rhodesian independence and, 13
  South Africa and, 12
    diplomatic efforts, 60–61
    guerrilla attacks, 20, 27–29
    Nkomati Accord, 28–30, 87,
      121, 161–66
    trade sanctions on, 97
  Soviet involvement in, 118–19
  trade routes through, 81–83, 89,
    90, 92–93, 96–99, 137
  U.S. involvement in, 28, 29, 118,
    122

Mozambique National Resistance (RENAMO), 28–30, 59, 61
economy disrupted by, 82, 83, 86, 89–90, 92, 93, 97–98
South African support of, 121
MPLA. *See* Popular Movement for the Liberation of Angola
Mugabe, Robert, 10, 12, 30–31, 76
anti-apartheid stance of, 26, 31, 95, 96
economy and, 82–86
election of, 14, 26, 115
Multi-Party Conference (MPC), 35–37
Muzorewa, Bishop Abel, 13, 26

Nacala, 93
Namibia
colonial, 6
guerrilla activities against, 20
independence of, 3, 59
negotiation process in
Contact Group, 14, 36–37
Cuban withdrawal from Angola and, 36–37, 55–57, 117, 121, 125
UN plan, 14, 34, 36–37, 56, 57, 59, 123, 126
South Africa's involvement in, 7, 9, 14, 15, 33–37
attacks on SWAPO bases, 34–35
ethnic battalions in, 49–50
multiethnic coalition and, 34–36
UN plan and, 34, 36–37, 56, 57, 59
superpowers' involvement in, 117, 129
whites in, 34
Namibian-Angolan peace accords, 21, 22, 111, 127, 129
effects of, 50, 62, 63, 64
National Front for the Liberation of Angola (FNLA), 10, 11, 114
Nationalist movements. *See* Independence movements; *and other specific topics*
National Union for the Total Independence of Angola (UNITA), 37–41, 111
foreign aid to, 117
peacemaking process and, 56, 59

South African support of, 38–41, 55, 56, 59, 117
transport sabotage, 97, 98
U.S. support of, 38, 120–21, 125–27
Nixon administration, 113
Nkomati Accord, 28–30, 87, 121
text of, 161–66
Nkomo, Joshua, 10
Northern Rhodesia, 4. *See also* Zambia
Nuclear weapons, 51–53
Nujoma, Sam, 7, 59
Nyasaland. *See* Malawi
Nyerere, Julius, 4, 6, 13–14, 80

Organization of African Unity (OAU)
goals and principles of, 5, 6, 10, 71
Harare Declaration of, 62
text, 174–80
Lusaka Manifesto and, 8
total onslaught concept and, 24
trade embargo against South Africa, 100
Outward movement strategy, 8, 9
Ovimbundu, 38

Pacavira, Manuel, 55
Pan Africanist Congress (PAC)
Chinese support of, 10
guerrilla forces of, 7–8, 33
outlawing of, 7
sanctuary in neighboring countries, 8, 96
People's Armed Forces for the Liberation of Angola (*Forças Armadas Populares de Libertação de Angola*) (FAPLA), 124
Pérez de Cuéllar, Javier, 111
Permanent Force, 48, 49
Political acceptability, South Africa's quest for, 20, 21, 64–65
Political prisoners, release of, 63
Popular Movement for the Liberation of Angola (MPLA), 24, 38
peacemaking process and, 59, 127–28
Soviet support of, 38, 114
Portugal. *See also* Angola; Mozambique
colonies of, 6–13

support of dissident movements, 20, 25
total onslaught and total national strategy concepts, 23–26
trade and investment, 99–102
transportation, 91–99
U.S. perception of, 121–22
as regional superpower, 19, 65
Rhodesia supported by, 8, 9
Soviet support of ANC in, 10
U.S. relations with, 47–48, 120–22
South African Transport Services (SATS), 94–95
Southern African Customs Union (SACU), 78–79
Southern African Development Coordination Conference (SADCC), 71–80
assessment of, 105–7
economic profile of member states, 78–90
founding of, 25–26, 76
goals of, 71, 76–77, 105–7
sectoral programs of, 76
structure of, 77
transport program of, 96, 98–99
Zimbabwe and, 26, 71, 76
Southern Rhodesia, 5. *See also* Rhodesia; Zimbabwe
South West Africa People's Organization (SWAPO), 7, 24, 33–37, 59, 63
Angolan bases of, 34–35
peacemaking process in Angola and, 57, 58
South African attacks against, 24, 34–35, 46
UNITA and, 38
South-West Africa Territorial Force (SWATF), 49–50
Southwestern Africa, agreements for peace in, 167–72
Soviet Union
ANC supported by, 58
Angola and, 111–29
African perception and, 115
early stages of involvement, 113–15
Mozambique and, 118–19
Rhodesia and, 10
Sino-Soviet rift and, 10

superpower rivalry and, 9–13, 64, 111–29
constructive engagement strategy, 116–19, 120–23
cooperation, 122–28
early stages of competition, 113–15
loss of interest, 129
points of agreement, 122–23
Third World support of, 114, 119
total onslaught concept and, 23, 24
State Security Council (SSC), 25
Superpower, South Africa as, 19, 65
Superpowers. *See* Soviet Union; United States
Swaziland
ANC sanctuary in, 26, 30
economy of, 78–79, 136
independence of, 6
refugees in, 134
South Africa's relations with, 8

Tanzania
defense against RENAMO in, 29
economy of, 79–80, 136–37
as Frontline State, 13
guerrilla bases in, 8
health care in, 132
independence of, 4–5
rail-port systems in, 4–5, 79–81, 93
refugees in, 134
Rhodesian independence and, 13
Tazara railroad, 79, 81, 93
Terrorism, 133–35
Third World, Soviet support of, 114, 119
Tolbert, William, 9
Total onslaught concept, 23, 24
Tourism, 72
Trade and investment
1980s increase in, 60
South African disruption of, 20, 31, 71, 72, 99–102
Transportation, 20, 91–99
bond requirements, 96
rail-port systems, 4–5, 30, 79–81, 92–94
sabotage of, 97, 98
South Africa's control of, 30–31, 71, 72, 94–98

AUTHORS

Michael Clough is the senior fellow for Africa at the Council on Foreign Relations, New York City. He is also a member of the board of directors of Africa Watch. In 1986–87 he was the study director of the U.S. Secretary of State's Advisory Committee on South Africa. He has taught at the Naval Postgraduate School, 1980–86, and the University of Wisconsin, Madison, 1985–86, and has worked as a consultant for CBS News. Dr. Clough received his Ph.D. in political science from the University of California, Berkeley, in 1983. Among his publications are *Free at Last? U.S. Policy Toward Africa and the End of the Cold War*, forthcoming; "South Africa: Challenges and Choices," *Foreign Affairs*, Summer 1988; "Beyond Constructive Engagement," *Foreign Policy*, Winter 1985–86; and *The United States and South Africa: Realities and Red Herrings*, 1984 (with Helen Kitchen).

Robert S. Jaster writes and lectures on southern African politics. He has been a Fellow at the Woodrow Wilson Center and the International Institute for Strategic Studies, and is a 1991–92 scholar-in-residence at the Arizona Honors Academy, a program of Arizona's three state universities, headquartered in Flagstaff. He is the author of several books, including the forthcoming *Voices for Change: South Africa's Other Whites*, written jointly with his wife, Shirley Kew Jaster. His home base is Rockport, Maine. Recent publications include *The 1988 Peace Accords and the Future of Southwestern Africa* and *The Defence of White Power: South African Foreign Policy Under Pressure*.

Moeletsi Mbeki, a journalist, is head of communications at the Congress of South African Trade Unions (COSATU) in Johannesburg, South Africa. He was previously on the staff of the *Herald* newspaper in Harare, Zimbabwe. He holds an M.A. in sociology from Warwick University in England and has been a contributor to several media outlets, including the BBC World Service, the *New African*, and *Africa Now*. In 1988–89 he was a Nieman Fellow at Harvard University.

Morley Nkosi was born in Johannesburg, South Africa. He earned his B.S. at New York University, an M.B.A. at Rutgers University, and a Ph.D. in economics at the New School for Social Research. He has taught economics and finance at the Graduate School of Management of Rutgers University, Hofstra University, and Upsala College, and has worked as an economic and development consultant. In 1989 he moved to Zimbabwe to direct research on regional economic integration and cooperation. He has since worked as a consultant on private sector development for the Preferential Trade Area for Eastern and Southern African States, based in Lusaka, Zambia, and on public policy and development management for the African Capacity Building Foundation, headquartered in Harare, Zimbabwe. He is presently executive director of the Management Leadership Development Center, a unit of the National African Federated Chambers of Commerce and Industry of South Africa. Dr. Nkosi has published articles on the labor structure in the Witwatersrand gold mines, structural changes in the South African economy, regional economic integration in Africa, and transnational corporations.

EDITOR

John de St. Jorre, a journalist and author, has been visiting and writing about South Africa since the mid-1960s. His book *South Africa: A House Divided* was published by the Carnegie Endowment in New York in 1977, and he was a senior writer for the study commission that produced *South Africa: Time Running Out* in 1981. Born in London and educated at Oxford University, he joined the British Foreign Service and spent three years in different posts in Africa. After resigning, he became the London *Observer*'s Africa correspondent, based first in Zambia and later in Kenya. He covered the Nigeria-Biafra conflict, and his book on that subject, *The Brothers' War: Biafra and Nigeria*, was published in Britain and the United States. He was subsequently the *Observer*'s Paris, Middle East, and New York correspondent. His other books include *The Patriot Game* (a novel), *The Insider's Guide to Spain*, *The Guards*, and *The Marines*.

South Africa UPDATE Series

John Marcum
Professor of Politics
Director, Education Abroad Program
University of California, Santa Barbara

Donald F. McHenry
University Research Professor
  of Diplomacy and International Affairs
Georgetown University
Washington, D.C.

Anthony Sampson
Writer and Journalist
London, United Kingdom

Howard D. Samuel
President
Industrial Union Department (AFL-CIO)
Chevy Chase, Maryland

Franklin A. Thomas
President
Ford Foundation
New York, New York

Leonard Thompson
Charles J. Stillé Professor of History Emeritus
Director, Southern African Research Program
Yale University
New Haven, Connecticut

Brian Urquhart
Scholar-in-Residence, International Affairs
Ford Foundation
New York, New York

Lynn Walker
Director
Rights and Social Justice Program
Ford Foundation
New York, New York

Each book in the **South Africa UPDATE Series** deals with a major topic related to South Africa and is written by one or more specialists. The series contains:

The United States and South Africa: The Reagan Years by Pauline Baker [1989]

All, Here, and Now: Black Politics in South Africa in the 1980s by Tom Lodge, Bill Nasson, Steven Mufson, Khehla Shubane, and Nokwanda Sithole [1991]

Adapt or Die: The End of White Politics in South Africa by Robert Schrire [1991]

The Last Years of Apartheid: Civil Liberties in South Africa by John Dugard, Nicholas Haysom, and Gilbert Marcus [1992]

Changing Fortunes: War, Diplomacy, and Economics in Southern Africa by Robert S. Jaster, Moeletsi Mbeki, Morley Nkosi, and Michael Clough [1992]

To order, please write: Foreign Policy Association, Dept. SA, c/o CUP Services, P. O. Box 6525, Ithaca, NY 14851, or call toll-free 800-477-5836. Credit card holders can fax orders to 607-277-6292.